Alternative Investment

Alternative Investment

A Guide to Opportunity in the Collectibles Market

Robin Duthy

Times
BOOKS

Published by TIMES BOOKS, a division
of Quadrangle/The New York Times Book Co., Inc.
Three Park Avenue, New York, N.Y. 10016

Published simultaneously in Canada by
Fitzhenry & Whiteside, Ltd., Toronto

First published in Great Britain in 1978
by Michael Joseph Ltd.

Library of Congress Cataloging in Publication Data

Duthy, Robin, 1939–
    Alternative investment.

    Includes index.
    1. Collectors and collecting.   2. Investments.
I. Title.
AM231.D88   1980   790.1′32   79-91669
ISBN 0-8129-0865-1

Manufactured in the United States of America

To my wife

Contents

List of Colour Illustrations

Picture credits

The following illustrations are reproduced by courtesy of:

Acknowledgements

I have been helped in many different ways by the people listed below and for their information, advice, readings of the manuscript and suggestions I record my deep gratitude.

BOOKS
Mr. Nicholas Poole-Wilson and Mr. Arthur Freeman of Bernard Quaritch Ltd. Mr. Hans Fellner of Christie's. Mr. George Lowry, Mr. Halberstam and Miss Kyles of Swann Galleries, New York. Mr. John Sausmarez-Smith of Heywood Hill.

CHINESE CERAMICS
Mr. Roger Bluett of Bluett & Sons. Mr. Julian Thompson, Mr. James Lalley, Miss Ann Roberts and Mr. Jonathan Robinson of Sotheby Parke Bernet & Co. Mr. Edmund Capon of the Victoria and Albert Museum.

COINS
Mr. Raymond Sancroft-Baker of Christie's. Mr. P. J. Seaby of B. A. Seaby Ltd. Mr. Patrick Finn of Spink and Son Ltd. Mr. Lester Merkin. Mr. Louis Vigdor of Manfra, Tordella & Brookes Inc. Mr. W. C. French of Glendining.

DIAMONDS
Mr. Richard Dickson and Mr. John Roux of De Beers Consolidated Mines Ltd. Mr. Eric Bruton. Mr. R. V. Huddlestone of Diamond Selection Ltd. Mr. Peter Hinks of Sotheby Parke Bernet & Co. Mr. Albert Monnickendam of A. Monnickendam Ltd. Mr. Terry Davidson of Cartier Ltd.

ENGLISH SILVER
Miss Judith Banister. Mr. Richard Came and Mr. Kevin Tierney of Sotheby Parke Bernet & Co. Mr. Anthony Phillips of Christie's.

FIRE-ARMS
Mr. Peter Hawkins of Christie's. Mr. John Hayward of Sotheby Parke Bernet & Co. Mr. Claude Blair of the Victoria and Albert Museum. Mr. Gill of the Center Firearms Company, New York. Mr. R. Butler of Wallis and Wallis.

GOLD
Mr. Christopher Glynn of Consolidated Gold Fields Ltd. Mr. David Fitzpatrick of Merrill Lynch Holdings Ltd.

MODERN PRINTS
Miss Judith Goldman. Miss Libby Howie of Sotheby Parke Bernet & Co. Miss Riva Castelman of the Museum of Modern Art, New York. Mr. Nicholas Stogdon of Christie's. Mrs. Pat Gilmour. Mr. James Ingram of P. D. Colnaghi & Co. Ltd. Mr. Alan Christea of Waddington and Tooth Galleries.

STAMPS
Mr. Ian Glassborow of Harmer's of London Ltd. Mr. Alan Bosworth of Robson Lowe Ltd. Mr. Abbott Lutz.

FRENCH WINE
Mr. Michael Broadbent of Christie's. Mr. Edmund Penning-Rowsell. Mr. Alexander McNally of Heublein Inc. Mr. R. L. O. Bridgeman of Justerini & Brooks Ltd.

I would also like to acknowledge my considerable debt to the authors of all the books recommended at the end of each chapter and of many others too numerous to mention. Lastly my thanks are due to the many people the nature of whose help was such that they did not wish to be acknowledged by name.

Introduction

This book has two main purposes. The first is to show how the values of the objects within each investment field have moved since 1950, to consider the market forces that have been responsible for those movements and to give the reader the information he needs in order to decide for himself what is likely to happen in the future. The second is to offer the reader a historical sketch of each field without which it is quite impossible to understand either the significance of the various objects to collectors or the development of each market to its present state. The choice of what to include has been personal and somewhat arbitrary, but I hope I have managed to convey something of the character of the objects which in many cases are capable of weaving such powerful spells over their collectors.

Many important aspects of each subject have had to be treated at summary length and others left out altogether. In such cases, I decided it would be tedious to repeat the formula 'Space unfortunately prevents me . . . etc' which, apart from being quite obvious in a survey of this kind, would only have restricted the available space even further. I hope therefore to be allowed the right usually accorded to anthologists to be judged by what I chose to put in rather than what I chose to leave out.

Although the ten fields of investment may not at first appear so, they are homogeneous in several important respects. Firstly, they are international in the sense that they can be traded in throughout Europe and America. Secondly, all the objects, with the possible exception of wine, are easily transportable, so that if an investment made in one country loses or looks like losing its attractions through taxation or for any other reason, it can be quickly removed (subject, of course, to existing legislation) to a more favourable location. Thirdly, whereas many hard and soft commodities require warehousing or refrigeration for long-term investment, none of those considered here calls for any special treatment. Fourthly, all the investments are sterile in that they produce neither dividend, interest nor rent. From this it follows that their sole investment attraction lies in the possibility of capital appreciation and this allows direct comparison between their performances to be made.

It is no accident that almost every collection that can now be seen to have risen spectacularly in value was formed by people who put into their collecting not just money but time, effort and even love. There does seem to have been a long period during the fifties and early sixties when it hardly mattered what

11

people bought. The position now is that the finer material in each field has become extremely scarce. Without knowledge, people are not merely less likely to make money, it is rather that without knowledge they are very likely to lose it. In several cases, leading dealers I asked to characterise the collectors in this or that field answered that they didn't think there were any! Of course there are, but what they were conveying was that months and even years can go by during which time many pieces scarcely touch the ground as they pass from one dealer's hands to the next before finishing up with a collector. Many of the fields of Alternative Investment might be compared to a game of snakes and ladders where the snakes represent the horde of unscrupulous dealers and the ladders represent knowledge, experience, judgement, taste and so on, whether possessed by the investor himself or by one of the many dealers of integrity who will share all these advantages with their clients. The knowledge of so much dark dealing I owe to a number of honest people in or connected with the trade who were highly sensitive to the damage being done to the reputation of their businesses.

Although I have thought it right to stress the dangers where they exist, it will be obvious from the performance of the indexes that it has been possible to make a great deal of money by buying wisely in many of the fields covered. The indexes are based in every case on a hypothetical portfolio of actual objects and have been compiled according to the following formula:

$$v(t) = \frac{1}{N} \sum_{j=1}^{N} v_j(t)$$

where $v(t)$ is the average value of the commodity considered in the year t, N is the number of components and $v_j(t)$ is the normalised value of the jth component in year t, the normalisation being such that $v_j(1975) = 1000$. The findings are shown on a 3 cycle logarithmic scale. The objects have been chosen not only because they are representative of their class but also because objects very similar to them have passed and continue to pass through the salerooms often enough to allow their values to be continuously monitored. The indexes have been compiled by or with the help of leading authorities in each field by reference to saleroom records and, as such, provide as accurate a price history as is possible.

I do not claim for them absolute precision. In some cases a high degree of accuracy has been possible from 1950 right up to the present day, while in others – especially for the earlier period of the fifties when auction-houses seldom took photographs and catalogue descriptions were often quite sketchy – the findings are generally more tentative. Although certain broad inferences may be drawn from the indexes about other objects in the same field, they should not be used as the basis of any commercial transaction or tax computation. Being based on auction-room hammer prices, they take no account of dealing expenses. Now that many auction-houses charge a 10%

premium to buyers on the hammer price as well as their selling commission, tax and insurance, the theoretical 'in and out' expenses of a saleroom investment are not far short of 25%.

Many people claim to find the whole business of art as investment very distasteful. Until recently it was fashionable, indeed almost mandatory, in certain circles to regard as impossibly vulgar any reference to art and money in the same breath. The expression of such a view which might have been calculated to offer a glimpse of a deeply sensitive and artistic nature, may well have masked a shrewdly-based opinion that art prices must move relentlessly but satisfyingly upwards. Nowadays with collapsing stock markets and high rates of inflation and taxation fresh in people's minds as well as some very bumpy rides in many of the areas of Alternative Investment, fewer people make the often expensive assumption that all art values will necessarily move higher. What most people are prepared to acknowledge is that the performances of almost all conventional investments over the last thirty years have varied between disappointing and disastrous while some sectors of the art market have seen spectacular rises. Such rises which look very enticing on paper are becoming progressively harder to achieve and the various reasons why this is so are discussed under the different headings.

All successful buying must be based on confidence whether in a dealer or in oneself, and the only basis for confidence in oneself is knowledge. It is not only that the acquiring of knowledge in the various fields discussed here is by common consent a pleasure, there still exists enormous potential for original personal research. That such activities should be enjoyable, cost nothing and also set the stage for a highly promising investment must give them a formidable appeal. Some of the objects discussed in the following pages are to me almost inexpressibly beautiful and others mean nothing at all. I have not thought it relevant in a book primarily about investment to say much about my personal preferences, firstly because they could have no bearing on future values, and secondly because, whatever may happen to their values, I hope for a more important result from this book which is that people may discover something new and beautiful for themselves.

Books

The earliest known written material consists of crude pictographs (cuneiform) incised on clay tablets found in Mesopotamia and dating from the 4th millennium B.C. These and the various forms of script that developed independently in different parts of the world – such as the Egyptian hieroglyphs (*c.* 2900 B.C.), the Indus Valley script (*c.* 2500 B.C.), the Minoan or Ancient Cretan script (2nd Millennium B.C.), the hieroglyphic writing of the Hittites and Chinese script (before 1500 B.C.) and the Mayan script of Central America (before A.D. 500) – were all used to record knowledge and ideas in more or less permanent form. Because the papyri, bones, codices, parchments and tablets, which are the vehicles for these writings, are not conventionally regarded as books and because, for the time being at least, they are of greater interest to museums and research establishments than to private collectors, the scope of this chapter is restricted to books dating from the invention of moveable type by Johann Gutenberg in 1455.

The impact of Gutenberg's invention upon the civilised world was as great as that of the phonetic alphabet by the Phoenicians in 1200 B.C. His invention was at once the result and the cause of a considerable growth in the literate populations of Europe.

At the beginning of the 15th century in England, the Church held a virtual monopoly of literacy. Lay literacy had more or less come to an end at the Norman Conquest when Latin replaced English as the official language of Church and State, and French became the vernacular for all but the humblest classes. But by 1400 English had, to a great extent, returned as the vernacular and was competing with Latin which remained the official language. Yet the continued use in 1400 of the 'benefit of clergy' test, whereby felons who could prove their literacy by reading a set verse from the Psalter were handed up for trial before an ecclesiastical court, bore witness to this monopoly.

The recent emancipation of vast numbers of serfs (who in 1350 had accounted for half the population), had been followed by a general drift towards the larger villages and towns where wages could be earned and the economic value of literacy quickly understood. The consequent demand for education resulted in the foundation of many new schools and colleges and a pressing need for books in English that could be understood by the newly literate classes.

The Church was utterly opposed to the growing use of English; the arguments paraded in favour of Latin – that it was stable, precise, international

15

and so on – were certainly strong but more compelling still, albeit unusable, was the argument that Latin maintained the closed shop. By excluding the majority, it helped to preserve the mystique of scholarship. This was also true of other professions, such as the Law, Medicine and Science, but it was the laxity and gross hypocrisy of most officials of the Church that made them apprehensive. If the teachings of Jesus were made available in English, the discrepancy between their life-style and that enjoined by the New Testament could only bring them into utter contempt with the people. The Church therefore zealously hounded the Lollards and their English Tracts, and Wyclif and his English Bible, although it nevertheless enjoyed a wide underground circulation.

Happily, the native language had just been kept alive since Anglo-Saxon times through sermons from the parish pulpit and later through the devotional writings of English mystics. It was to these that the continuity and development of English prose owes far more than to the monastic and academic institutions. Translations into English for the benefit of the new readers formed a significant part of the literature of the first half of the 15th century but the demand for instruction and education was far outrunning the supply of books, all of which still had to be laboriously copied by hand. It was into this newly dynamic cultural climate that Caxton introduced in 1485 Gutenberg's revolutionary method of printing with moveable type.

It is strange that the relatively minor step from the Phoenician invention of alphabetic script – that is, the use of interchangeable components to write a word – to the use of interchangeable components to print a word should have taken 2,600 years. The idea first struck Gutenberg in the 1430s. If such a process could be made to work, its advantages over woodblock-printing were obvious. The letters could be set up in any order whatever, mistakes could be corrected at the proof stage and when the printing was finished, the types could be dismantled and used again. Gutenberg also realised that if his invention was to be successful, it would have to stand comparison with the finest manuscript. For this reason he experimented in secret in Mainz for some twenty years until he was satisfied with the results. The precision needed for cutting the metal type was so great that many of the first printers were goldsmiths.

It was Gutenberg's tragedy that when he was finally ready to bring his great labours to fruition, his backer, Fust, sued him for the return of a loan and Gutenberg, being unable to pay, was ordered by the court to forfeit his equipment. Fust then engaged Gutenberg's former assistant and calligrapher Schoeffer, and together they set up in business. Using all Gutenberg's presses and dies they were very soon able to publish the great 42-line Bible. Gutenberg was thus robbed not only of the credit for his invention but of the financial reward too. This Bible, now justly known as the Gutenberg Bible, was published in an edition of probably 200 of which 47, only some complete, have survived. For many people it is the most beautiful book ever printed. The type-setting is remarkably fine and the gothic type successfully matches the finest manuscript. Fust and Schoeffer were unable to protect their invention and by 1460 three other printing-presses were operating in Mainz. The process rapidly became known throughout Europe and by 1500 many thousands of titles had been printed.

The first few decades of printing were much concerned with typography. Gutenberg's gothic type was followed by the first humanistic miniscule adopted by two German monks Pannartz and Sweinheim when they settled in Rome in 1467 – the first version of the style known ever since as roman. Venice, being a more important commercial city than Rome, soon became the centre of the European book trade and it was there that Nicolaus Jenson, a Frenchman, brought out an improved roman style free of all gothic traces. The definitive style of roman was evolved much later by Simone de Colines in 16th-century France. Also in Venice, the great scholar and printer Aldus Manutius designed the type known as italic. He was the first to publish pocket editions of the Latin and Greek classics, and became particularly famous for his five-volume *Aristotle* (1495–9).

The subject matter of most of the early publications was religious. Printers cautiously confined themselves to known best-sellers in the earliest days starting with the Bible, the Psalter, Lives of the Saints and a little later venturing forth with the classics. Christianity had always been vitally dependent on the written word – Christian books were regarded as the most powerful weapons of God and most other books as the weapons of the Devil. Such was the reasoning that justified the destruction (with the exception of three Codices) of the entire literature of the Mayan people of Central America by the Spaniards in the early 16th century. By imposing censorship or burning books, authoritarian regimes have, from time to time, tried to suppress ideas or even destroy a whole culture. Yet only in the single tragic instance of Mayan literature do they appear to have been wholly successful. In the 1590s, Bodley extended the library at Oxford to house the heavy artillery of Protestantism and it is significant that half of all the works in the *Short Title Catalogue* (STC) which lists books published in England between 1475–1640 are religious in content or purpose.

By reviving interest in classical antiquity and especially in Plato and Greek philosophy, the Italian Renaissance led to a general reassessment of the role of man in relation to the universe. It thereby raised man's estimation of his achievements and aspirations, and created eventually throughout Europe an unprecedented demand for books on every subject but particularly those that were based upon the new view of humanity. Throughout the 15th and 16th centuries, this thirst for knowledge was satisfied by a flood of brilliant writing never surpassed at any period in history.

Illustrations by copper-engraving and by woodblock were both older than printing and although the illustrations to accompany the earliest printed books were usually done by hand, both mechanical processes were soon in general use together. Book-illustration was raised to an art-form by Albrecht Dürer whose

17

wood-cutting led German artists towards the Renaissance.

During the 16th century, the influence of manuscripts upon printing gradually waned. The title page of a book made its first appearance for the good commercial reason that people might know where it was to be bought. Artists were attracted to the possibilities of the frontispiece which also appeared for the first time, often taking the form of a classical portico framing the title of the book decorated with arabesques, vases, putti and other Renaissance motifs.

In the 17th century, the Netherlands rose to be the most important printing centre in Europe. Whereas in the 15th and 16th centuries, the Christian Church had seen humanism as a force to be assimilated rather than crushed, the publication of books containing independent ideas in the 17th century began to take place increasingly in the Netherlands to avoid religious and political censorship.

Amongst these were Kepler's *Astronomica Nova* (1609), which explained the motion of the planets round the sun; Hugo Grotius's *De Jure Belli et Pacis* (1625) which was the forerunner of *The Rights of Man*, and William Harvey's *Exercitatio Anatomica de Motu Cordis* (1628), the first accurate description of the circulation of blood. There were too a host of works on philosophy,

From Plautius (Caspar 'Honorio Philipono'): *Nova Typis Transacta Navigatio. Novi Orbis Indiae Occidentalis*, Munich, 1621.

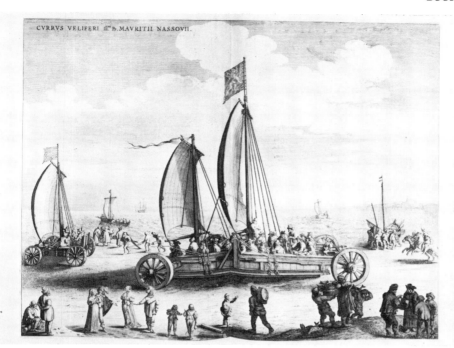

CVRRVS VELIFERI IIᵐᵇ. MAVRITII NASSOVII.

From Blaeu (Jan): *Novum Ac Magnum Theatrum Urbium Belgicae Foederate*, Amsterdam, 1645. It shows one of the many sports invented by Prince Moritz of Nassau.

architecture, archaeology, geography, topography, cartography and travel. Those on travel sometimes included what claimed to be accounts of exotic native customs in distant lands which were in some cases lifted straight from classical texts, although as the century wore on, a more scientific spirit emerged. The great names in Netherlandish printing were the Blaeus in Amsterdam, the Elzevirs at Leyden – who published some two thousand titles during the 17th century usually in editions of one to two thousand – and Plantin-Moretus in Antwerp, a firm which published mainly vernacular Bibles for religious propaganda in Europe and elsewhere, for whom Rubens drew seventy frontispieces. The Netherlands also provided a natural refuge for the Jews – in Amsterdam alone there were two hundred Hebrew publishers in business at one time or another during the 17th century.

Meanwhile, a press set up in Rome in 1622 was turning out Roman Catholic propaganda in forty-four languages for missionary work all over the world. In France, apart from a good many counter-Reformation salvoes, there were very grand publications on natural history and travel appearing in typically Baroque style with long florid introductions leading up to lavish illustrations often held together by a rather flimsy text. The 17th century was also a time when people were taking stock of the vast increases in knowledge that had recently taken place and publishers were producing the first great alphabetic vernacular encyclopaedias.

There were two very important developments affecting books in the 18th century. Firstly, the great stimulus to reading provided by the appearance of large numbers of political pamphlets, many of which sold five to ten thousand copies compared with top circulations of three to four thousand in the 17th century; and secondly, the growing concept of reading for entertainment. The role of a book in medieval times was seen as essentially instructive and usually morally uplifting. This proto-Victorian attitude persisted well into the 17th century and even during the 18th, the shelf of books in countless middle-class homes would have been of a primarily religious character. During the mid-18th century in England, a spate of light novels appeared. With them appeared circulating libraries throughout the country and quite suddenly the habit of reading among women.

In the field of collecting, a group of English noblemen, Devonshire, Roxburghe, Harley, Sunderland, Blandford and Pembroke, were suddenly seized around 1700 with the desire to collect *incunabula*, books printed before 1500. They were the first of their kind in Europe and assembled in a remarkably short time very fine collections, all of which have now been dispersed. Their taste was much concerned with the physical qualities of binding and printing although a little later English collectors became more interested in early English literature, first in Caxtons and then in the productions of Shakespearian times. As the century wore on, book collecting became the favourite pastime of the less indigent scholar. It was a period of great reverence for the classics after which collectors went for the masterpieces of the early printers and next the important illustrated works of their own time.

For most of the 18th century, France dominated Europe in literature and book illustration, and the rococo style was copied extensively. Although censorship was still strictly enforced, the effect was often counter-productive. Proscribed works had the benefit of free publicity and their prices would rise sharply as soon as they were condemned. Voltaire wrote to a friend in Paris in 1786 asking him to make a special effort to get his *Processe de Babylone* condemned by the Sorbonne because, he said, it would greatly please his publisher in Geneva.

It was still a time when fine collections could be formed for very little money. Early printed books were held in such low esteem that John Ratcliffe, a chandler in Southwark, only became interested because the pages were used to wrap up his wares. He became an eager collector and owned fifty Caxtons by the time he died in 1776. Book-auctions had been going on in England since 1676 although the earliest were usually more in the nature of trade sales than the dispersals of private libraries.

The Roxburghe sale in 1812 was an important milestone. The highest price – $4500 – for Boccaccio's *Decameron* printed by Valdarfer in Venice in 1471. This volume (sold again in 1819 for $1800) exemplified the taste of a generation and thereafter interest tended to be focussed on a book's literary qualities. The sale was also the occasion of the founding of the Roxburghe Club which owners of

54

great libraries or distinguished librarians might be invited to join. The club which still exists has about forty members, each of whom is supposed to publish in turn some important bibliophilic work for the benefit of the other members.

As the 19th century progressed, collectors following the fluctuations of literary taste began to buy the Elizabethan and Jacobean dramatists. By the middle of the century, the trend had started towards the cabinet collection. This was partly because books had become so much more expensive and partly because collectors began to pride themselves on what John Carter has called '. . . a sort of microcosmic elegance, an ability to express a refined eclecticism within the confines of a single bookcase'. Towards the end of the century, the question of chronological priority became increasingly important. Author-bibliographies began to be published which introduced collectors to the notion of completeness of an author collection while the precise descriptions of the individual works intensified the demand for original condition.

During the last fifteen years of the century, the cult for modern first editions developed fast. In 1894 William Roberts wrote in the *Fortnightly Review*: 'The craze for first editions is not by any means a recent one although it may be said to have now reached its extremest form of childishness. Time was when the craze existed in perfectly rational form and when first editions in demand were

From Plante (Franciscus): *Mauritiados Libri XII*, Amsterdam, 1647. Parayba being a province of Brazil.

books of importance and books with both histories and reputations while their collectors were scholars and men of judgement. Now every little volume of drivelling verse becomes an object of more or less hazardous speculation and the book market itself a stock exchange in miniature.'

Until the late 18th century, most great English collectors had thought in terms of eventual public ownership of their books. This may have been influenced by the fact that no national library existed until the British Museum was founded in 1753. The greatest collector of *incunabula* the world has ever seen was the 2nd Earl Spencer (1758–1834) who bought whole libraries in Hungary and Italy and elsewhere and, by becoming known as the most generous buyer in Europe, was given the first offer of any important book to come on the market. His library which included nearly all the rarest *incunabula* and no less than fifty-six Caxtons, the finest Bibles, the first editions of all the great Italian authors and many Elzevirs and Aldines, passed in its entirety to the Rylands Museum, Manchester in 1892.

The greatest bibliomaniac of all time was Richard Heber (1773–1833). He began to buy at auction through his father at the age of ten, and during his life he accumulated a colossal collection of which the early English poetry and drama was his finest achievement. The library ran to between two and three hundred thousand volumes and was stored in houses in England and on the Continent. It was sold in sixteen sessions between 1834–7 but the market was flooded and the prices realised were far below those he had paid. William Henry Miller (1789–1848), who was present at these sales, saw his opportunity and bought by the cartload. Those books and the ones bought by his heirs went on to form the greatest private library ever brought together – the Britwell House Library which was eventually sold between 1916 and 1927 for a million dollars and mostly bought by Henry Huntington of California. Among the great books was a volume containing Shakespeare's *The Passionate Pilgrim* and *Venus and Adonis* bought by Huntington for $30,000. The *Venus and Adonis* had been ordered to be burnt by Bishop Bancroft in 1599 and only one other copy was known to exist. That was the one presented to Trinity College, Cambridge, in 1779 by Edward Capels who had written in it 'not quite perfect so it cost but $1\frac{1}{2}$d'.

During most of the 18th century when it was antiquaries and other scholars who were assembling their libraries, the guidance of experts had not been needed. But when at the beginning of the 19th century, book collecting became the hobby of the rich dilettante, booksellers saw their chance and exerted a powerful influence on many great collections. So there came into being a more enlightened breed of booksellers who began a tradition of expertise and integrity which, with a few exceptions, has continued up to the present day.

The greatest collector of manuscripts was Sir Thomas Phillips (1792–1872). On his tours of Europe, he would buy whole libraries at a time and by the time he died he had amassed 60,000 manuscripts and 50,000 printed books. In the

23

end, he admitted openly that he gave any price he was asked. He was, he explained, so horrified by the unceasing destruction of vellum manuscripts by gold-beaters, gluemakers and tailors that his object was not only to secure good manuscripts for himself but also to raise the public estimation of them. For, as he said, nothing tends to the preservation of anything so much as making it bear a high price. By the end of his life he had come to hate the Roman Catholic Church (perhaps for their imposing record of book-burning) and his son-in-law James Orchard Halliwell with equal passion. In a venomous will, he stipulated that neither his daughter, nor Halliwell nor any Roman Catholic 'shall ever be admitted to the inspection of my library of books and manuscripts'. As it turned out, eighteen sales of his collection took place between 1886 and 1928 and a second series beginning in the sixties recently completed the dispersal.

In 1884 the Grolier Club was founded in the U.S.A. dedicated to the encouragement of book-production and to the preservation and appreciation of

From Scheuchzer (Johann Jacob): ΟΥΡΕΣΙΦΟΙΤΗΣ *Helveticus, sive Itinera per Helvetiae Alpinas Regiones Facta.* Leyden, P. Vander Aa, 1723.

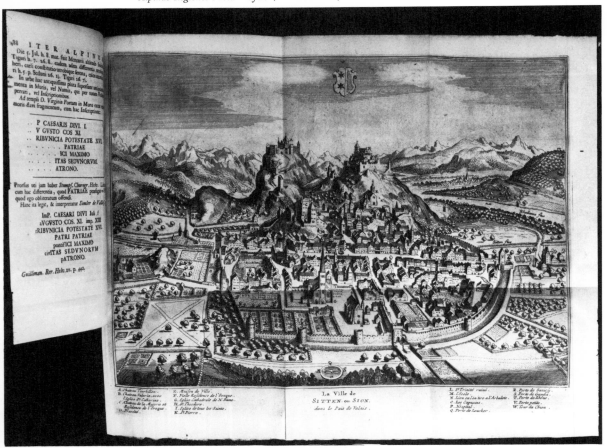

24

old books. The date roughly marks the entry by the Americans into the world of book collecting. It is a field that has been more or less dominated by Americans ever since. There is no doubt that the great resources and appetites of American collectors and institutions has resulted in a one-way flow of fine books almost ever since. During the twenties, there was another bout of wild speculation in England and America started by a group of New York dealers. Much deplored by the more conservative dealers, it was brought to an end with the Depression and the book market remained flat until well after the war.

Of the great American collectors, the most formidable were Huntington and Morgan. Henry E. Huntington (1850–1927) gave up his business interests when he was fifty-seven and devoted the last twenty years of his life to his library. In that space of time he built a most spectacular collection. He bought the entire libraries of many European noblemen, large parts of the H. W. Poor and Robert Hoe collections, twenty-five Caxtons from the Duke of Devonshire, the Bridgewater House Library of great Elizabethan books and large quantities of Americana. In this great buying programme he was helped by George D. Smith and A. S. W. Rosenbach, two of the most aggressive booksellers of all time. The 300,000 rare books that now form the Huntington Library in California are permanently available to scholars. For Pierpont Morgan (1837–1913), books were just one branch of a massive art-acquisition programme. He set out to buy autograph manuscripts of great authors, the finest manuscripts and the most important *incunabula* and the fruit of his collecting is housed in a remarkable building in New York whose interior is designed to resemble that of a Renaissance palace.

Forgeries

The forgery of books presents fiendish problems. To imitate every detail of an existing book so convincingly that even laboratory tests would not reveal minute differences in the composition of the paper, ink, binding etc. was a labour of the greatest complexity. For this reason, most of the forging activities of the book trade have been confined to doctoring books in poor condition, adding missing leaves and so on.

Thomas J. Wise (1859–1937) was revered for most of his life as the greatest bibliographer of his time. Created honorary M.A. Oxford, honorary fellow of Worcester College, Oxford, President of the Bibliographical Society, member of the Roxburghe Club, he was the first to apply lateral thinking to the problem of forgery. He had assembled a fine collection of early editions of the Romantic Poets and was watching their values climb in the last decade of the last century with growing satisfaction. It dawned on him that one way to avoid a comparison between a genuine first edition and a forgery of that edition was to print a whole new edition that predated the one hitherto regarded as the first. It was not at all unusual for a struggling poet to have a very small edition of his work printed for private circulation to close friends. If the poet subsequently became famous, these very earliest editions were always the hardest to trace if they had not been lost altogether.

Wise saw his opening and in all had fifty entirely spurious editions printed. In the stories he concocted to explain his discovery of these long-lost treasures he allowed his imagination full rein although it was notable with hindsight that the people from whom he claimed to have bought these precious editions had almost invariably died just after the sale. It was also strange that none of the 'first' editions contained any dedication or message in the handwriting of the poet which might have been expected if many of them had been given as presents to friends. Wise not only made a lot of money from his enterprise but received much credit for his generous presentations of rare books to the British Museum. It was only three years before he died that two ingenious booksellers, John Carter and Graham Pollard, published *An Enquiry into the Nature of Certain Nineteenth Century Pamphlets* in which they proved beyond all reasonable doubt by dating the paper from its chemical composition and identifying the printers by some unique peculiarities of type that the 'first' editions were forgeries. Wise was by this time conveniently under doctor's orders not to engage in controversy and he died before the actual documentary evidence of his forgeries had been discovered.

The standard of scholarship is much higher today, but so too is the standard of the 'doctored' or 'sophisticated' books. Although experienced collectors cannot easily be taken in by the forger, there are real dangers for the novice. Certainly almost all the 19th century and pre-war 'improvements' look remarkably clumsy today. Almost every field of interest is now covered by a specialist bibliography giving full details of the internal and external make-up of any edition, so that almost any volume can now be collated – that is the right number of its leaves, illustrations and other points verified.

The motives of collectors

A book may appeal to a collector for one or more reasons at the same time. A collector of books whose outstanding features are fine binding or illustration or printing is obviously concerned with their physical appeal. A collector who spots a good copy of a first edition of Emily Brontë's *Wuthering Heights* in a junk shop and having bought it for a dime takes it at once to a saleroom knowing that he may get several hundred dollars for it is interested in the book's financial appeal. More difficult to explain is the collector who buys the first edition of *Wuthering Heights*, the appearance of which is to say the least uninteresting, for several hundred dollars when the text may be bought for a dollar or so in paperback.

This sort of appeal may as well be called numinous – it is certainly irrational, arcane and mysterious. Ever since men could read and write, literacy has been closely associated with power and established religion. From the time of Aristotle to the Age of Reason, almost every library in Europe was built on holy ground. Human beings naturally tend to worship the source of power as seen for example in the Roman practice of deifying their Emperors some of whose qualifications for such an honour might otherwise be considered rather slender. Literacy to most literate people nowadays is altogether unremarkable and it is largely forgotten that the ability to communicate by making marks on a piece of paper still seems in a primitive society like pure magic.

There remains a deeply implanted respect if not awe for the printed word and the desire to own books may be, at least in part, a manifestation of a desire to own the instruments of power. For many people, one particular book may have provided a momentous experience and the collecting of books may be an unconscious attempt to recreate that experience. For others, the observation that some highly intelligent people have read a great many books may even lead them to believe that the accumulation of books will actually confer on them a high degree of intelligence. Others may recognise that their minds have been shaped to some extent by the books they have read and their book collecting may be an attempt to possess the forces that created them and by extension an attempt to possess or control themselves.

The burning desire to own autograph manuscripts or first editions may also be an attempt to sense an affinity with the author at the moment of the book's creation and so a wish by the owner to be associated with the creative force that brought the book into existence. The current obsession with original condition is based on this wish. Most book collectors prefer to think of themselves as the most normal of people and of course it would indeed be abnormal if a man invariably threw books away once he had read them. Yet there is a point at which book collecting takes on an obsessive quality which amounts to a neurosis.

For this reason book collectors on the whole have a peculiar public image. They are variously thought of as venerable, eccentric, cliquish, doddery, rapacious, boring, fastidious and even miserly. They have often been ridiculed as for example by Jules Renard who saw them as 'these men who know that one must turn the pages of a beautiful book by the top and who always have both hands ready in case you should drop the book they are presenting for your admiration'. The advice given by Seymour de Ricci, the great chronicler of English book collecting, on how collectors should behave at auctions is particularly revealing. '. . . the most sacred duty of every collector is to overpay . . . Every great collection in the world has been made by men who had foresight enough to secure for themselves, to snatch away from others, objects that they understood to be really significant and desirable.' This emphasis on denying possession to others, although perhaps necessary in the sense de Ricci suggests, has a rather desperate ring to it. As for overpaying, this with hindsight happened all too frequently in the 19th century, many libraries being sold for only half what their owners had paid for them.

Frederick Locker, the poet who first conceived the idea of the cabinet collection, complained to Bedford his bookbinder that a book he had bound did not shut properly at which Bedford exclaimed, 'Why, bless me sir, you have been reading it.' This accusation that book collectors do not read the books they buy is certainly justified in most cases. They may well have read the books they buy in another edition where spilt drinks and fatty biscuit crumbs would not do serious damage to its value but Bedford certainly put his finger on a sensitive issue.

Value in books is closely related to rarity and needs to be considered carefully. There are several kinds of rarity to examine. Firstly, deliberate rarity where a publisher advertises that a limited edition is to appear. This has to be treated cautiously on the basis that a publisher will not ordinarily appeal to a small readership if he can be confident of a larger one. Publishers can create rarity but they cannot do much to create interest in a book where very little exists – that is, they have no control over demand. Rarity has a fairly clear meaning – it means there are not many about. But how many are about? If the answer is six and, of those, five are in national museums then the book may be said to be very rare indeed. If the book in question were Swinburne's *Siena* of 1868, then it would be in very great demand. But rarity has no value in itself. If the North Thames Gas Board had published on vellum and in an edition of six its 'Standing Instructions for Meter-readers' the publication would of course produce not a flicker of interest.

A book's rarity therefore must be related not only to the number of copies originally printed or the number believed to have survived but also to the literary quality of the text. Another special feature that can raise the status of a particular book is its associative interest; that is where either the book is inscribed in the hand of the author with some personal message or when a book has passed through the hands of a number of famous collectors and acquires a kind of pedigree. It is well known and considered interesting for example that the only complete copy of Malory's *Morte d'Arthur* printed by Caxton in 1485 was owned by Dr. Bernard in 1698, Thomas Rawlinson, the Earl of Oxford, Thomas Osborne, Bryan Fairfax, the Earl of Jersey, Mrs Abby Pope and Robert Hoe, before ending in the Pierpont Morgan Library.

Rarity can also be temporary and if a book not seen in the auction-rooms for twenty years makes a spectacular price, this may well bring on to the market a few more copies which can depress the price as well as adding to the stock of known survivors. Rarity can also be localised in the sense that a first edition of Molière's *Tartuffe* might be harder to get hold of in London than Paris although the arbitrage activities of booksellers have gone a long way to eliminate the differences in price that used to exist between different centres.

Market trends

The constant activity of dealers buying for American institutions over a long period has masked a general fall-off in the U.K. of purchases by private collectors. It is not only that books in the highest price range are now beyond the reach of most U.K. collectors, it is rather that young people are not turning to book collecting as fast as the old collectors die off. Poor economic performance and high taxation in the U.K. have taken a heavy toll on the buying-power of collectors and as a result on the numbers of important books leaving the country. There are still plenty of collectors buying books up to $500 but there has been a considerable drop in the number that could once have spent $2000 or more on a book and now only a very small handful who will spend over $10,000.

Those few that can, tend to go for 'safe' established material – Colour Plate and Natural History Books such as Gould's *The Birds of Europe* or Audubon's *Birds of America*. These sold for $360 and $400 respectively in 1950, fetched $20,000 and $5,000 in 1974 but dropped to $10–14,000 and $3,000 in 1976. At one time, this field was regarded as the most dependable of investments but since the setback in 1976, must be treated more cautiously. In the same field, some books of lesser standing have fared better – for example Gerning's *A Picturesque Tour along the Rhine* which was selling at $30–40 in 1950, fetched $2,800 in 1977.

Ceratophrys dorsata. Fem

From Maximilian zu Wied-Neuwied (Prince): *Abbildungen zur Naturgeschichte Brasiliens.* Weimar, 1822–31.

It is often difficult to identify quite why a book rises or falls sharply in value. A plausible explanation of the case of the Gerning might be that it is a fairly rare and beautiful book that had been undervalued in relation to others in the topography department. On the other hand, it might not be a re-rating but rather the fact that German libraries have, particularly over the last ten years, been paying higher and higher prices for Germanica as they try to replace the catastrophic loss of books through bombing and looting during the last world war.

Another powerful influence in the book market was Japan until its recession in 1973/4. The Japanese dealers were highly selective but ruthless bidders going for Graphics, Maps and Atlases, Science and Medicine and William Faulkner. Faulkner spent some time in Japan and there are several Japanese Faulkner scholars who, for a time, set new records for his first editions.

Interest in a book will usually be greatest in the country in whose language it was published, although in America the competition of certain ethnic groups for their own material will establish world market prices. For instance, there is considerable demand for the little Armenian material available. With their background of persecution, there are a few rich Armenians who are trying to gather together the remnants of their culture and are prepared to pay increasingly high prices to do so. Similarly, the demand for Hebraica – books written in Hebrew – and Judaica – books on the subject of the Jewish people – is very strong in New York. On the other hand, interest in Black history is very limited throughout America with slave narratives etc. having little appeal to the tiny literate and wealthy black minority. And curiously enough, Arab oil money has so far had little impact on the prices realised for Arabica sold in Europe or America.

Book prices fluctuate according to literary taste and the fortunes of a nation's economy. Dealers are by no means agreed on what is going on in the book world and often hold conflicting views. The hammer-prices of particular books can be a long way from the true market-prices because dealers often decide to support their own market to protect the 'value' of their existing stock. For instance, if a leading dealer already has two copies of Newton's *Optics* on his shelves priced at $8,000, he can scarcely afford to allow another copy to be seen to be sold at auction for $4,000, for what chance would he then have of disposing of the two in his stock. Equally, hammer-prices will not reflect the true market value of lots during the bidding for which the ring has operated successfully. Nor will dealers' catalogue prices be a sound guide since the presence of the book in the list obviously indicates that the book remains unsold and the price is the one the dealer hopes to get. It may well sell the next day but all dealers know that books can take a very long time to sell – Quaritch of London, for example, is not alone in having books in stock bought during the last century.

The influence of American buying was paramount until 1972 in almost every department of the rare book market. American university librarians were

From Smith (Captain John):
The Generall Historie of Virginia, New England and the Summer Isles, with the Names of the Adventurers, Planters and Governors etc.
London, 1632.

receiving large appropriations and were using them to buy any material that offered an advantage in research or teaching to the staff or students. Librarians tended to buy in the same way as other collectors, that is they preferred to buy a first edition with a dedication even though that might not be strictly necessary. The sectors particularly affected by American institutional buying were

Modern Literature, English Books of the 17th–19th centuries, Science and Medicine, and Americana.

In the Science and Medicine sector, sometimes referred to as the History of Ideas, it is noticeable that, whereas in literature the works of second league writers are valued in an understandable relationship to first league writers, second league contributions to science are accorded a very low value compared to the milestones marking the great advances in human knowledge. People have no interest at all for instance in what some obscure scholar might have written about the Origin of the Species or the Interpretation of Dreams; it has to be Darwin or Freud and no one else. It is a field where the great names – Euclid, Ptolemy, Copernicus, Galileo, Newton, Einstein etc. – will always fetch great prices. Demand for this sector has grown particularly fast in the last fifteen years, notably in the U.S. and the U.K., but in Japan too where there has been a special interest in Economics and Music. Since the U.S. recession which resulted in allocations to some university libraries being cut to nil and had a serious effect on private collectors too, the running has been taken up in Germany and to a lesser extent France. Values of many 17th-century English books of secondary importance have actually dropped during the last five years as have some of the great 16th- and 17th-century Bibles, some by as much as half over the same period.

Modern first editions in general also suffered in the recession. This was always a risky sector for the investor because the literary world operates like a team of coroners performing endless autopsies on the work of dead authors (as well as some preliminary vivisections), pausing from time to time to announce a revised verdict. The revised verdicts mean changes in status, popularity and so in value. But it is also a more exciting field in which the buyer can back his own judgement, although first edition runs of established and even many unestablished writers are now so long that any real scarcity must lie a long way in the future.

The last thirty years have shown a steady growth in the values of Thomas Hardy, T. S. Eliot, Ezra Pound, James Joyce and Yeats, Hemingway and Faulkner. A disappointing showing has been made by Bernard Shaw, partly because he wrote so much, partly because the first editions of his works were themselves so large and partly because the autograph manuscripts and letters of a vast correspondence help to sate the appetites of Shaw specialists. Galsworthy and Kipling have been disappointing since 1950, not surprisingly since their work enjoyed an enormous vogue in the 1930s which has not been equalled since. The literary coroners have been able to announce more favourable findings in the cases of E. M. Forster, Conrad and George Eliot, whose works have increased in value strongly during the last ten years. D. H. Lawrence and T. E. Lawrence have both in their different ways been cult figures. There was a surge of interest in D. H. Lawrence's work following the *Lady Chatterley's Lover* trial in 1959 but has since shown a below-average rate of growth. T. E.

ANAS SUPERCILIOSA.
BLACK DUCK.

Lawrence values seem to fluctuate with the historical status of his *Seven Pillars of Wisdom*. As researchers come close to proving that large sections of his magnum opus were hallucinated, Lawrence naturally loses status and his cult following tends to thin out.

Each writer and even each book he has written has a price-history for which detailed, although often conflicting, explanations may be offered. But whatever justification there may be for a writer's rating in the literary world, the concern collectors now show for the condition of books has become obsessive and is tending to become ever more so. The Stockhausen collection sold in the U.S. in 1975 was famous for the immaculate condition of its books and some of the prices realised were four times higher than the next best price for the same volume ever recorded. In another U.S. sale in 1977, a copy of the *Wind in the Willows* was auctioned with its dust-jacket in perfect condition for seven times the price realised for a comparable copy without the dust-jacket. In

33

this case it was not the general condition of the book but the humble dust-jacket that accounted for the difference in price and the absurd situation was reached where the book was in theory valued by the market at around $500 and the dust-jacket at $3000.

Private Press books are a special branch of publishing in which the greatest effort and expense is concentrated on the appearance of the book involving the highest printing skills, hand-made paper, special type, binding and so on. The famous U.K. publishing names in this field – the Kelmscott, Ashendene, Doves, Golden Cockerel and Nonesuch Presses – have produced editions which will always rank amongst the finest accomplishments in printing. The Kelmscott Chaucer used to be regarded in the early part of the century as the barometer of prices for the whole book market.

The growth in value of Private Press Books as a whole has certainly been steady although less dramatic than other sectors of the book market. They may now be rated a dependable but less promising sector than before since many younger collectors regard them as rather corny and because several editions, such as the Nonesuch Dickens, have been textually superseded. Many American Press Books that appeared after 1900 published by Grabhorn, Gehenna and Limited Editions Presses have not yet by comparison with English Press Books made market-prices that their quality and textual interest would seem to warrant.

Children's books and juvenilia have become an important sector where original condition is naturally even harder to come by. First editions of children's classics such as *Winnie the Pooh, Babar, The Flopsy Bunnies, Tom Sawyer* and hundreds more have for long been growing in value, but during the last five years other children's publications such as comics and 'Penny Dreadfuls' have risen sharply in value. This is a typical reaction where collectors and investors feel they have missed the big rise in the mainstream of a market, in this case children's books, and begin feverishly buying up peripheral material that has been 'left behind'. But this can be a dangerous activity for the peripheral material has often been ignored by serious collectors for good reasons as in this case where there is very little of textual or typographical or any other interest to justify a high price. In 1975, a first copy of *Superman* comic sold for $8000 and many dealers forecast, and have so far been right, that it would never fetch such a price again.

Children's books is certainly a field where investors can back their own judgement. It would have been quite difficult to be unaware over the last fifteen years of the cult growing around the work of J. R. R. Tolkien. That accumulating interest resulted in the sale of a first edition of *The Hobbit* in 1977 for $1000. Anyone wishing to take a position in this market has only to establish which children's books out of the annual avalanche have been regularly reprinting over the last ten or twenty years; in other words, those that may be on their way to becoming classics, and begin searching for the first editions.

The field of early printed books of the 16th and 17th centuries still holds a lot of interest and potential. It is scarcely believable that only twenty years ago many of these books, particularly those published in Latin, were actually being dumped. Ten years ago they were fetching a dollar apiece and now can still be bought for between $20 and $40 depending upon the language, subject, condition etc. Although they remain generally inexpensive throughout Europe and America, they vary in price, ignoring other criteria, according to the language they are printed in. They are most expensive in German, next most in English, a long way cheaper in French, Italian and Spanish and cheapest of all in Latin. These differentials merely reflect the degree of interest shown in them in different countries. A beautifully printed 16th-century folio of English sermons in superb condition may still be bought in a New York saleroom for as little as $50. In no other field does a 400-year-old object of unquestioned beauty command so little interest.

Important changes in the book trade have taken place over the last thirty years. Although the catalogues of one or two dealers have ever since the last

From Newcastle (William Cavendish, duke of): *Méthode et Invention Nouvelle de Dresser les Chevaux.* J. van Meurs, Antwerp, 1657.

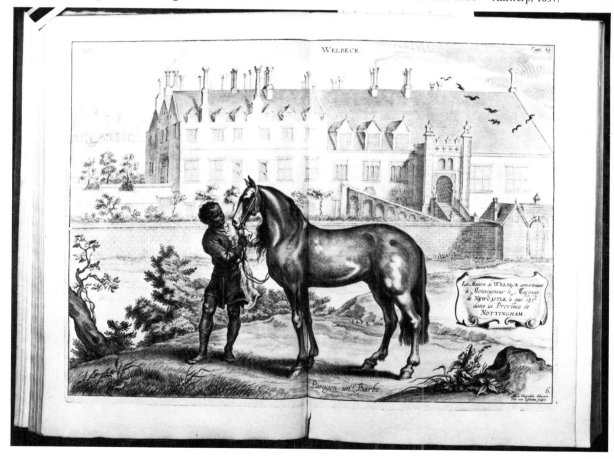

century – particularly those of Quaritch – been impressive bibliographical achievements, the advances in the general standard can be seen by comparing the pre-war lists of a second-league bookseller with those he produces today.

Another change for the better is the manner in which auctions are conducted. Until around 1960 book-sales in London were a straightforward carve-up between a handful of dealers. Now the presence of so many international dealers, the increase in the number of postal bids and the refusal of several leading dealers to take part in any bidding agreement have enabled much more realistic prices to be achieved in the auction-rooms. The ring certainly operates at every London auction if it can (usually affecting 15–20% of the lots in a typical sale) but its members are said to be old and tired; young bookdealers are showing no interest in joining and don't trust the book-keeping. Occasionally the ring pulls off a major coup but, for the most part, the prices reached at the settlement, that is the second auction that takes place among the ring-members, are in the $200 area for a book that may have sold for $150. Not big money in the book world and so fewer and fewer dealers can be bothered with the hassle.

Private collectors nevertheless do not participate in the auctions to any great extent, usually preferring dealers to buy for them on commission. These commissions range between 5 and 10% depending on the price of the lot and how often the dealer has performed this service for a client. In America, auctions are mercifully free from the activities of the ring although even there it is customary for collectors to commission a dealer to buy for them at auction. The antiquarian book trade in America is generally very buoyant. Attendances at the New York Book Fair more than doubled in three years. Membership of the American Antiquarian Book-dealers' Association has grown strongly with many younger dealers building reputations in highly specialised fields and some, with heavy financial backing, beginning to establish new price-levels for certain modern first editions.

Dealers' mark-ups work on a sliding scale and are determined by their overheads, by how cheaply or expensively they believe they have bought the book, by how quickly the book is sold and by the absolute cost. On a book priced under $20, the mark-up will be in the 100–300% range, between $20–100 around 100%, between $100–200 about 50–100% and so on until on a book bought for $2000 the mark-up might be only 10–30% and at the lower end if it were sold quickly.

For nearly a century, dealers have been complaining that the best quality material is becoming harder and harder to get. Although this is true to the extent that very many important books disappear every year into libraries and museums from which they are never likely to reappear (although some American museums have taken recently to de-accessioning duplicate or unsuitable material), the complaint is also a natural salesman's gambit to get people running in to buy. Book-collectors sometimes sell their collections during their life-time but more often their heirs, unless they are collectors

SCENOGRAPHIA FABRICÆ ✝ S. LAVRENTII IN ESCVRIALI

From Blaeu (Jan): *Atlas Maior, sive Cosmographia Blaviana*. Amsterdam, J. Blaeu, 1662–5.

themselves, find books easier to part with in settlement of taxes than any other portion of the estate. So the cycle of dispersing and collecting begins all over again.

Edmond de Goncourt, the great French collector, specifically directed that his library should be sold at an auction after his death in order to renew for his fellow collectors the pleasure he had received in assembling it.

Book list

CARTER, JOHN. *ABC for Book Collectors* rev. ed. (Illus.) 1963, Knopf

MUNBY, A. N., compiled by. *British Book Sales Catalogues 1676–1800: A Union List* 1977 (pub. by Mansell, England), Merrimack Book Service

QUAYLE, ERIC. *Old Cook Books: An Illustrated History* 1978, Dutton

RAY, G. *The Illustrator and The Book in England 1790–1914* 1976, Oxford University Press

THOMAS, ALAN G. *Great Books and Book Collectors* (Illus.) 1975, Putnam

VERVLIET, HENDRIK D., ed. *Annual Bibliography of the History of the Printed Book and Libraries* 1978 (pub. by Martinus Nijhoff Publishers), Kluwer, Boston

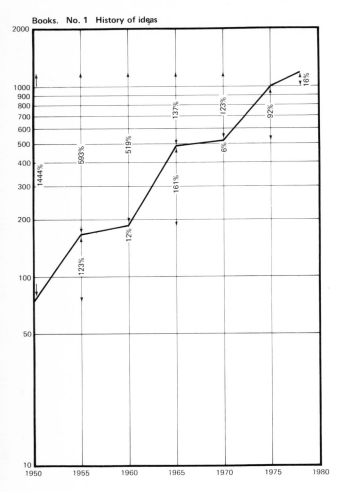

Books. No. 1 History of ideas

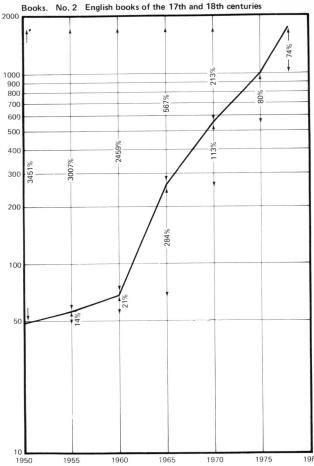

Books. No. 2 English books of the 17th and 18th centuries

INDEX NO. 1 HISTORY OF IDEAS.

1. Galileo Galilei. Dialogo . . . sopra i Due Massimi Sistemi del Mondo Tolomaico e Copernicano. Florence. 1632.
2. William Harvey. Exercitationes Anatomicae de Motu Cordis et Sanguinis Circulatione. 1653.
3. Sir Isaac Newton. Philosophiae Naturalis Principia Mathematica. 1687.
4. Charles Darwin. On the Origin of the Species. London. 1859.
5. Albert Einstein. Die Grundlege der Allgemeinen Relativitätstheorie. Leipzig. 1916.

INDEX NO. 2. ENGLISH BOOKS OF THE 17/18TH CENTURIES.

1. John Donne. Biathanatos: A Declaration that Self-Homicide is not so Naturally Sinne. London. 1647.
2. John Locke. An Essay concerning Humane Understanding. London. 1690.
3. Adam Smith. Inquiry into the Nature and Causes of the Wealth of Nations. 2 vols. 1776.
4. James Boswell. Life of Samuel Johnson. 2 vols. 1791.

38

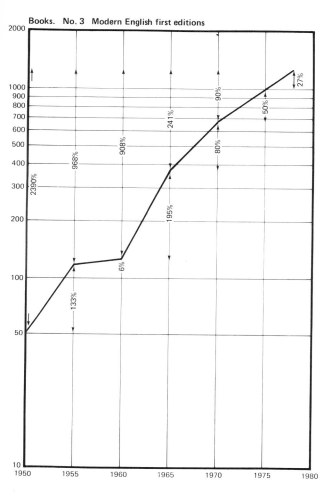

Books. No. 3 Modern English first editions

INDEX NO. 3. MODERN ENGLISH FIRST EDITIONS.

1. Aldous Huxley. Brave New World. London. 1932.
2. Joseph Conrad. The Secret Agent. London. 1923.
3. W. B. Yeats. The Celtic Twilight. London 1893.
4. T. S. Eliot. Prufrock and Other Observations. London. 1917.
5. James Joyce. Ulysses. Paris. 1922.

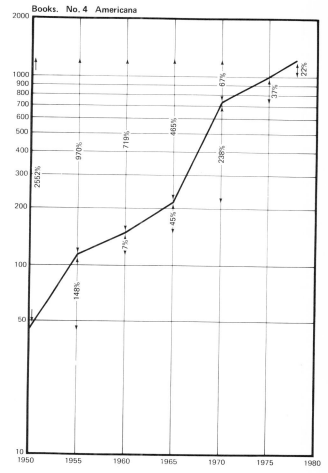

Books. No. 4 Americana

INDEX NO. 4. Americana.

1. Captain John Smith. The Generalle Historie of Virginia, New England and the Summer Isles. 1624.
2. Captain John Knox. An Historical Journal of the Campaigns in North America. 2 vols. 1769.
3. Thomas L. McKenney and James Hall. History of the Indian Tribes of North America. 3 vols. 1836–44.
4. Alexander MacKenzie. Voyages from Montreal on the River St Laurence through the Continent of North America. 1801.
5. George Catlin. Letters and Notes on the Manners, Customs and Condition of the North American Indians. 2 vols. 1841.

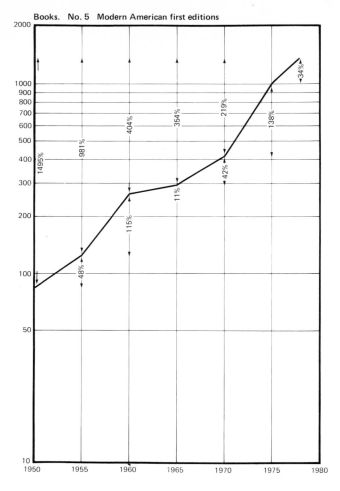

Books. No. 5 Modern American first editions

INDEX NO. 5. MODERN AMERICAN FIRST EDITIONS.

1. Sherwood Anderson. Winesburg, Ohio. 1919.
2. Sinclair Lewis. Main Street. 1920.
3. William Faulkner. The Sound and the Fury. 1929.
4. Ernest Hemingway. A Farewell to Arms. 1929.
5. John Steinbeck. The Grapes of Wrath. 1939.

Chinese Ceramics

Chinese dynasties and periods

NEOLITHIC		*c.* 7000–1600 B.C.	
SHANG		1600–1027 B.C.	
CHOU		1027–221 B.C.	
Western Chou 1027–771 B.C.			
Eastern Chou 770–221 B.C.			
CH'IN		221–207 B.C.	
HAN		206 B.C.–A.D. 220	
SIX DYNASTIES		A.D. 220–589	
Three Kingdoms A.D. 220–265			
Western Chin A.D. 265–316			
Eastern Chin A.D. 317–420			
Northern & Southern A.D. 420–581			
SUI		A.D. 581–618	
T'ANG		A.D. 618–906	
FIVE DYNASTIES		A.D. 907–960	
SUNG		A.D. 960–1279	
LIAO		A.D. 916–1125	
CHIN		A.D. 1115–1234	
YÜAN (Mongol)		A.D. 1279–1368	
MING		A.D. 1368–1644	
Hung-wu	1368–1398	Hung-chih	1488–1505
Chien wên	1399–1402	Chêng-tê	1506–1521
Yung-lo	1402–1424	Chia-ching	1522–1566
Hsûan-tê	1426–1435	Lung-ch'ing	1567–1572
Chêng-t'ung	1436–1449	Wan-li	1573–1619
Ching-t'ai	1450–1457	T'ai-ch'ang	1620
T'ien-shun	1457–1464	T'ien-ch'i	1621–1627
Ch'êng-hua	1465–1487	Ch'ung-chêng	1628–1644
CH'ING (Manchu)		A.D. 1644–1912	
Shun-chih	1644–1661	Tao-kuang	1822–1851
K'ang-hsi	1662–1722	Hsien-fêng	1851–1862
Yung-chêng	1723–1735	T'ung-chih	1862–1875
Ch'ien-lung	1736–1795	Kuang-hsü	1875–1908
Chia-ch'ing	1796–1821	Hsüan-t'ung	1908–1912

The first Chinese porcelain to be exported can be dated from finds at Samarra in Mesopotamia to the 9th century A.D. but it was during the Yüan (Mongol) dynasty in the 14th century A.D. that the trade is known to have extended to East Africa, the Middle East and India. Thereafter, the establishment by the Portuguese in the mid-16th century of their trading centre at Macao gave Europeans their first glimpse of the objects first referred to as Chinaware and soon to be known simply as china.

By the beginning of the 17th century the English, Dutch and French East India Companies had become involved in the trade which continued to flourish throughout the 18th century and only began to decline, due to a deterioration in quality, towards the middle of the 19th. The Chinese exports to Europe had throughout this period been geared to the tastes and customs of the importing countries and so it was that very little was known until towards the end of the 19th century of what might be called native Chinese classical wares.

A side-effect of the construction of the Chinese railways in the 1880s and 1890s had been the excavation and appearance on the market of quantities of these early classical wares. The condition of the Celestial Empire after the war with Japan of 1894–5 was of such chronic weakness as to provoke another indecorous scramble by the Great Powers for 'spheres of influence' in China, and resulted in the occupation by Europeans of the key ports along her seaboard.

The social upheavals which preceded and followed the collapse of the Manchu dynasty in the Revolution of 1912, brought about the dispersal by one means or another of many private Chinese collections and it was no doubt in these circumstances that a great deal of early Chinese ceramics passed for the first time into foreign hands. The finest of these early pieces came to be more highly regarded by many Western collectors than much of the later Ming and Ch'ing export wares with which they were already quite familiar.

The whole field of Chinese ceramics only began to be systematically researched even by the Chinese themselves in the present century. Much work remains to be done, yet it is apparent that as new documentary and archaeological evidence enables experts to ascribe dates and provenances to different pieces with greater assurance, so the circle of collectors and investors steadily widens.

To understand the appeal of Chinese ceramics it is essential to have some knowledge of the evolution of the materials, techniques and processes available to the Chinese potter, and if an understanding of the Chinese mentality itself proves too elusive, it will be valuable to have at least some acquaintance with the religious and philosophical ideas which influenced his life and work.

Neolithic period c. 7000–1600 B.C.

Large areas of the earth's surface are covered with clay. The discovery that clay

Vase, reddish-buff earthenware painted in purplish-red and black. Yang-shao type, 4th–3rd millennium B.C.

when heated to around 1112°F becomes hard seems to have been made independently by people all over the world at different times. In China, jars dating from the Yang-shao culture, which covers the period 4200–3500 B.C., have been excavated. At these early dates, the clay was usually worked into the shape of a pot by coiling a long roll of clay round and round on itself. Then, by holding a pad inside as a cushion and beating the outside with a kind of bat, the inner and outer surfaces were made smooth. The finished object was then baked over an open wood fire.

When a kiln is open to the air, the wares are said to be fired in an oxidising atmosphere, which means that the oxygen combines with the iron in the clay to form ferric oxide, which gives earthenware fired in this way its characteristic red colour. When objects are fired in an enclosed and, therefore, smoke-filled kiln, it is called firing in a reducing atmosphere or reduction firing. In this case, a weaker metallic oxide, ferrous oxide, is formed which turns the baked clay

43

grey or, when very little iron is present, almost white. Very early pots and jars were sometimes decorated with a point or comb while the clay was still soft and then painted white, red or brown, these colours being obtained by grinding chromate of iron, manganese dioxide and other natural minerals.

In the last thirty years, archaeological discoveries suggest that the Yang-shao may have been but one of a number of neolithic cultures in China not only related to each other but to other neolithic cultures as far apart as the Middle East, Ukraine and Thailand. They probably ran from around 4200 B.C. down to the beginning of the Shang dynasty, and therefore embracing the legendary Hsia dynasty *c.* 2200–1600 B.C. and the even earlier age of semi-divine hero-rulers who were believed to have provided the Chinese people with their language, customs, calendar and much else that constituted their first civilisation.

Shang dynasty 1600–1027 B.C.

During this period, the potter's wheel came into general use throughout China. A wide range of cooking pots, funerary and ritual wares were being produced, some quite elaborately decorated. The shapes of the grey pottery seem to be trying to imitate the sharp outline of the bronze vessels whose manufacture the Chinese had just mastered.

Shang potters were the first to be able to make stoneware. This became possible because improvements in kiln design had enabled a temperature of 1832°F to be reached. At about this point the silica present in clay, or the sand that may have been deliberately added to it, becomes vitrified giving the object a hard, dense, glass-like consistency. Another important technical advance made, albeit accidentally by the Shang potters, was the discovery of glazing. They had noticed that if any ash from the fire gathered on the body of the object being fired, a shiny coating was left where the ash had been. They then no doubt experimented and found that lime and potash acted as a flux or fusing agent creating a smooth glaze on the surface of the fired clay. Although other methods had been used to enable porous earthenware to hold liquid, this was and remains even now the most effective.

Chou dynasty 1027–221 B.C.

Many people tend to suppose that any object of aesthetic value in good condition and being two or three thousand years old must be very rare and expensive. Nothing could be less true of the funerary wares of the Chou period.

The Chinese burial custom from the earliest times had been to inter with every corpse whatever it might be expected to need in the after-life. Even the lowliest were supplied with dishes of food and jars of wine. The higher the status of the dead man, the more elaborate the equipment. An important official might be expected to need, as well as food and drink, horses, chariots, weapons, servants, musicians and so forth. The practice of burying pottery models of servants and household goods developed from the earlier practice of sacrificing the actual servants and burying them along with the actual household goods. This was, of course, most repugnant to Confucius (551–479 B.C.) and his followers, and it may be partly due to their teachings that human sacrifice appears to have ceased in his life-time. During the Sung dynasty, wooden effigies were often used but these have not survived, while even now the same basic ritual can be observed at Chinese funerals in the burning of paper images.

Fine pottery of the Chou period can be found in public and private collections all over the world, yet since 1965 over 100,000 objects of the pre-Han era have been excavated in Honan Province alone. Although they cannot by law leave the People's Republic of China, and are therefore not likely to disturb the supply pattern in the markets of West, it is nevertheless a significant enough factor to deter many collectors.

The major technical advance under the Chou was the use of feldspar as a glaze. This material, which is a form of decomposed granite, when applied to the clay body and fired in an oxidising atmosphere, turned a rich golden colour, and in a reducing atmosphere turned green. Some pottery of these periods is exquisitely decorated with real or mythological animals, leaves, birds' heads and geometric patterns. Yet most is simple and unpretentious exerting the same powerful, earthy appeal that is common to so much primitive art. Because it lacks the refinement of form and colour which distinguishes so much later Chinese pottery, it remains for most people of greater archaeological than aesthetic interest.

Ch'in 221–207 B.C. and Western Han 206 B.C.–A.D. 12

The most familiar ware of these periods is of a clear light silvery-grey colour showing a well-controlled firing atmosphere, while a few pieces are of a deep blue or almost black colour. Some of these curious effects are thought to have been achieved by introducing particular kinds of smoke into the kiln during the firing. Lead-glazing was introduced to China at this time, possibly from Egypt or Syria. The glaze was made from a mixture of lead-ore, silica and limestone, and offered the advantage that it could be fired at the relatively low temperature of 1112°F.

The range of mortuary wares widened considerably to include shapes that are basically unceramic in character such as boats, houses, pigsties, machines, wells, etc. The glazes on these objects have often acquired, as a result of their

Water-pot in the form of a
lion, in porcellaneous
stoneware. Ch'in dynasty.

Hill-incense jar,
earthenware with green
glaze. Han dynasty, 20
B.C.–A.D. 220

long burial, a silvery-grey or golden iridescence which is highly prized by collectors.

One Taoist theme which recurs frequently in Han pottery is the so-called hill-jar, the lid of which symbolises the magic mountains of the Chinese immortals, to which one emperor sent expeditions in search of the elixir of immortality. These and other wares decorated with animals and personages of Taoist mythology are particularly bizarre. Many of the tombs of this period have yielded great treasures, and there are certainly more to be unearthed. In 1965 a single tomb at Hsien-Yang was found to contain a collection of three thousand statuettes of horsemen, musicians and dancers.

The tomb of Shih-Huang-Ti, the first Emperor of Ch'in, which he had built by seven hundred thousand workmen during his own lifetime is only now being properly excavated. It still stands 90 yards high and 525 yards in diameter. In spite of a system of bows and arrows that were supposed to fire automatically on intruders, the tomb was rifled six years after Shih-Huang-Ti's death. No one knows the extent to which it was then pillaged but recent excavations have yielded many hundreds of life-size ponies and human figures which are the finest of the whole period.

Eastern Han A.D. 25–220; Six Dynasties Period A.D. 220–589; Sui A.D. 589–618

These were periods of almost incessant dynastic warfare in China during which tens of millions of people were killed. Perhaps, not surprisingly, as a reaction against this, it was also the period which saw the introduction from India, and widespread adoption by the Chinese, of the Ch'an sect of Buddhism (Indian dhyana, Japanese Zen).

Not a great deal of authenticated material is known of the Eastern Ch'in although some so-called proto-porcelain stonewares with greenish or dark brown glaze have recently been excavated which can be dated to this period. There exist, too, some very fine figures from northern China where Buddhism was adopted as the state religion under the Northern Wei, which have a remote and contemplative aura which is unmistakably Buddhist.

T'ang A.D. 618–906

In many ways the T'ang period, at least until A.D. 850, was the most culturally distinguished in all Chinese history. It was one of those periods during which the doors of China were thrown open to receive all kinds of cultural influences – Hellenistic, Indian, Sassanian and many others, while the three existing religious systems of Confucianism, Taoism and Buddhism were joined by Islam,

Figure of a horse, earthenware with coloured glazes. T'ang dynasty, A.D. 618–906.

Nestorian Christianity, Zoroastrianism, Judaism and even Manichæism. It was a time when the arts of painting, poetry and prose shook themselves loose from the rigid stylistic forms to which they had descended.

In ceramic art it was also a period of vitality and freedom, for here the Chinese revealed their greatness as modellers of the animal form. The most famous T'ang figures are horses and camels, the best of which combine liveliness, grace and strength. This is unfortunately by no means true of all T'ang figures, and they need to be chosen with the greatest of care. Indeed, so many were made that an Imperial decree of 741 was needed to restrict the number that could be placed in each grave.

Many technical developments giving greater control of kiln operations took place under the T'ang. It may therefore seem rather strange that what enchants most collectors about the san t'sai or three-colour glazes that were applied to so many vases and ewers at this time, apart from the sheer beauty of the colours, is the deliberate way in which the glazes were allowed to splash and dribble into each other during the firing and so create haphazard patterns which, to the uninitiated, can appear no more than an unsightly mess. It is often these accidental effects and the impurities which give each piece its own special character, and enable the collector to sense a link with the person who created it.

The most important development of all under the T'ang was the discovery of true porcelain. Unfortunately the Chinese use the same word *t'zu* to describe their finer stonewares such as those made in the Shang dynasty as well as what

48

is defined as true porcelain in the West. According to the Western definition, porcelain consists of two natural substances called in Chinese *kaolin* and *petuntse* and in English china-clay and petuntse. Kaolin is a fine, white, relatively infusible clay produced by the decomposition of feldspar while petuntse is a white earth consisting of pulverised granite. When the mixture of the two is fired to a temperature of around 2372°F the petuntse acts as a cement which holds together the particles of kaolin.

This true Chinese porcelain is fine-grained, hard, brilliant white, impervious sonorous and translucent, and was for long regarded as a semi-precious substance. Its importance in the history of ceramic art is paramount. The date of its first appearance is still in dispute, but no expert dates it later than the 8th century A.D. It was therefore about a thousand years before the secret of its manufacture was eventually discovered by Johann Böttger in Germany in 1709, where he started the famous Meissen factory the following year.

Five Dynasties A.D. 907–960; Sung 960–1279; Yüan (Mongol) 1279–1368

These three periods are usually taken together as forming one continuous period for the purpose of ceramic studies. Although the low-temperature lead-glaze wares continued to be made, they were not patronised by the Emperor or

Vase (mei-ping), buff stoneware with painting in brown over creamy-white slip. Tz'u-chou type. Sung dynasty, A.D. 960–1279.

the intellectual aristocracy who interested themselves chiefly in the high-fired stonewares and porcelain. The attitude of the period seems to be one of refined aesthetic indulgence, conservative and rather backward-looking of the kind that so often in Chinese history followed a period of adventurousness and achievement. So a cultured antiquarian tendency was expressed in celadon ware which sought to imitate jade.

Jade occupied a unique position in Chinese culture similar to that of gold or diamonds in the West. Although its opaque and soapy appearance is by no means instantly appealing to Western eyes, its beauty, like so much else that is Chinese, seems to reveal itself by degrees. Celadon was the name of a languorous gallant in a 17th-century play *Astrée* by d'Urfé who wore ribbons of a pale willow-green colour, and his name was taken to describe any ware that corresponds to jade-green in any of its shades.

Celadon ware was only one of a magnificent range of colours and styles. The

other famous 'families' of ceramics of this period, the Ju-ware, Chun, Tz'u Chou and Ting show a refinement of form and colour which is powerfully impressive. It is the power of understatement, and to appreciate it makes it possible to understand how the extensive use of blue patterns in the early Ming period was at first considered garish and vulgar.

The Sung had for long been under pressure from the Tartars and Mongols in the North, having had to cede much territory and move their capital south to Kai Feng in 1127 and later to Hang Chou. Eventually Khublai Khan, probably the grandson of Genghis, overran the rest of China and established the Yüan dynasty in about 1260, with its capital at Peking. The truth about the state of China at this time will probably never be known. There are some perhaps naturally tendentious contemporary Chinese accounts of the sufferings and privations of the people, yet it was also the time when Marco Polo, admittedly in the service of the Emperor, was extolling not only the beauties of the city of

51

Bowl, porcelain with
carved lotus flowers under
ivory glaze. Ting ware.
Sung dynasty.

Peking but also the order and justice of society and the thriving state of commerce and industry. Cultural activities also flourished, particularly poetry and drama. The administration of the Mongol Empire was so efficient that according to a 14th-century manuscript in Florence, which amounts to a vade-mecum for the route from the Levant to Peking, travellers could cross the whole of Central Asia in complete safety by day or night.

During the early part of the 14th century, China received its first cobalt oxide from Persia. At first the new blue colour was used almost entirely to decorate export ware destined for the Near Eastern market, but by the end of the century it had become popular in China too. The Chinese had assimilated from the Mongols a whole new range of forms which were made continuously throughout this and the Ming period. After many popular uprisings the Mongols were finally overthrown in 1368, and a native dynasty was re-established by Hung-wu.

Ming A.D. 1368–1644

Many people consider that the ceramic art of China, and indeed of the whole world, reached its zenith during this dynasty. One reason why Ming porcelain is so well liked in the West may be because there is on the whole more for the Western eye to identify with than in the case of earlier wares. The flowers and animals that decorate many pieces, even where their symbolic meanings are not understood, are easier to appreciate than the more abstract concepts of shape, and even more esoteric qualities of glaze where, for example, a texture giving the effect of an orange-peel or chicken-skin can delight a connoisseur.

The whole ceramic production of the Ming dynasty divides itself, by no means neatly, into two kinds. There are on the one hand the wares in the Imperial or official style which are so highly civilised as to give an impression of being almost inhuman, and on the other hand the more robust and spirited work which somehow shows that it has been modelled and fired by a man in close touch with nature. While the majority of collectors prefer the more rarified pieces of the first category, others find a stronger appeal and better value in the second.

In 1369 the establishment of the Imperial Porcelain Factory at Ching-tê Chên quickly set the standard and became the centre of production for the whole of China and remained so until the end of the 19th century. Very little can be attributed with certainty to the reign of Hung-wu but the reign of Yung-lo (1402–24) was famous for its plain white porcelain, now extremely rare; also for blue and white porcelains often decorated with flowers and fruit and leaf-scrolls, the rims of dishes frequently covered with a stylised wave motif which was to remain popular throughout the Ming period.

The art of painting for the Chinese was, from the beginning, a means of symbolic expression closely related to calligraphy. Hsieh Ho first formulated

Dish, porcelain painted in underglaze blue. Ming, 14th century.

the Six Principles by which painting should be judged in the 5th century A.D. These principles, although constantly re-interpreted, were still being applied in art criticism in the 19th century. Five of the principles dealt with questions of technique, while the first and most important principle laid down that a painting should have *Ch'i-yün shêng-tung* but, as so often with the Chinese language, this is an evocative rather than analytical statement. It might be rendered in English 'the vitality and life-breath of nature resounding in harmony with the cosmos', and if the meaning there seems a little opaque, Hsieh Ho would not have been disappointed for he well knew that such matters can be understood but not expressed.

Hsüan-tê who reigned from 1426–35 took a personal interest in the Imperial Factory and during his reign the practice began to grow of marking ceramics with the *Nien-hao* or Imperial Mark. The reign of Ch'êng-hua (1465–87) saw the first polychrome enamel painting, often of Buddhist and Taoist emblems over underglaze blue. His and the following reigns of Hung-chih (1488–1505) and Chêng-tê (1506–21) form a great classical period of blue-and-white ware. In the reign of Chia-ching (1522–66) the blue of the blue-and-white has a brilliant rich shade, in some cases almost violet.

A record survives of the designs which were to appear on the porcelain ordered for the Emperor in 1529 which gives an idea of the great variety of decoration in use. The motifs were to include dragons pursuing pearls, dragons among clouds, dragons coiling through lotus flowers, dragons flying with phoenixes and cranes, lions flying and playing with embroidered balls, the eight famous horses of the Emperor Mu Wang, the waterfalls of Sau Ch'uan, the eight Taoist Immortals, playing children, peacocks and fishes, the bamboo, the sacred fungus, the flowers of the seasons, the Indian lotus, the flowers celestial and fairy, the precious emblems, mystic diagrams and the characters for health, peace and longevity.

The reign of Chia-ching is also known for the particularly fine and rich tomato colour derived from iron used in monochrome or with other colours. Not many pieces of the short Lung-ch'ing (1567–72) period are known, but during the reign of Wan-li (1573–1619) there was difficulty in getting the best quality clay and even the blue colour has a pale silvery quality compared to earlier shades. Towards the end of Wan-li's reign and under the last two Emperors T'ien-ch'i (1621–27) and Ch'ung-chêng (1628–44) the ceramic art seems to have gone into decline. The same shapes were endlessly repeated, the decoration began to lose vitality which only reflected, it was said, the increasingly effete behaviour of the Imperial Court which had gradually fallen under the power of the eunuchs. In recognition of what used to be regarded as a lowering of standards during the reigns of the last two Ming Emperors and the first reign and a half of the Ch'ing dynasty, this period came to be known as the Transitional Period and until a recent revival of interest prices remained low.

Of the many other famous and beautiful families of ceramics of the Ming period at least two must be mentioned. Firstly the blanc-de-Chine family made at Tê-hua in the southern province of Fukien. Although it is known that this was a major centre of production as early as the Sung period and produced a good deal of coloured wares, it has become identified with the very fine cream-coloured and white pieces. Various objects such as libation cups, brush jars and tea-pots were made but perhaps the statuettes of Buddhist deities are the best-known, if only because they have been so extensively copied ever since.

Secondly and less well known in the West are the equally striking Swatow 'enamelled wares' which were and still are most sought-after in Japan. They were indeed made with the Japanese market, and to a lesser extent the Indian market, in mind. The decoration on the red and green wares was often of dragons, birds and flowering plants quickly painted with great zest and freedom, while the green and blue variety was often painted with sea motifs such as crabs, crayfish and ships, all rendered in the same carefree style.

Ching (Manchu) 1644–1912 and later

Another unsettled period of China's history began at the end of the 16th century with coastal raids by the Japanese warrior-tyrant Hideyoshi and continued throughout the long dynastic struggle between the decadent Ming Emperors and the Manchu claimants from the north. The return to stability only came in 1680 when a final rebellion was suppressed and the position of K'ang-hsi, the second Manchu Emperor, was consolidated.

K'ang-hsi was a poet and calligrapher, and an enlightened patron of the arts and sciences. The Imperial Factory at Ching-tê Chên had felt keenly the absence of patronage from the Ming Court although it had been compensated to some extent by increased demand from Europe and Japan. In the rebellion of 1673 the Factory was badly damaged and looted and it was K'ang-hsi who organised its reconstruction in 1683. By this date Europeans had for long been visiting and trading with China. An important thread running through Chinese ceramic history since 1600 is the continuous but varying influence on form and decoration of European taste. Recent Chinese contact with Europeans went back to the beginning of the 16th century, but the European motive for this contact was the promotion of trade, not of cultural or scientific knowledge.

It was the Jesuits, the first of whom, Matteo Ricci, arrived in 1582 who set themselves this task. Ricci had brought with him clocks, globes and mathematical instruments which had intrigued the more intelligent Chinese, but he had antagonised them by showing a map of the world with China insignificantly placed at the edge. Fortunately he managed to repair the damage by drawing a hemispherical map in which China filled the whole central area but it took him until 1600 to engineer an audience with the Emperor. The Chinese, in spite of an ancient and brilliant civilisation, remained

55

in some respects suspicious and naive. The success of the Jesuits in improving relations with the Chinese can be judged from the fact that the last two Ming Emperors were actually converted to Roman Catholicism. K'ang-hsi himself had two Jesuit priests as tutors in science and mathematics, and received another two who were also painters at court in 1699. Their style and technique impressed the Chinese deeply and there were requests for new designs from Europe to be copied on to porcelain to present as novelties to the Emperor.

What European influences brought about was a gradual departure from the traditional Chinese style in its broadest sense. Whereas the influx of foreign forms and ideas seemed wholly beneficial to Chinese ceramics under the T'ang, the results now seemed, at their worst, to be unsuccessful attempts by the Chinese to bring together their great ceramic art, the beauty of which had depended to a great extent on simplicity and purity of form and colour, with the Western style of painting.

Figure of a seated European merchant. Painted in Holland in Japanese Imari style, first half of the 18th century.

Punch-bowls, for example, were sometimes painted with a party of half-castes in Western dress (for the Chinese never quite managed to make Europeans look like Europeans) on a pheasant shoot in a most improbable landscape and these show the Chinese potter absurdly out of his element. Such objects are very popular among some collectors but should be valued as curiosities rather than as great examples of ceramic art. At their best, and there are many who esteem the porcelain of the reigns of K'ang-hsi and Ch'ien-lung higher than any other, the wares made for the home market show the result of Western influence in an exquisite lightness and femininity deriving from the European rococo style but which have retained their essential Chinese-ness.

The French were the first to study Chinese ceramics seriously, with the result that many French phrases are still used to describe certain kinds of porcelain. 'Famille verte' for example, usually refers to the family of wares enamelled in several different colours, but in which the dominant colour is green. Similarly in the cases of famille noire, jaune and rose. The famille rose came into being only about 1720 when a rose-pink colour derived from gold was introduced into China from Europe.

The most famous Director-General of the Imperial Factory, T'ang Ying who worked at Ching-tê Chên from 1728–49, recalled in his autobiography that he was instructed by the Emperor Ch'ien-lung to reproduce most of the porcelain treasures in the Imperial Palace. His brilliance in accomplishing this task was such that his copies of early wares have caused much dispute and confusion among ceramics experts ever since. To run such a factory must have been a formidable assignment, for a Jesuit, Père d'Entrecolles, has left a detailed account of the Factory's operations based on his visits to Ching-tê Chên in 1713 and 1714. He relates that 3,000 kilns were in operation and that the town's population reached about a million, most of whom were directly or indirectly engaged in the production of ceramics.

As might be supposed, a vast range of ceramics in every form and colour was produced to satisfy every taste. Even in 1713 production-line methods were in operation, and over the course of the next two centuries the artist-potters, if they could still be so described, ceased to stand in the same relation to the material they worked with. They made the clay perform new tricks simulating wood, lacquer, silver and so forth. In the main, standards declined, popular forms were repeated *ad nauseam*, decoration became banal, vulgar or both. Objects were smothered with brilliant enamel flowers and animals until not a pin-prick of the white ground could be seen. The Imperial Factory was sacked in the Taiping rebellion of 1853, and although rebuilt in 1864 most of the production remained weakly imitative.

Even during the chaotic years of the Republic, immediately following the Revolution in 1912, production continued at Ching-tê Chên. Hung Hsien, who seized power and proclaimed himself Emperor in 1916, found time before he was deposed after only eighty-two days to order a service of 40,000 pieces from the Imperial Factory. Some of these pieces were completed, but it is difficult to see them with an innocent eye, and by this date the interest of most collectors is already waning fast.

Copies and forgeries

Copies generally fall into two categories: those that are intended to deceive and those that are not. In the case of the Chinese, however, it is not known whether their inveterate practice of applying to ceramics reign-marks of long-dead Emperors always sprang from the genuine desire to venerate antiquity or from less exalted motives. It must be said in their defence that they have habitually described pottery by its place of origin, colour, form, decoration, and lastly if at all by its date – the question of assigning a date to each piece being very much a Western preoccupation.

Whatever the motive of the copyist, it is the date of production which will fix the price in the Western market-place. Considerable numbers of copies are in circulation, and there are several ways in which the collector can safeguard himself. Firstly, by training his eye. By studying and handling genuine and fake pieces, a feeling can gradually be gained of the ceramic language in which the Chinese potter communicated. Anything alien to that language will eventually draw attention to itself. Secondly, a knowledge of the pieces that have most frequently been copied and the differences or weaknesses by which they betray themselves. Thirdly, in the case of forgeries of very early pieces, by the thermoluminescence test.

This test, which many dealers will have carried out as a matter of course, works as follows. The minerals present in clay (and in many other substances) contain traces of radioactive material such as uranium and thorium. These minerals store the energy produced by this radioactivity but the energy will escape in the form of light if the clay is heated to a temperature of 500°F. When the temperature drops, the minerals gradually begin to rebuild the store of energy. So when a piece of clay is first fired, all the energy escapes. The scientist can now take a tiny specimen from a piece of pottery, heat it to 500°F and by measuring the light it gives off tell for how long it has been rebuilding that energy or, in other words, how long it is since it was first fired or made. Although the margin of error is as much as 20% either side of the true age, this is accurate enough to determine whether or not an object claimed to be of the T'ang or an earlier dynasty is genuine. For since T'ang and earlier pieces were only copied in the last hundred years, the test will always show that the piece is either about a hundred years or a thousand plus years old and must therefore be quite conclusive.

Tomb-wares of the Han period are not particularly difficult to reproduce, for they were often quite crudely modelled. The forger can also produce the crackle effect of burial on unglazed wares but not the characteristic minute crazing. But the most obvious danger-signs to the collector are when the objects are of uncharacteristic shape, excessively brightly painted or when the colours are the wrong shade for the period.

T'ang reproductions are very plentiful. Orvar Karlbeck first reported in 1912 that he had visited a factory at Peking where he saw hundreds of newly-made figures which he compared with genuine originals and was unable to tell apart. The age of glazed figures could usually be established more easily because the dampness of the tomb worked its way under the glaze, which took on a particular iridescence. However, it is said that certain operators in Hong Kong have now devised a way of producing almost instant iridescence on their wares.

The very high prices paid for the most interesting T'ang horses have encouraged forgers to take genuine unglazed animals and upgrade them by adding flowing manes, elaborate harnesses etc., and even by changing the horse's posture. Standing horses, for instance, are the least valuable, prancing ones more expensive, while those at full gallop fetch the highest prices of all.

T'ang Ying in the 18th century made superb copies of Sung and Yüan wares, considerably better than those made by the Japanese this century, although they too are good. Taken together, the copies are thought to outnumber the originals so that much care needs to be taken in this field, although the Japanese copies often give themselves away simply by being the wrong shape. The Japanese Imari potters of the 17th century copied the later Ming blue-and-white quite well and sometimes added reign-marks. The 18th century Chinese copies of Ming ware are often rare and beautiful objects in their own right, indistinguishable from the originals (and hence disputed) by many experts. The 20th-century Japanese copies of Ming blue-and-white are quite pleasing but the 20th-century Chinese copies are too crude to be at all convincing.

In the 19th century, copying in Europe and Asia developed on a grand scale but it was usually left to the Europeans, mainly the English, French and Dutch, to copy Chinese export ware. European copies of these wares which include figures or landscapes often give themselves away by an un-Chinese mastery of shade and perspective.

In dating, special attention must always be given to the paste, the glaze and the decoration, and only lastly to the reign-mark. Reign-marks first came into use in the early Ming period, and there probably exist more Chinese ceramics now carrying the wrong reign-mark than the right one. All reign-marks therefore need special study and experts usually consider the style and quality of the calligraphy before venturing an opinion.

Market trends

The field of Chinese ceramics is one where only the very rich can now expect to acquire even a small collection of the finest wares. The buying power in the market of the 1950s was largely American, in the sixties and early seventies the running was taken up by the Japanese and more recently it is the Hong Kong Chinese who have competed furiously and successfully against all bidders for some of the finest pieces.

Until now, the four most important dynasties for collectors have been T'ang, Sung, Ming and Ch'ing. Human and animal figures of the T'ang period appeal strongly to European, American and Japanese tastes for their sculptural qualities. But the Chinese themselves, in their reverence for ancestors, take no more interest in these mortuary wares, ransacked from the tombs of their forefathers than Americans might be expected to take in collecting fragments of 18th-century shrouds. During the fifties, T'ang figures overall rose in price by around 700% and then through the sixties, having by then passed out of reach of many collectors, more steadily by a further 250%.

Sung wares are the most esoteric and intellectual of the four principal groups and as such for a long time attracted a smaller following. Taken as a whole, Sung wares actually fell in value during the early fifties although over the whole decade climbed a moderate 100%. During the sixties they doubled again and although the rate of appreciation picked up in the 1970s, they hardly shared at all in the hectic rise in 1972–4. There are for example tens of thousands of Sung celadon bowls and dishes in circulation. Many of them are kiln wasters thrown away by the potter and later excavated, others undistinguished examples or in poor condition. It may not be difficult for an amateur to say which of two similar pieces he prefers but it takes great experience to appreciate why one may be worth fifty rather than ten times more than the other.

Even though Ming wares have for centuries been widely appreciated and collected in the West, they rose in value by around 400% during the 1950s. The pace slackened in the sixties to an average of 20% a year before the next surge forward in the early seventies. A solid advance in knowledge of the Ming dynasty had accounted in the 1950s for a steep rise in early Ming blue-and-white. It had been supposed that early Ming blue-and-white of the late 14th and early 15th centuries were merely less accomplished forerunners of the much finer late 15th and early 16th century wares. The discovery that certain of the finer pieces could be firmly dated to the earlier period had set off this furious competition which was resumed in 1972–4 for the few examples that reached the saleroom.

So fast was the rise in values for all Ming blue-and-white between the end of 1972 and July 1974 that for once in this market the nimble investors were able even to buy retail and sell at auction with a large profit. But for those that held on the cost was heavy. London and Tokyo were then, as they are now, the key centres for dealings in oriental ceramics. Japanese buying had been serious since 1969 but became even more so in 1972 and early 1973 when, with a soaring Tokyo stock market and accelerating inflation, Japanese collectors were anxiously switching out of the yen. Sotheby's began to hold auctions in Hong Kong in 1973. Then the immensely rich Hong Kong Chinese made their impact on the market, particularly for Imperial porcelain of the Ch'ing dynasty.

At the same time in London, some dealers were forcing prices upwards as they become involved in speculative buying for non-collectors. One particular dealer was buying on behalf of Portuguese clients at prices that have never been equalled since. $840,000 was paid for a 14th-century blue-and-white bottle $16\frac{1}{4}''$ high and $460,000 for a Mei Ping or blossom vase also of the 14th-century. In a historic sale at Sotheby's in April 1974, 29 lots fetched over $40,000 each and it was forecast that the ceiling was still a long way off.

But events turned the market with astonishing speed. The Japanese economy had reeled under the impact of quadrupled oil prices late in 1973. Many of the great Japanese collections were effectively being formed by industrial corporations for tax benefits or prestige and their buying programmes were for the time being brought to a standstill. Towards the end of 1974, the nosediving stock market in London left those who had speculated in the Chinese ceramics market unable or unwilling to make any further commitment. In April 1974, the coup d'état in Portugal had left one legendary collector behind bars and seriously altered the financial outlook for several others. During the second half of 1974, prices began to fall fast and one London dealer later had to write down his stock by over $2m. A 20'' famille rose dish that might have been bought for $6–8,000 in 1971 reached $50,000 in 1974, dived to $10,000 the following year and even now might only have climbed back to $30–40,000.

From the point of view of Chinese art history, the 18th-century Chinese export porcelain dinner services, goose tureens etc. are quite unimportant. This was material to be shipped away to the barbarians who apparently liked it and even paid for it. The serious side of ceramics to the Chinese was the production of Imperial wares and it is these whose beauty was reappraised in the late sixties and for which the Hong Kong Chinese have paid astonishing sums. A pair of tiny famille verte stem-cups fetched $320,000 at the height of the market and although the general collapse of confidence affected this area of the market too, the revaluation was partly based on a rediscovery of a branch of Chinese art, not on speculation, and for this reason has recently proved most resilient.

In the past, collectors have been, to say the least, fastidious about damage. Depending on its size, a chip could reduce the value of a piece by up to 90%. Cracks are generally regarded as even more serious since there is always the danger that they may turn into a full break. Yet the more rare and beautiful a piece, the more tolerant the market is of its imperfections. There are signs too that the disdain collectors have expressed through saleroom prices for damaged pieces may now be moderating. Prices for perfect pieces have soared so high that imperfect pieces now seem real bargains and a more reasoned attitude is evolving which values the overall quality of each piece which can be quite unimpaired by minor damage.

Being so fragile, ceramics are very expensive to insure. While it is true that unlike many other works of art they are not vulnerable to fire and water, insurance companies do not regard this as a compensating bonus and the rates for full cover are punitive. Usually the rates will vary according to the circumstances in which the collection is kept, i.e. locked cabinet, children's playroom etc. and the classes of risk to be covered theft, breakage etc.

Although research is continuously throwing new light on different aspects of Chinese ceramics, the field as a whole has now been very well explored. Much work remains to be done, yet it is unlikely that any major discoveries remain to be made. Sotheby's and Christies are again the most important auction-houses, holding regular sales between them in New York, London and Hong Kong. But the sales are not so frequent as in the early seventies; less top-quality material is on the move and a growing proportion has found its way into public ownership or private collections which are destined eventually to become public.

Principal public collections

CANADA	Toronto	Royal Ontario Museum
CHINA	Honan	Chang Sha Provincial Museum
	Kuantung Province	Guan Tong History Museum
	Nanking	Kiang Su Provincial Museum
	Peking	Imperial Palace Museum
	Shanghai, Kiangsu Province	Art and History Museum
	Sian	Shensi Provincial Museum
DENMARK	Copenhagen	Kunstindustrimuseet
FRANCE	Paris	Cernuschi Museum
		Musée Guimet
GERMANY	Berlin	Museum für Ostasiatische Kunst
HOLLAND	Amsterdam	Rijksmuseum
JAPAN	Kyoto	Kyoto National Museum
	Nara	Yamato Bunkakan
	Tokyo	Idemitsu Art Gallery
		National Museum
		Nezu Art Museum
SWEDEN	Stockholm	Museum of Far Eastern Antiquities
TAIWAN	Taipei	National Palace Museum
TURKEY	Istanbul	Topkapi National Museum
U.K.	Brighton	Barlowe Collection
	Bristol	City Art Gallery
	Cambridge	Fitzwilliam Museum

	Durham	Gulbenkian Museum of Oriental Art and Archaelogy
	Edinburgh	Royal Scottish Museum
	London	British Museum
		Percival David Foundation of Chinese Art
		Victoria and Albert Museum
	Oxford	Ashmolean Museum of Art and Archaeology
U.S.A.	Boston	Museum of Fine Art
		Fogg Art Museum, Harvard University
	Chicago	Art Institute
	Cleveland, Ohio	Museum of Art
	Kansas City	William Rockhill Nelson Gallery and Atkins Museum of Fine Arts
	New York	Metropolitan Museum of Art
	Philadelphia	Museum of Art
		University Museum
	San Francisco	Center of Asian Art and Culture, Avery Brundage Collection
	Seattle	Museum of Art
	Washington, DC	Freer Gallery of Art

Book list

BEURDELEY, CECILE and BEURDELEY, MICHEL. *A Connoisseur's Guide to Chinese Ceramics* Watson, Katherine translated from French 1974, Harper & Row

GARNER, H. *Oriental Blue and White* 3rd ed. 1970 (pub. by Faber & Faber), Merrimack Book Service

GOMPERTZ, G. *Korean Pottery and Porcelain of the Yi Period* 1968 (pub. by Faber & Faber), Merrimack Book Service

JEYNS, SOAME. *Later Chinese Porcelain.* 4th ed. (Illus.) (pub. by Faber & Faber), Merrimack Book Service

MEDLEY, MARGARET *A Handbook of Chinese Art* (Icon Editions) (Illus.) 1974, Harper & Row

WILLIAMS, C. A. *Outlines of Chinese Symbolism and Art Motives* 1976, Dover

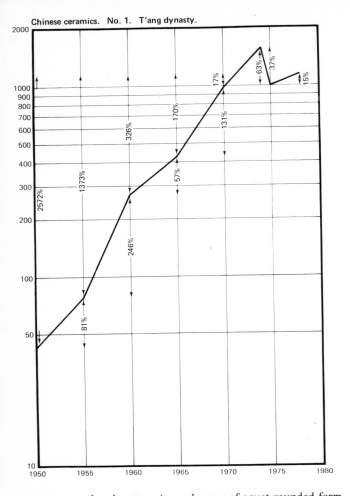

Chinese ceramics. No. 1. T'ang dynasty.

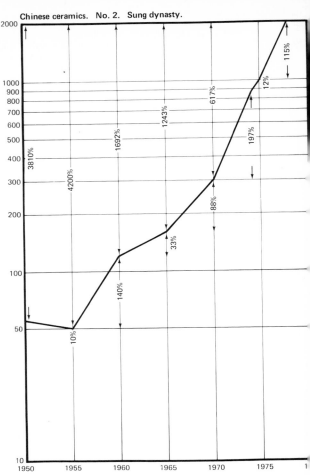

Chinese ceramics. No. 2. Sung dynasty.

1. A green glazed pottery jar and cover of squat rounded form, tapering towards the slightly splayed flat base and surmounted by a short flared mouth, the domed cover with a button knop set on a circular seat, the bright green glaze unevenly applied falling short of the base on one side, with areas of iridescent incrustations on the lower part of the body, the cover similarly glazed. 8¾in. T'ang dynasty.

2. A brown glazed pottery figure of a Fereghan horse, standing four-square on the unglazed rectangular base, its head turned slightly to the near side, held in with mouth open, nostrils flared and ears pricked, the strong arched neck with a groove for the attachment of the mane and the hind-quarters with a socket for the tail, the elegantly proportioned body covered overall with a brown glaze of rich tone apart from a cream-coloured blaze of greenish tint on the head and similarly coloured hooves. 19¾in. high. T'ang dynasty.

3. A dish of pinkish white earthenware with a flat base, rounded profile and everted rim, on three cabriole feet and decorated with deeply impressed designs of a central hexagonal floral medallion surrounded by six formal leaves (recalling those of the sacred fig-tree) linked together: the ornament lead-glazed blue and green, the rest creamy-white. 7¼in. 8th century.

4. A white stoneware amphora with ovoid body, slender neck, cup-shaped mouth, everted foot and high-looping handles of dragons' necks and heads attached to the mouth; covered with a light green feldspathic glaze reaching to a line just below the mid-point of the ovoid body. 10¼in. 7th–early 8th century.

1. A splashed Chün Yao dish (p'an), of shallow form with evert rim, standing on a short foot and covered overall with a thick applied glaze of soft pale blue colour of richer tone on t underside, and with irregular reddish and purple splash some crackle and the body showing through on the well a rim, the base with a central shallow concavity and three sp marks. 7¼in. Sung dynasty.

2. A carved Ting-Yao conical bowl with copper-bound rim, interior decorated with a curved lotus stem bearing a large op flower and a single naturalistic leaf, seen side on, with crink edge, luxuriant conventional foliage and a blade of arrow gra with combed details on the larger leaves and petals, withi faint incised ring, the underside plain. 7¼in. Northern Su dynasty.

3. A stoneware ovoid vase with broad base, rounded should narrow neck and spreading mouth. Painted in brownish-bla over a cream slip, with two flowering sprays, two butterf and other insects with scratched detail; around the neck oblique petal pattern. Covered with a colourless glaze includ the recessed base. Tz'ü-chou ware. 9½in. Sung dynasty, 1 century.

4. A greyish stoneware jar with broad mouth and two lo handles at the shoulder, covered with a lavender-blue g showing purplish splashes shading into crimson, and wit small foot ring burnt brownish. Chün ware. 4¾in. high. Su dynasty, 12th century.

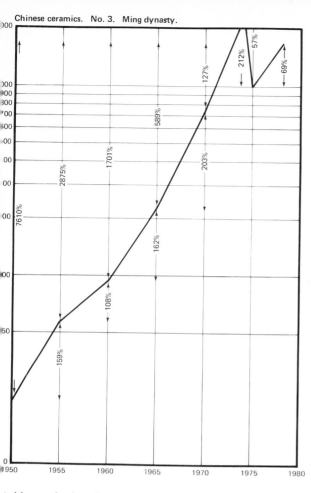

Chinese ceramics. No. 3. Ming dynasty.

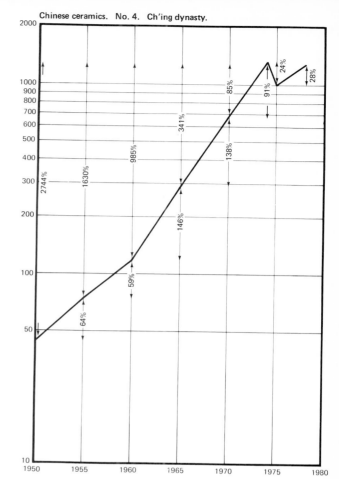

Chinese ceramics. No. 4. Ch'ing dynasty.

A blue and white bowl painted both inside and out with a flower scroll, including lotus, pomegranate, camellia and peony, between a border of lotus petals encircling the base and key-fret under the flared rim, the interior with a bunch of scrolling lotus in a central medallion and a scroll of single chrysanthemums around the lip, the footrim edged with a classic scroll. 7¾in. Six character mark and period of Hsüan-tê 1426–35.

A white bowl, the steeply rounded sides springing from a cylindrical foot of slightly tapering shape, the interior decorated in *an hua* with a continuous scroll of peonies and chrysanthemum, the exterior with a band of slender upright lotus petals below a band of key-fret on the rim, covered overall with an even glaze of faint bluish tint. 8¼in. Six character mark of Hsüan-tê in underglaze blue and of the period.

A dish with rounded sides and everted rim, painted in underglaze blue with a flower spray in the centre and sprays of lotus, pomegranate, loquat and vine against an overglaze yellow ground. On the plain glazed base the six character mark of Hung-chih. 1488–1505. 10¼in.

1. A 'Famille Verte' dish of saucer shape predominantly enamelled in tones of green with a pair of song birds and butterflies in flight beside a gnarled tree bearing blossom in 'rouge de fer' growing among yellow and aubergine peony flowers and rocks in blue and green, the lipped rim with a band of yellow and green bordered floral vignettes on a seeded ground decorated with stylised peony scrolls. 14½in. Conch mark K'ang-hsi. 1662–1722.

2. A Ruby Back plate, the centre superbly enamelled in 'famille rose' palette enriched with gilding, with a maiden and three boys, each elaborately attired in loosely draped robes, seated in front of precious objects set on a tall bamboo table, and two large jars each holding a *ju-i* sceptre, all within a narrow yellow-ground trellis border reserved with floral vignettes encircling the well. 8¾in. Yung-chêng 1723–35.

3. Jardinière with celadon glaze. Shaped distantly after the form of an archaic bronze *tsun*, with a wide-flaring mouth, hexagonal lobed body with rather straight sides and a domed foot. Pierced in the base are two holes for drainage. Porcelain covered with semi-opaque celadon glaze of light bluish-green tint. 8½in. Six character seal mark of Yung-chêng.

4. Famille Noire Jar and Cover. The jar of *potiche* form with broad base short, wide neck and low domed cover. Porcelain painted in 'famille verte' enamels on the biscuit with magnolia, tree peony and hydrangea growing among rocks on a lustrous 'famille noire' black ground. Height 23½in. K'ang-hsi 1662–1722.

Coins

The names Bronze Age and Iron Age rightly suggest the great importance of metal to primitive man. The attainment of the skills required to forge metal into farming implements, weapons and domestic utensils marked important stages along the road to civilisation. These metal objects were men's most valued possessions and it was natural that men should come to associate metal through farming implements with the production of food and through weapons with strength and security. If comparatively dull-looking metals such as copper, iron and tin should have acquired this status in men's minds and were firmly identified with the fundamental necessities of life, it was hardly surprising that at the first appearance of silver and gold, metals which were generically similar although scarcer and more pleasing to look at, they should have seemed instantly desirable.

The only condition necessary for the success of a currency is that it should be generally acceptable in the society within which it circulates. This has enabled currencies based on cowrie shells and even cows to function effectively in different parts of the world. Yet the universal appeal and convenience of silver and gold offered advantages that were soon recognised. The need for a coinage develops when the economic progress of a society has reached the stage where specialised production has created surpluses which call for a generally acceptable medium of exchange. An illuminating example of the transition from barter to coinage is provided by the Chinese system of the 7th century B.C. Although ancient Chinese authorities dated the use of metallic coinage to the 20th century B.C., modern research has not been able to substantiate a true coinage earlier than the 7th century B.C. in which case its first circulation would have coincided with the introduction of different coinages in India and the West. The coinage the Chinese evolved consisted of small-scale reproductions in bronze or copper of objects such as spades, hoes and knives which had earlier been used in barter. It was as though the acceptance of 'coins', even though these were stamped with a guarantee of weight, was not yet general enough to ensure the viability of the currency so that the concept of bartering had to be maintained in their design.

In the West, gold, silver and electrum objects had circulated on a barter basis long before the 7th century B.C., but if coins are defined as objects of standard weight guaranteed by a distinguishing mark, then the first true coins in the West were those issued during the reign of King Ardys of Lydia 652–625 B.C.

Chinese hoe, knife and spade money, *c.* 7th C. B.C.

He found it profitable to issue and the merchants found it convenient to use lumps of electrum, a natural alloy of gold and silver, already weighed and guaranteed by the lion's head device of the Mermnad dynasty. This was only a short step from the earlier practice of weighing the pieces of metal each time they were offered in exchange, and even in those days some merchants had made punch marks in the metal signifying their personal guarantee.

Almost all the coinage of the ancient and medieval world was die-struck. Blank pieces of metal were placed on a kind of anvil called a pile on which a design was engraved. A second piece of engraved metal, usually of cylindrical shape and known as a puncheon, was placed over the blank and struck with a hammer squashing the metal and forcing it into the engraved parts of the die. The pile side of the coin is known as the obverse and the other the reverse. Although this method was capable of reproducing the finest detail, it could not ensure the centering of the design and it was not until the introduction of mechanical striking in the 16th century that perfect centering and control over the shape of the coin was achieved.

For obvious aesthetic reasons, accurate centering and roundness are important factors in the valuation of ancient and medieval coins. Croesus, who became king of Lydia in 560 B.C., introduced the bimetallic system into coinage setting the relative value of gold at ten times that of silver – an exchange rate that spread after the conquest of Lydia throughout the Persian Empire. As the trade routes from Asia passed through Lydia, it was natural that the cities of Ionia and the Greek islands should quickly copy the new invention and soon

Aegina, 600–480 B.C. Silver *stater* showing a turtle, the city emblem.

coinages were issued throughout the Greek world. Aegina was one of the first to follow Lydia in issuing silver *staters*, showing a turtle, their city emblem, whose value was related to an earlier iron and copper currency. Then came Corinth in 575 B.C. and Athens about 525 B.C. after the discovery of the silver mines at Attica.

In Sicily the art of coinage soon reached a height that has never been equalled since. Such was the prestige of the men who engraved the dies that their names actually appear on the coins. While many Sicilian cities took animals as their emblems, Syracuse took a four-horsed chariot for its obverse and the figure of Artemis Arethusa for its reverse. Of the many variations on these themes, perhaps the greatest are the dies engraved by Euanetos and Kimon for the large *decadrachms* used as prizes in the games commemorating the deliverance of Syracuse from the Athenians' siege in 413 B.C. Taken as a whole, the Sicilian series of coins is rated the most beautiful ever struck although the Ionian silver *tetradrachm* of 370 B.C., showing the full-face Apollo signed by Theodotus, is held by some to be the finest individual piece of all time.

Almost all the city-states of Greece displayed ingenuity and great artistry in their coinages, except Athens which, after the defeat of the Persians in the 5th century, became the foremost commercial power in the Mediterranean. For two hundred years the Athenian coinage showed no artistic progress and in 250 B.C. coins were still being struck in a degenerate archaic style. This pattern of long artistic stagnation has been seen in the coinages of countries at different periods of history and is supposed to result from a fear of damaging the confidence that had been built up in a particular coinage by changing its appearance.

The Macedonian Empire, which reached its zenith under Alexander the Great (336–323 B.C.), stretched from Greece to N.W. India and from the Black Sea to Egypt. Alexander used the gold and silver mines in Thrace and other conquered territories to mint the first great uniform coinage of the ancient world based on the gold *stater* and silver *tetradrachm*. Every large city east

68

Syracuse *tetradrachm* signed by Kimon. 480–400 B.C. Obverse, Arethusa. Reverse, Quadriga (four-horsed chariot).

Calabria, *Tarentum* gold *solidus c.* 340–330 B.C. Obverse, Hera. Reverse, the boy Taras appealing to his father, Poseidon.

Attica, Athens *Tetradrachm* 480–400 B.C. Obverse, Athena. Reverse, owl.

Ionia, Magnesia ad Maeandrum. *Tetradrachm*, 2nd C. B.C. Obverse, Artemis. Reverse, Apollo.

69

of Greece issued coins of Alexander the Great and almost all the independent Greek coinages except that of Athens were swamped. After the death of Alexander, the division of the Empire between his generals did not affect the coinage until the turn of the century when the dynasties founded by his generals began to mint their own so-called regal coinages. Ptolemy I, who had taken Egypt as his share of the Empire, was deified when he died after the custom of the Pharaohs. His son Ptolemy II issued silver *tetradrachms* bearing his father's portrait on the obverse and his own and his wife Arsinoe's portrait on the reverse. With this honour, previously reserved for immortals, began the long history of portraiture on coins which in many instances provides the only knowledge we have of the appearance of ancient kings and emperors.

Macedon, Alexander the Great, 336–323 B.C. Gold *stater*. Obverse, Athena. Reverse, Nike holding a wreath and naval standard.

Egypt, Ptolemy I, 323–285 B.C. Silver *tetradrachm*. Obverse, Alexander the Great. Reverse, eagle on thunderbolt.

Egypt, Arsinoe, *c.* 270 B.C. Silver *octodrachm*. Obverse, Arsinoe, deified wife and sister to Ptolemy II. Reverse, double cornucopia.

70

Rome, *aes signatum*, *c.* 289 B.C.
Elephant and pig.

The Roman coinage is traditionally divided into the Roman Republican period (*c.* 289–31 B.C.), the Roman Imperial period (31 B.C. to A.D. 476) ending with the deposition of Romulus Augustus and the period of the Byzantine Empire – that is, the Eastern part of the Roman Empire not conquered by barbarian invaders until the sack of Constantinople by the Ottoman Turks in 1453. The date of the issue of the first silver *denarius* is still disputed although the evidence now seems to point to the end of the 3rd century B.C. Along the coast in the south of Italy, the great cities which had been founded as Greek colonies had issued series of fine coins during the 6th century and the Etruscans to the north of Rome had issued coins in the fifth.

It was not until the beginning of the 3rd century that Rome made its first issue of rectangular bronze bars each weighing five pounds which, because of their uniform weight, may be regarded as coins. These bars were known as *aes signatum* because they were cast with a device on each side. One type bears the device of a bull which refers to the use of cattle as currency in earlier times. It also provides the derivation of the Latin word for money – *pecunia* from *pecus* meaning cattle – while the word money itself derives from the location of the first Roman mint in the temple of Juno Moneta. Another type of *aes signatum* depicts an Indian elephant on one side and a sow on the other recalling the failure of Pyrrhus's invasion of Italy at the battle of Beneventum in 274 B.C. when his elephants were routed by having driven towards them pigs whose smell they could not bear.

The earliest Roman coinage proper came in 269 B.C. when the growing power of the city and its increasing contacts with Greek cities to the south called for something more than the basic series of bronze coins based on the *aes signatum*. The result was a series of silver coins which, although Hellenistic in style, carried the motifs of Roman mythology – Janus, the wolf and the twins, the war goddess Bellona, Castor and Pollux, etc. The silver *denarius* which first appeared about 211 B.C. was supposed to be worth 10 bronze *asses* but soon the Senate reduced its silver content in order to finance the growing expenditure of the public sector and the bronze *as* was transformed into a fiduciary coin – that is one whose face value bears no relation to its weight or intrinsic value. Later, because its value could not be re-established on an acceptable basis, it was withdrawn and the gradual debasement of the coinage continued until 155 B.C.

The Roman series grows more interesting during the last century of the Republic when the three officers responsible for minting the coinage threw off their Republican inhibitions and began to introduce religious themes into the design as well as subjects of family or personal interest. Although the coinage had always been produced by the authority of the Senate (and often bore the letters SC – *Senatus Consulto*), generals in the field or in the provinces took to issuing their own coinages during the Civil War. Once they had been started, the provincial coinages grew in importance and the first indications can be seen of the use of coinage for propaganda purposes which was to assume such importance under the Empire.

Soon after the beginning of the Roman Imperial period, Caesar's adopted son Octavian took the title Augustus and began to strike the first great series of the Imperial coinage. In a generally illiterate world, the symbols used on coins could be highly evocative and Augustus recognised their full value as a means of communication with his people. In his various coinages, he stressed the Roman character of his régime by using the earlier Republican symbols such as the crown of oak leaves while successes in the field such as the capture of Egypt, the extension of influence over Armenia and the triumphs of his heir Tiberius in Pannonia and Germany were also celebrated. Later emperors from Claudius to Caracalla encouraged the cult of the Imperial family by portraying themselves and various relations on the obverse side of the coins they issued which, artistically, are the greatest achievements of Roman coinage. The reverses were used to draw attention to every sort of achievement from the invasion of Britain by Claudius in A.D. 43 to the completion of the Colosseum as well as conceptual motifs such as the morale of the legions and the virtues of the emperor.

The coins in issue during the Roman Empire were the gold *aureus*, the silver *denarius*, the brass or orichalcum *sestertius*, the brass *dupondius* and the copper *as* and *quadrans*. Many were issued at mints throughout the provinces as well as at Rome itself. The weight, fineness and rate of exchange of these coins fluctuated with the fortunes of the Roman economy. The costs of administering the Roman Empire were partly borne by the revenue from issuing coins and

(*Left*) Roman Republic, silver *denarius*, c. 133–126 B.C. Obverse, Fostlus. Reverse, wolf and twins.

Roman Republic, *denarius*, 44 B.C. Obverse, Julius Caesar. Reverse, Victory in biga.

Roman Empire, Tiberius. *Denarius* (tribute penny) A.D. 14–37. Obverse, Tiberius. Reverse, probably Livia, widow of Augustus and mother of Tiberius.

Roman Empire, Caligula. *Sestertius*, A.D. 37–41. Obverse, Caligula. Reverse, Caligula addressing his troops.

(*Far left*) Roman Republic, *aureus*, 42 B.C. Obverse, Octavian. Reverse, Aeneas carrying his father Anchises on his shoulder as they escape from Troy. Octavian's family, the Julians, claimed descent from Aeneas.

Roman Empire, Constantine the Great. *Solidus*, A.D. 306–337. Obverse, Constantine the Great. Reverse, motif symbolising Constantine's victories.

73

increasingly by debasing those issues to a point where the State actually demanded bullion in payment of taxes, refusing even to accept its own coin. By the time of Caracalla (Emperor A.D. 211–217) the silver content of the *denarius*, which had always been the cornerstone of the coinage system, was down to 40%. Under Gallienus (259–268) at a time when the Empire had lost several important provinces and was on the verge of economic collapse, *denarii* were minted containing practically no silver at all.

The gradual reconstruction of the Empire was achieved by Diocletian, Aurelian and Constantine. Diocletian carried out a complete monetary reform based on the gold *aureus* with a guaranteed weight of 60 to the pound (0·2 oz) and a silver coin guaranteed 96 to the pound. Further major reforms took place under Constantine (306–337), the first Christian Emperor, who removed the capital of the Empire to Byzantium which he renamed Constantinople. He introduced in 313 the gold *solidus* at 0·165 oz and a bronze coinage to replace the previous issues which had fallen steadily in weight.

The style of government of the Roman Emperors after the move to Byzantium became more despotic and eastern in character and this is strangely reflected in the portraiture of their coins on which the figure becomes very stylised suggesting that the office of Emperor had become more significant than the man. By the time Rome fell in 476, the western provinces of Britain, Spain, Gaul and Italy had also fallen to barbarian invaders and the coinages of those regions became those of medieval Europe while the eastern part of the Roman Empire, henceforth known as the Byzantine Empire, and its coinage was to survive until the traditional end of the Middle Ages, the fall of Constantinople to the Turks in 1453.

The gold *solidus* remained the cornerstone of Byzantine coinage until the 11th century. Its weight and purity were so widely accepted that its very name has passed into many of the languages of Europe. But by and large, the Byzantine coinage did not match up to the brilliance of much other Byzantine art. The sterile iconoclast controversy over the representation of images which simmered on for several hundred years was reflected in the appearance and disappearance of members of the Holy Family from successive coinages and the alternating Latin and Greek legends are amongst the only high points of interest in an otherwise conservative tradition.

In the newly emerging kingdoms of the West, there was a proliferation of coinages mostly imitating, even in the style of portraiture, the gold *tremissis* of the Roman Empire which lasted until the 8th century. Gold then largely disappeared from the coinage of Western Europe and was replaced by the silver penny known in different countries by variations of the term *denier*. This one denomination lasted until economic growth in the 13th century called into existence the larger silver groats, equivalent to four pennies, as well as bringing about the return to European coinages of various gold coins. Although many medieval coins hold a powerful almost primitive historical interest, it was not

(*Left*) England, gold thrymsa, *c.* 650–700. Obverse, a bust. Reverse, two busts facing orb, between and above another head and two wings.

England, Mercia. Silver penny, 774–796. Obverse, Offa with name and title. Reverse, floreate cross.

England, Wessex, Alfred. Silver penny, 871–899. Obverse, Alfred. Reverse, monogram of the name of London.

England, William I. Silver penny, 1066–87. Obverse, William crowned and holding a sceptre. Reverse, a cross with the letters PAXS in the angles.

for nothing that this period had been called the Dark Ages and the barbarous and ugly portraits are in astonishing contrast to the great artistry of the early Greek and Roman series.

Although in the late Middle Ages some coins displaying the highest Gothic art were issued, of which a fine example is the *masse d'or* of Philip IV of France (known as the 'roi faux monnayeur' for his debasement of the coinage), it was not until the Renaissance that a return to really fine design and workmanship was seen again. Pisanello's portrait of the Byzantine Emperor John VIII of 1438 was one such case which was to have a profound influence on coin design.

Since the 13th century, the Florentine *florin* and the Venetian *ducat* had been the most important coins in Italy as well as becoming the international currency of Europe and the Mediterranean world. Yet the issuing authorities had stuck to their archaic designs for fear of lowering the coins' reputation and it was only at the beginning of the Renaissance that many of the great ruling families of Italy such as the Sforzas, Gonzagas and d'Estes began to revive the tradition of portraiture on coins.

During the 15th century, as gold came to be in increasingly short supply, the

75

France, Philip IV 1285–1314. *Chaise d'or*. Obverse, Philip IV enthroned. Reverse, a decorative cross with *lis* in the angles.

Bohemia, Louis I. Gold *thaler*, 1516–25. Obverse, St Joachim, patron saint of Bohemia. Reverse, a lion.

silver mines of the Tyrol, Erzgebirge and Schwarzwald began to be worked more intensively. Larger silver pieces began to be struck in the Tyrol in the late 15th century, equivalent in value to the Florentine gold florin. These culminated in the issue in 1520 by the Counts of Schlick in Bohemia of the famous Joachimsthaler named after the mines that provided the silver. Coins of this type whose issue marked the beginning of the modern period of coinage in Europe came to be known as *thalers*, a name that survives today in the form dollar.

The great influx of American gold and silver in the 16th century brought about a considerable increase in the money supply and with it high rates of inflation. The relationship between these two phenomena was actually expounded, perhaps for the first time, by the political writer Jean Bodin in 1568. Another result of the great numbers of coins being minted was that a significant part of them were so badly struck that they were relatively easy to forge or clip. It therefore became urgent to invent machinery that would produce coins of uniform weight and size. Leonardo da Vinci had produced drawings of a machine for cutting the blanks and Bramante his contemporary designed a screw press for striking the coins. Both the machines used by Benvenuto Cellini (1500–1571) in striking the coinage for Pope Paul III were

76

similar to these but they left unsolved the problem of producing perfectly round edges.

Henry II of France heard reports of a workman in Augsburg who was said to have invented such a machine and he sent an agent, Aubin Olivier, to buy the invention. Olivier returned to Paris with various machines which were erected in 1554 on the Ile du Palais where they could be powered by the river Seine. The coins they produced were far finer than those struck by the established moneyers who, fearing for their jobs, contrived to postpone the introduction of the mechanical press for nearly a hundred years.

The story was similar in England where Elizabeth I employed Eloye Mestrelle from the Paris mint to set up the new screw-type presses driven by horse and water-power at the Tower of London. The sixpences he produced were of excellent quality but again the moneyers themselves raised objections and it was not until the middle of the 17th century that England got its first milled coinage. Mestrelle himself was dismissed in 1572 and hanged a few years later for counterfeiting. The clippers of coins were finally defeated by a machine invented by Pierre Blondeau in the mid-17th century which rolled each coin between two bars forcing its edge to receive the impression of an inscription or design engraved on one of the bars. The vertical lines often seen on the edge of a coin arrive there by this process and are generally known as milling or graining.

The Industrial Revolution in England created an unprecedented demand for money. Paper money and credit were used for large transactions but the payment of wages to a vast new work-force and the transaction of a correspondingly larger retail business required quantities of money which could not be provided by the manually operated and horse-driven equipment which was still in use at the Royal Mint.

Matthew Boulton, a manufacturer of metal buttons in Birmingham, who had been associated with James Watt in the development of the steam engine, built a steam coining-press capable of much faster production but it was not until 1797, long after his machines had minted coins for the American colonies and after years of badgering the Government that he was granted permission to strike 20 tons of copper twopenny pieces and 480 tons of pennies. As the English law then stood, the coin of the realm had to contain its own intrinsic value in metal so that the twopenny piece, known as the cartwheel, weighed a full two ounces. The Boulton and Watt machines very soon became standard equipment for most European mints and were kept in production even after the change to electric power in the late 19th century.

The coinage of the world is so vast and so complex that collectors almost without exception specialise in one particular series. They do so because even now it is possible to achieve a good coverage or even a complete collection of a small field and because it is more satisfying to study the chosen field in depth than to acquire a shallow knowledge of the coinage of the entire world.

Furthermore, when the time comes to sell, a collection formed with judgement and careful study of its theme will generally fetch more at auction than the sum of its parts sold individually.

The most usual form of specialisation is to go for coins of one country or one period. People sometimes choose quite obscure fields such as the coins of Pomerania or the coins struck during the joint reign of King Bogislav II and King Casimir II of Pomerania (1187–1219) or just the paper-thin bracteates struck during their reign. More normal choices are:

Emergency coins struck during sieges
Coins issued by revolutionaries
Sicilian and other Greek coins signed by the artist
Coins issued by ecclesiastical rulers
Coins with animal designs
The Gold Eagles of America

Forgeries

There are two kinds of coin forgery. Firstly, the contemporary forgery which is the forgery of current coinage of whatever date and, secondly, forgeries of old coins intended to deceive collectors. Of the first kind none so far as is known is attempted today, the criminal fraternity now tending to concentrate on banknotes because of their higher denominations. Forgery of current coins was certainly going on until gold went out of circulation in the 1930s.

Of the second kind there are two methods. The first method is to make a cast copy by pouring molten metal into a mould taken from an existing coin. Results look quite impressive to the untrained eye but, under a microscope, minute air bubbles caught in the mould show up as tiny pock-marks all over the surface. An Egyptian dentist achieved an improvement by placing the mould between the two poles of an electromagnet so drawing the metal back into the recesses of the mould to force out the air bubbles. These so-called pressure casts are very much more difficult to detect.

Perhaps the greatest coin forger of all time was Carl Wilhelm Becker (1772–1830) who perfected the second method. He faithfully engraved new dies from existing coins and struck some very fine and beautiful copies. He was a most prolific forger and the dies he engraved for his 360 forgeries, including Greek, Roman, Visigothic, Transylvanian coins and even siege pieces, are preserved in the Berlin Museum. Many of Becker's pieces are believed to be undetected even today and are no doubt highly regarded by their owners. Now that they are at least 150 years old, they have acquired the patina collectors prize so highly and the only way they can be recognised is by their style.

The style of a coin is the total effect of the engraver's creative ability. This can be very marked in genuine coins but in forgeries the restrictions of imitation manifest themselves to the experienced eye, both in detail and in the overall effect. The style of a coin is also very important in assessing its value particularly in the Greek series. For example, if two coins of the same size, date, material, rarity and condition are compared, the style – that is the conception and execution of the design – can make one of them five or even ten times more valuable than the other.

A recent advance made by forgers was in Sicily where, to foil the electrolytic analysis test, they took to using old coins as blanks on which to strike the new dies. Forgeries can range in subtlety from the finest Sicilian productions to the silver *denarii* of Julius Caesar seen recently on sale to tourists in an Istanbul market bearing the date 48 B.C.

Since 1974, the Lebanese forgers have expanded their operations. The quite rare British £5 pieces of 1887 with a catalogue value of $1400 began to be seen in surprising numbers. The counterfeits were struck from exceptionally well-engraved dies and one or two experienced dealers were taken in by them. More recently, greatly improved counterfeits of valuable coins from twenty-three countries in the world have caused havoc in the market. The International

England, Edward III. Gold noble. Obverse, royal title. Reverse, abbreviation of *Jesus autem transiens per medium illorum ibat.*

England, Elizabeth I. Silver crown.

United Kingdom, Victoria. Gold five pounds. Reverse, St George and dragon. 1887.

Bureau for the Suppression of Counterfeit Coins was set up to gather in and circulate counterfeit reports. These reports contain blown-up photographs of the counterfeits, together with meticulous descriptions of the details by which they may be recognised. The forgers have shown such ingenuity so far, it is likely they will have been able to procure from some nefarious member of the trade the complete dossier of the IBSCC and so take steps to improve the dies even further.

Although these are worrying developments, most doubts can be dispelled by the forgery detection service of the International Association of Professional Numismatists who for a small fee will supply a signed opinion on any piece.

Valuation

The value of a coin is affected by its condition, rarity, material, popularity and style. The following scale of condition is more or less internationally accepted, although in the U.S. there is no such description as FDC and their standards are usually a whole class higher than the European, i.e. EF in the following scale would be equivalent to VF in the U.S.

Fleur-de-coin (FDC): absolute perfection, as it left the mint and even without the minute imperfections that can occasionally be seen on modern mass-produced coins even though fresh from the mint.

Uncirculated (UNC): a coin newly issued from the mint which may nevertheless have tiny imperfections.

Extremely Fine (EF): a coin with its design and inscription still sharp and clear but showing under the eye glass faint traces of wear.

Very Fine (VF): a coin with the design and inscription still clear but with some rubbing or minor damage.

Fine (F): a coin with obvious signs of wear, or badly centred, with visible marks of minor damage such as faint scratches although with design, inscription and date easily distinguishable.

Fair: design inscription and date still distinguishable but serious wear, damage or faulty striking.

Poor: so worn or badly struck or damaged that very little detail can be made out.

Collectors very often buy an example of a coin in each category as a control group so that they can always refer to them when assessing a possible acquisition.

The following scale is often used to specify degrees of rarity:

N Normal	R2 Very rare	R5 5–10 in existence
S Scarce	R3 Extremely rare	R6 3–4 in existence
R Rare	R4 11–20 in existence	R7 1–2 in existence.

Coins can be rare for several reasons. There might have been a small issue in the first place or the ruler appearing on the coin might have died or been killed or deposed during the minting. Or a coin might be one of a small number of patterns struck as samples of a proposed coin not ultimately issued. Or, as sometimes happened when the coins of a particular issue were gathered in and melted down to make a second issue in less fine metal to enable the authorities to take a profit on the debasement, then any that remained of the earlier issue might be rare. A coin can also be very rare in EF condition although quite plentiful in inferior condition. Coins can also exist in reasonably large numbers yet be hard to procure, or at least very expensive in relation to their number because they are so popular. Of the many that have caught people's imaginations are the tribute penny of Tiberius, the shekel of Simon Maccabeus, the denarius of Antony and Cleopatra, the Queen Anne farthing, the 1794 American cent and the Spanish pillar dollars known to every schoolboy as 'pieces of eight'.

The mystique of gold still exerts its power over collectors in that where two coins, one gold and one silver, which otherwise are closely comparable in terms of rarity, workmanship, design, etc., the gold coin will usually be more valuable than the bullion price relationship of the two metals would suggest.

U.S.A. silver dollar, 1795. Draped bust type, small eagle reverse.

(*Left*) U.S.A. copper cent, 1794. Liberty cap type.

(*Below*) U.S.A. gold dollar, 1853. Obverse, Liberty head. Reverse, wreath of olive leaves.

81

The market

The U.K. market for coins has been dominated by three London firms: B. A. Seaby, Spink & Son, and A. H. Baldwin. Although these firms deal in the rarest and most expensive coins in the world, they are always ready to help and spend time with beginners, particularly if they show a real interest in the subject. It is worth remembering that dedicated numismatists have strong reservations about investors. They feel their civilised circle is disrupted by cheque-book-waving vulgarians. They do not wish beautiful coins to fall into unappreciative hands, let alone into bank vaults, and may retaliate in the form of extremely high prices or even refusing to sell exceptional coins at all.

There are many hundreds of lesser dealers – perhaps between five hundred and a thousand, many of whom carry on their business by post. They circulate lists of coins to their customers, often giving fairly inaccurate descriptions. Although these postal dealers usually offer coins on a 'money with order' basis, they will almost invariably return the money to a customer who is not satisfied.

The International Association of Professional Numismatists was formed by dealers to protect themselves and collectors as well as for the dissemination of knowledge and advice. Dealers can be and have been expelled for malpractice and the names of dishonest customers are circulated to members.

The specialist coin auctioneers in London, Glendinings, are part of Phillips, but Christies and Sotheby's also hold coin auctions about once a month. The expertise available in these auction-houses, and hence the high standard of cataloguing together with the absence so far of any buyer's commission on the hammer-price, assures London of its position as capital of the world coin trade.

The Royal Numismatic Society and the British Numismatic Society are the two leading learned bodies of the U.K. coin world both largely concerned with research. The British Association of Numismatic Societies organises conferences and seminars and coordinates the activities of some fifty provincial numismatic societies. These societies hold lectures, discussions and meetings after which some dealing and swapping usually takes place.

The leading numismatic publications in the U.K., mostly available on subscription, are:

British Numismatic Journal
Coin and Medal Bulletin
Coin Monthly
Numismatic Chronicle
Numismatic Circular

And in the U.S., the following are available:

Coin World
Coin World News
The Numismatist

The best annual guides to the values of particular coins are:

Coin Market Values (published by Link House)
Coin 1978 Yearbook (Numismatic Publishing Co.)
A Guide Book to United States Coins (Western Publishing Company Inc.)
Seaby's Standard Catalogue of British Coins
Standard Catalog of World Coins (Krause and Mischler)

Why do people collect?

It is the spell that coins weave over collectors that cannot be very precisely defined. Collectors often account for the attractions of coins by reference to their great value as historical documents. It is true that coins do contain a great deal of information that would not have reached us without them. Together with sculpture they tell us of the appearance of many ancient and medieval rulers. But for all that, a coin cannot in isolation provide as much information as a single paragraph in a history book, although there are cases where that paragraph could not have been written without coins. It is usually that they evoke history rather than that they are pieces of history and it is their powerful associations with historical figures or events that make them so desirable.

A man might reflect that the tribute penny of Tiberius in his collection was the same as the one that Jesus held in his hand when he said 'Render unto Caesar the things that are Caesar's'. The aesthetic appeal of many coins is quite evident yet others with no such claim are often equally valued by collectors.

The unconscious motives for coin collecting will vary from one collector to another. It is nevertheless very noticeable that the feature common to most coins is the representation of a figure of considerable power, usually a king or queen or dictator and, even before mortals were portrayed, a god or goddess frequently appeared on Greek coins. The coin collector then is collecting symbols of power and his ownership or control of them may be enough to remove for him the threat of their authority or it may enable him to feel part of their power has transferred itself to him. He has them as it were in his pocket. The lack of interest shown by collectors generally in most Middle Eastern coins can be explained not only by the difficulty in understanding the inscriptions but also because they very seldom carry the head of a ruler which creates that essential interest. Coin collecting may also be a rationalised form of miserliness where, because the actual hoarding of coins would be socially unacceptable, it takes a ritualised form and can be passed off as the most civilised of pursuits.

ALTERNATIVE INVESTMENT

Market movements

In 1950, the market for coins in the U.K. and the U.S.A. was very small indeed. Old coins were generally looked upon as useless scraps of metal that no one could quite bring themselves to throw away and the people who actively collected them were considered cranks. The circle of dealers was similarly small and at an important sale at Glendining's in May 1954, 90% of the lots were bought by just two dealers, Spink and Baldwin, the remaining 10% going to four other dealers. Those six dealers would probably have been the only people attending the sale. At a sale of comparable importance at Christies in 1977, forty-eight different buyers were recorded.

In these changed circumstances, the ring cannot operate even at a normal sale in the U.K. or U.S.A., let alone an international sale. Many coins are anyway so standardised that it would not be in the interests of dealers to form a ring and depress the prices in the saleroom unduly because many collectors would know the prices the dealers had paid and would refuse to pay what the ring-members were charging in their shops.

The market rate for proof coins, where there can be no argument over condition, is so well-known that the margins dealers have to work on are fairly tight and this represents a major benefit to investors. If a dealer paid $1000 at auction for a proof set, it would probably be offered the next day with a mark up of only 10–20%. If a dealer is offered the same proof set privately, he will naturally tend to offer less than he would expect to have to pay in a saleroom and, if he succeeds in buying it, he will offer it at the same price as the one bought in the saleroom, giving himself in this case a higher margin. It is extremely unwise to take a rare coin to a dealer unless you know him and the market very well indeed. There have been successful prosecutions against dealers who have knowingly offered absurdly low prices for rare and valuable coins and subsequently sold them for many times the prices they gave.

Descriptions of condition in saleroom catalogues tend, by tradition, to be conservative because buyers generally are suspicious of attempts to overgrade coins. The question of condition is paramount in the coin world and the concept of a buying and a selling condition is well understood. Over the last ten years, the obsession with condition has been promoted by unscrupulous dealers to take advantage of collectors. Some numismatists estimate over half the coin-dealers operating in the U.S.A. and U.K. are living by perpetrating a massive confidence trick on collectors.

To accept that this is happening, it is first necessary to understand the almost unimaginable gullibility and ignorance of most coin-collectors and investors. In the U.S.A. there are otherwise intelligent professional people who will instruct a dealer to put $1000 a month in coins with no knowledge of the subject at all. Not only do they have no knowledge, they have no wish to acquire any

84

knowledge and it is quite usual for the investor to have the dealer mail the coins direct to his bank without ever seeing them. Presumably, in such cases, the investor supposes coins to be a fungible commodity like a Stock Exchange security whereas the difference between the condition of two otherwise identical coins can make one a hundred times more valuable than the other. The American Numismatic Association is in the process of establishing a new official grading system using numbers and precise descriptions of the appearance of a coin in different states. Unfortunately, many people expect the new system to provide unscrupulous dealers with just one more means of confusing collectors.

Most coin collectors find all modern coinage – that is, post 1945 – considerably less interesting both in design and material than any that has gone before. The circumstances of each issue are what makes a coin interesting to a true numismatist: the portrait, the artist, the legend, the value, the process of manufacture etc. Modern coinage, it seems, may even be designed to be unappealing or at least to deter hoarding. The five-franc piece issued by the French Government in the late 1950s was so heavy and shiny it caught the public imagination and was hoarded away up chimneys and into mattresses in such quantities that its primary function of circulating as a medium of exchange could not be fulfilled without extra minting.

The American market for modern coins has developed in its own quite unique way. The market for investment was initiated by promoters in the 1930s. It was then that investors seriously began to buy cents, nickels, dimes, quarters and halves by the roll. The mintages were sometimes quite small in those days and the rationale of these purchases was, as it still is today, that future generations of coin-collectors, of which there will have to be quite a number, will need these coins to lay the foundations of their collections. These bags and rolls are quoted in the U.S.A. on teletype circuits in the same way as any other commodity. Commemoratives, silver dollars, proof and mint sets are dealt in the same way.

Circulated coins are graded G – good, VG – very good, F – Fine, VF – very fine, XF – extremely fine and AU – about uncirculated. Bright uncirculated coins (BU) are graded MS 60, 65 and 70 – Mint State with the numbers indicating the state of the lustre or the presence of bag marks. Speculation in coin rolls is now on a smaller scale than in the early seventies. Many people dropped out simply because they lost money, others because the dealer's spread between buying and selling prices was too wide and yet others developed into serious coin-collectors.

The mintage of U.S. proof sets which had been only 3837 in 1936 grew in response to demand from investors to become quite big business for the Government and to reach a first peak of 3·9 million sets in 1964. Thereafter, demand settled back until a new peak of 4·1 million sets were issued in 1976. The issue prices for 1964 and 1976 were $2.10 and $7.00 respectively and market values are now $5.00 and $7.75.

Many countries have tried to cash in on the buying-power of coin collectors by minting a special class of commemorative coins known as non-circulating legal tender coins. In the sixties, promoters began to approach officials in various countries such as Haiti, Ghana, Andorra, Costa Rica, Ivory Coast, Ecuador and prevailed upon them by one means or another to arrange the issue and cooperate in the marketing of series of coins conceived entirely to exploit collectors. The number of these issues reached a peak in 1974 when unfavourable publicity over the losses suffered by collectors when they sold this type of coin made buyers generally more wary and most issuing authorities careful not to market unacceptably large numbers nor offer coins at excessive premiums.

The silver and copper series, for example, issued by the Argentine Government in connection with the 1978 World Cup Soccer may circulate as legal tender and have been issued in small enough numbers for there to be a good chance of their later market value comparing favourably with their issue price.

Many private organisations in the U.S.A. and U.K. profited by the surge of interest in coins in the sixties and began to market series of medallions through newspapers and periodicals. The medallions were sometimes well struck but invariably the intrinsic value of the metal was no more than a small fraction of the price the investor was invited to pay, the balance being for the artistry and production costs. In many cases, the editions were said to be strictly limited but, on closer enquiry, the limit usually turned out to be strictly limited to the number of people who sent in their cheques. When all the cheques were in production began and this explained the 'Allow six weeks for delivery' or 'Orders are handled in strict rotation' or whatever nonsense was put in the advertisements to create an impression of scarcity.

Salerooms in London and New York are frequently having to explain to people who bring in such medallions with a view to realising their 'investments' that, with rare exceptions, they stand no chance of recovering more than the scrap value of the metal from which they are made. It is unfortunate that the people to whom these offers usually appeal are those least able to stand the loss. For a similar price they might so easily have bought a real collector's piece such as a Henry VIII groat or a Saxon penny which would very likely have proved a sound investment.

The psychology of the coin market is partly concerned with fear. Many collectors regard coins as a form of insurance, explaining that when the dollar is worth nothing they will have them at least to fall back on. At coin fairs, dealers notice people are reluctant to part with their coins. They ask how much a coin is worth and if told $1 they tend to say they will give it to their son and if told $100 they say they had better keep it.

Coin price-movements have been quite volatile recently. The sharpest rise in values came in 1973 and 1974 when the values of many conventional securities were collapsing. Prices of the classic series of coins rose very fast and this focussed attention on neglected areas such as early commemorative coins, trade tokens etc. But back in 1970 in the U.K. there was a rush to buy the coins of the pre-decimal series which drove prices unreasonably high as people scrambled to complete their sets before decimalisation. Prices for quite common coins shot up with people paying for instance $50 for a mint 1959 half-crown which can now be had for $2.

Other random examples will give an idea of the price-movements that can occur. Scottish gold coins shot up in 1974 by as much as 150% but could be bought in 1976 for half the prices they had fetched two years earlier. Byzantine gold coins, for which a typical price was $15 in the early 1960s, reached $300–400 in 1973/4 but were back to $200 in 1977. English gold coins too made new highs in 1974 but as 1975 wore on, even though their prices did not fall as far as the Scottish and Byzantine series, there was a very obvious lack of interest as collectors switched their attention to silver coins which were beginning to climb in value. Roman and Greek gold coins too had a dramatic rise in 1974 and following the sharp setback in 1975 are now holding steady. There are fewer younger collectors with a knowledge of Greek and Latin nowadays and interest in the ancient series is expected to wane slightly for this reason.

Several other series rose sharply to their peaks in 1974 and slumped to half or less of their value the following year. German coins of the Weimar Republic went through this experience although they have been recovering strongly in the last year. An exceptionally steep rise in classic United Kingdom coins took place in the second half of 1974 when the Financial Times Index was falling sharply. In mid 1974, a 1937 U.K. proof set – always an accurate barometer of the market – was fetching $500 but by the end of the year, as the U.K. stock market moved towards its twenty-year low, people were paying $1300 for the same set. Numismatists have been appalled at the disruptive effect of investors on the coin market. The steady trends of the last thirty years have been broken and, even after a period of consolidation, it is quite possible that falling stock markets will again produce a wave of speculation in coins.

The discovery of hoards can upset the price of coins and will always be bad news for someone. The William I silver penny, for example, used to be the rarest of all Norman coins until a hoard of 8640 was unearthed in Hampshire in 1833 which overnight made it one of the most common. Greater archaeological and construction activity has increased the rate of discoveries and there are many instances of coin values being affected in this way. Medieval coins of Cyprus were comparatively rare, the silver gros of 1380–1400 selling for $30–40 until discoveries in 1975/6 brought the price back to $2–4. The Prestwich hoard of English pennies brought too many on to the market and a Colchester penny of King Stephen 1135–54 made $500 at the first sale in 1975 but two years later an almost identical coin was sold at $300.

In 1957, a 1927 $20 Double Eagle minted in Denver, one of only eight accounted for out of the 180,000 minted, was worth $1,200. In a 1969 sale it made $32,000; in 1972, another specimen changed hands for $60,000, in 1973 for $90,000 and in 1974 for $175,000. The regular 1927 Double Eagle minted in San Francisco and therefore missing the tiny D on the Denver-struck coins is not uncommon and worth $300. In this case extreme rarity alone accounts for the massive premium one coin commands over another almost identical.

It is said there are no more coin collectors now, just investors. Coins have become a fairly rough business since 1974 which makes it all the more urgent for the novice to find a dealer he can really trust. To buy coins with no knowledge obviously amounts to an act of faith in the dealer, apparently quite often misplaced these days. The literature now available to help the amateur is vast and even a few weeks' study on one theme will provide an investor with the basic survival kit to venture cautiously into this complex market.

Book list

CARSON, R. A. *Coins of the World: Ancient, Medieval, Modern* (Illus.) 1962, Harper & Row

HOBSON, BURTON. *Coins and Coin Collecting* (Illus.) 1971, Dover

LINECAR, HOWARD A. *The Commemorative Medal: Its Appreciation and Collection* (Illus.) 1974, Gale

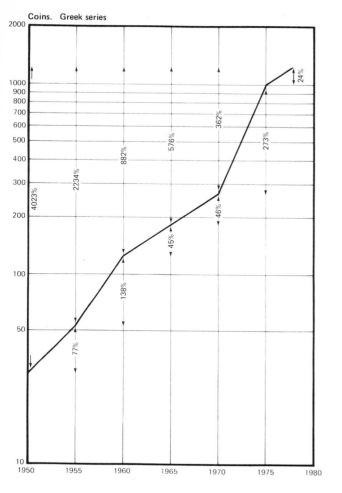

Coins. Greek series

INDEX NO. 1. GREEK.

1. Sicily.   Syracuse.   c. 470 B.C.   Tetradrachm. R
2. Attica.   Athens.   c. 440 B.C.   Tetradrachm. R
3. Macedon.   Alexander III   336–323 B.C.   Stater. N
4. Lucania.   Metapontum.   330–300 B.C.   Stater. R
5. Egypt.   Ptolemy II   285–246 B.C.   Octodrachm. N

N = gold R = silver

CONDITION – Extremely Fine.

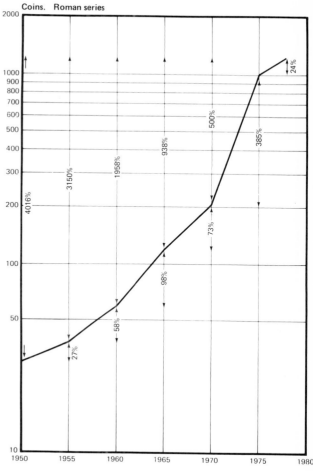

Coins. Roman series

INDEX NO. 2. ROMAN.

1. Julius Caesar. c. 47 B.C.   Denarius. R
2. Caligula.   37–41 A.D.   Sestertius. $Æ$
3. Otho.   69. A.D.   Denarius. R
4. Hadrian.   117–138 A.D.   Aureus. N
5. Constantine I. 307–337 A.D.   Solidus. N

N = gold R = silver $Æ$ = copper

CONDITION – Extremely Fine

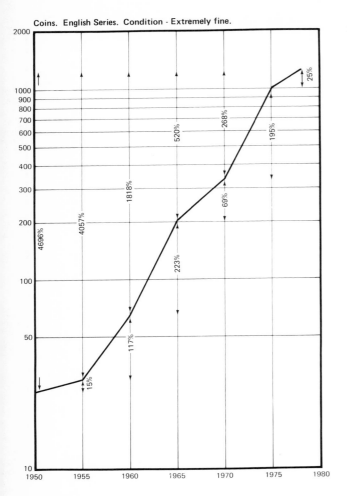

Coins. English Series. Condition - Extremely fine.

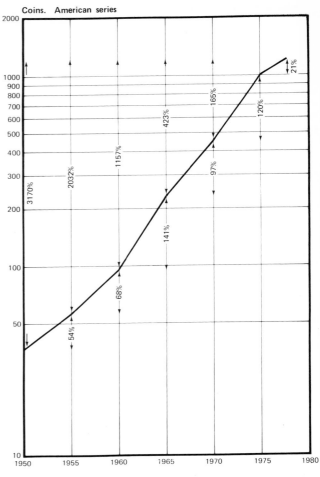

Coins. American series

INDEX NO. 3. ENGLISH.

1. Edward III Treaty Period.	1361–69.	Noble. N
2. Elizabeth I	1601.	Crown. R
3. Commonwealth.	1653.	Unite. N
4. Cromwell.	1658	Crown. R
5. Victoria.	1887	Five pounds. N

N = gold R = silver

CONDITION – Extremely Fine

INDEX NO. 4. AMERICAN.

1. 1794.	One Cent. $Æ$
2. 1795.	One Dollar. R
3. 1835.	Five Dollars. N
4. 1853.	One Dollar N
4. 1870S	One Dime. R

N = gold R = silver $Æ$ = copper

CONDITION – Extremely Fine.

90

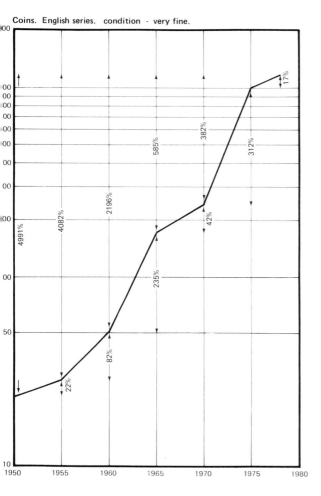

Coins. English series. condition - very fine.

4991% 4082% 2196% 235% 585% 82% 382% 42% 312% 22% 17%

INDEX NO. 5. ENGLISH

1. Edward III Treaty Period.   1361–9.   Noble. N
2. Elizabeth I.   1601.   Crown. R
3. Commonwealth.   1653   Unite. N
4. Cromwell.   1658   Crown. R
5. Victoria.   1887   Five pounds. N

N = gold R = silver

CONDITION – Very fine.

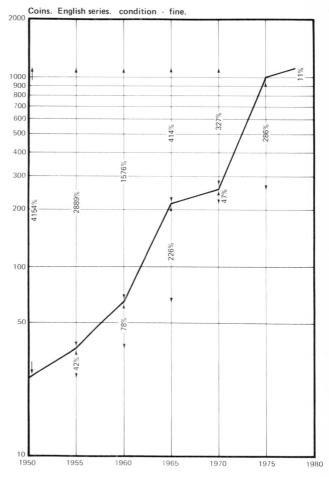

Coins. English series. condition - fine.

4154% 2889% 1576% 414% 226% 327% 47% 286% 78% 42% 11%

COINS. INDEX NO. 6 ENGLISH.

As above except

CONDITION – Fine.

91

Diamonds

Human beings have decorated themselves with teeth, stones and *objets trouvés* in general since the Palaeolithic Age (25,000–18,000 B.C.). But diamonds, which in their natural state look rather like soda crystals to most people, may well have been ignored in favour of prettier stones such as rubies and emeralds at least until the first millenium B.C. when some rudimentary polishing skill began to be learnt.

Diamonds are composed of carbon which is one of the commonest substances on earth. It is found in combination with other atoms in trees, plants, their residues, coal and oil, and many kinds of rock, but it only occurs in crystal form as graphite and diamond. Graphite is the soft black mineral used as the lead in a pencil, and diamond the hard, transparent and shiny substance once the rarest, now the most widely owned gem-stone in the world.

The word diamond derives from the Greek *adamas* meaning invincible, because it was believed in ancient Greece that diamonds were unbreakable. In A.D. 77 Pliny wrote in his *Natural History* that if a diamond were hammered on an anvil, the hammer would bounce back from the diamond and the anvil would split in two. Most of Pliny's information on diamonds is wrong, yet in this he is strangely close to the truth. A diamond is extremely brittle and if struck as he suggests, it would shatter immediately. Yet being the hardest substance known, if it were squeezed gradually in an iron vice, it would keep its shape and impress itself into the jaws.

India was the world's only source of diamonds until 1725 when deposits were discovered in Brazil. The Indian diamonds were probably in circulation by about 800 B.C. and although there is a reference in Exodus XXVIII which suggests that they were known in 1200 B.C., this, from the context, is probably a mis-translation for corundum. The next reference in the Bible is in Jeremiah XVII about 600 B.C. which fits with the knowledge that iron tools with diamond tips for cutting other stones were common by this date.

The origin of diamonds is still a mystery. Current theory has it that diamonds were formed about 120 miles below ground in a part of the earth's mantle composed of the ultra-basic rock peridotite. Carbon is thought to have turned by slow precipitation into diamond in the molten peridotite, at temperatures between 1292–4532°F and at pressures between 500,000 and 1,300,000 pounds per square inch. Some 120 million years ago, these diamonds were forced to the surface of the earth by an explosive drive of carbon dioxide gas which explains

92

the geological structures known as pipes in which many diamonds are found. Over a period of millions of years, rivers washed away the top layers of these pipes taking with them the diamonds. The diamonds first found in India were discovered in the beds and banks of rivers.

The most famous of these alluvial deposits, Golconda, was the great gorge of the river Kristna in Hyderabad. Pliny offers a most exotic account of the recovery of these diamonds which has survived in the legend of Sinbad. They were to be found, he claimed, only in the East, lying on the floor of one deep inaccessible valley which was guarded by venomous snakes. From the heights, the natives threw down pieces of carrion flesh to which the diamonds stuck. Mountain eagles would then swoop down to the bait and carry it off, with the diamonds attached, to their rocky nests. The diamond-gatherers then climbed to the nests and collected the diamonds from the droppings round about.

Whatever the precise method of extraction may have been in those days, the first eye-witness acount to reach Europe was not until Jean-Baptiste Tavernier, a French jeweller, published an account of his six journeys to the East. On his second visit to India in 1638, he recounts that some 60,000 men, women and children were at work in the valley at Golconda. The men in those days shovelled the mixture from the riverbed into pans. The soil was then washed away with water by the women and children who sifted the diamonds from the sand and heavy minerals that were left behind. Some of the largest diamonds ever found came from India, and many of these still exist among the family jewels of Indian princes.

The appeal of diamonds

Diamonds have many curious properties which have taken thousands of years to discover. For this reason they have been valued for different reasons at different times. Diamonds were traded by the Arabs and Persians throughout most of the Middle East as early as the 4th century B.C. The Romans are known to have bought them for their magical powers, while Indian Buddhists believed that some impure souls which could not yet be united with the great universal soul were temporarily animating various minerals, including diamonds. Such beliefs no doubt accompanied the diamonds as they spread west and we find Theophrastus actually classified them into male and female. The medicinal value of powdered diamond, according to Hindu tradition, depended on the quality of the stone. The powder of a flawed diamond was supposed to bring on a variety of diseases, whereas the powder of a top quality stone brought long life, health, happiness and so forth.

A list of a diamond's powers, published by Leonardus in Europe in 1502, included curing lunatics and those possessed by devils, winning lawsuits, taming wild animals and conquering enemies. As late as 1532 diamond powder was prescribed to the ailing Pope Clement VII, but he failed to survive the fourteenth spoonful. Even today people are inclined to believe in the magical and sometimes maleficent power of certain diamonds – successive owners of the 44-carat Hope diamond, for example, having succumbed to a sequence of disasters.

Cutting and polishing

The discovery of the art of diamond-polishing was probably made in India soon after the discovery of diamonds themselves. Diamond-polishers have always tended to be secretive about their trade; their skills were handed down from father to son and no written record of their art has survived. The basic tools involved in diamond-polishing have barely changed in the last five hundred years and were probably much the same in the earlier two thousand.

The only substance hard enough to polish a diamond is a diamond's own dust. The arrangement of the atoms in a diamond is such that some faces of the diamond are hard and some soft. Each stone therefore has what is known as a hard direction and a soft direction, rather like the nap on the surface of velvet. Diamond chips were ground up in a pestle and mortar, and the resulting dust, mixed with olive oil, was then worked into a wooden or cast-iron wheel, now known as the scaife. The soft face of the diamond was then pressed against the rotating wheel on which some of the diamond dust particles would be presenting their hard direction to the diamond and in this way a highly-polished facet was created.

The shape in which a diamond most frequently occurs in its natural state is an octahedron – that is, the shape of two pyramids stuck base to base – while most of its other natural shapes are related to this. The art of cleaving a diamond, which is based on a knowledge of these shapes, may also have been known in ancient India, although its origins remain mysterious. If a diamond can be cleaved, and this can only be done along a plane parallel to a face of the octahedron, two usable pieces may result from a single rough stone. The operation, which always carries a certain risk, is done by laying a metal blade in a groove cut parallel to the chosen plane of the octahedron, tapping the blade with a hammer and so causing the diamond to fall cleanly into two.

The art of cutting and polishing diamonds developed slowly, and although the Brilliant Cut with its fifty-eight facets was first used in the 17th century, the angles were not cut in such a way as to return the most light to the beholder. It was only at the beginning of this century that optical science showed the diamond-cutter how to maximise the return of light from a diamond and even now there are disagreements over the angular relation of one facet to another. Hitherto cutters had been preoccupied with maintaining weight even though at the expense of brilliance.

94

The invention of bruting, or cutting as it is now known, was probably made about 1400. The process which was used to give a diamond its preliminary shape before the polishing or faceting began, involved placing the diamond to be shaped in a stick which was then vigorously rubbed by another diamond in another stick, while the dust was collected in the cleaving box underneath. The skills of cutting and polishing may have originated in Venice in the 14th century, but had certainly spread to most of Europe during the course of the 15th.

The first shape into which diamonds were made was the Point Cut, where the stone's natural octahedral shape was simply polished up. Such diamonds can be seen on the sleeve of Henry IV of England (1399–1413) in a portrait in the National Portrait Gallery in London, and there is little doubt that at this stage the diamond was being worn as an amulet to ward off evil spirits or to endow the wearer by a process of sympathetic magic with its own primary characteristic of hardness.

The Table Cut was the next most natural development, in which one point of one pyramid was ground away. Next came the Lozenge Cut, which exposed the cubic plane and was the easiest surface of all to polish, and thereafter a large number of variations decided upon firstly by the shape of the original uncut stone, and secondly in an attempt, mostly by trial and error, to maximise the light that the diamond returned.

The determinants of value

The four most important determinants of the value of a diamond are its cut, clarity, colour and carat (weight) – known as the four Cs.

CUT: The cut is important because it must take advantage of the diamond's three optical properties: refractivity, reflectivity and dispersion. All transparent substances are refractive – that is, when light enters them at any angle other than the perpendicular, the path taken by the light deviates. In glass, the refractive index is expressed numerically as 1·5, while in diamond it is very high indeed at 2·42. If, then, light enters a diamond and meets a face at an angle greater than $24\frac{1}{2}$ degrees, it does not pass through it but is reflected internally as though that face were a mirror. So the important effect of the diamond's high refractivity is what is known as its total internal reflection. By perfect faceting, most of the light that enters a diamond can be made to bounce off the facets and back in the direction from which it came.

The reflectivity of materials is closely related to their refractivity and the reflectivity of a diamond is therefore high. Whereas light falling perpendicularly on glass would reflect only 4% of that light, diamond reflects 18%.

The third and most important of its optical properties – dispersion – concerns the way in which the different components of light are refracted. White light is composed of different colours and a diamond has a slightly higher refractive index for the blue component of light than for the red, and so on. This means that as the light moves through the diamond, it is broken up into all the colours of the spectrum which return separately to the looker. This gives the diamond its spectral 'fire', the glittering effect for which it is so highly prized.

CLARITY: No diamond is absolutely flawless, and the clarity of a diamond is often even now a matter of subjective judgement. All diamond grading systems try to quantify and qualify the imperfections in a stone. Various terminologies are used, of which the Scandinavian Diamond Nomenclature system (Scan. D.N.), the Gemological Institute of America (G.I.A.) and the Confédération

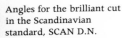

Angles for the brilliant cut in the Scandinavian standard, SCAN D.N.

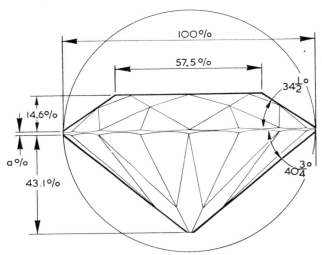

(Opposite) A pair of porcelain covered jars enamelled in the famille rose palette with a continuous scene of ladies at play on horseback in a garden, one lady throwing her whip to an admiring gentleman spectator who stands among others on the balcony of a pavilion, another lady seen adjusting her coiffure; the covers painted with large peony blooms and both jars and covers with decorative borders of diaper patterns; the knops on the covers embellished with gold enamel.
Yung-cheng period 1723–35
Height: 25 inches.

Augustus 31 BC—AD 14

Tiberius 14—37 AD

Caligula 37—41 AD

Claudius 41—54 AD

Nero 54—68 AD

Vespasian 69—79 AD

Domitian 81—96 AD

Trajan 98—117 AD

Hadrian 117—138 AD

Antoninus Pius 138—161 AD

Marcus Aurelius 161—180 AD

Caracalla 211—217 AD

(Actual sizes c. ¾")

Internationale de la Bijouterie, Joaillerie, Orfèvrerie. (C.I.B.J.O.) are the most widely recognised. Scan. D.N. makes use of the following terms:

F.L.   Flawless
I.F.   Internally flawless
V.V.S.   Very, very small inclusions
V.S.   Very small inclusions
S.I.   Small inclusions
P.   Piqué

(*Opposite*) A selection of Roman coins.

Anything that interferes with the passage of light through the stone, whether internal or external, diminishes its value and is graded according to this or a similar scale. The jeweller's loupe, an eyeglass with a ten-times magnification, is used for this purpose, although to place a stone in the last category in the Scan D.N. scale or any other scale would signify the presence of a flaw visible to the naked eye. Each of the last four categories is subdivided into two or more sub-categories, so precise classification is difficult enough to give rise to serious disagreements from time to time. Some diamond dealers now use a slit lamp with a graticule set into the eye-piece which measures the size of any inclusion and relates it to one or other clarity scale.

COLOUR: Scientific equipment can also be used to measure the colour of a diamond. There are at least a dozen colour-grading systems in use throughout the world using letters, numbers, adjectives and even the names of mines to describe the range of colours from pure white to yellow. Diamonds are so nearly pure carbon that the purest give the impression of being quite white. Yet in nearly all gem diamonds, there are traces of nitrogen and other impurities (0·2–0·0001%) which absorb some of the colour in white light giving each stone a more or less yellowish tinge. A traditional method used by dealers to grade a diamond's colour is by relating it to a set of perhaps ten master stones which range from pure white to light yellow. Even an untrained eye can soon match a stone to its counterpart in the master group. Yet not everyone's eyesight is the same and differences can become specially apparent when a selling-price is being negotiated.

The visible spectrum can be measured in Angstroms, each of which is equivalent to one ten millionth of a meter. At around 4150 Angstroms, the nitrogen present in all diamonds will absorb a small amount of light. A system in growing use, known as reflectance spectrophotometry, measures how much light each diamond absorbs and hence the intensity of its colour. This scientific method can, when properly used, partly eliminate subjective judgement and with it one major hazard for investors.

CARAT: A diamond is usually weighed according to an ancient unit of weight, the carat. The word is taken from the Greek name of the locust-tree Keration (in Latin, *Ceratonia siliqua*) whose fruit was a black pod in which were beans filled

97

with a sweet syrup. The tree is common throughout the Middle East and it was the ancient pearl-traders who noticed that when these beans dried out they were remarkably uniform in weight, and adopted them as the unit of weight for pearls. As the trade in pearls and diamonds spread, various countries related the carat to their own weighing systems.

Eventually the carat came to signify different weights in different places until it was internationally standardised in the early part of this century as equivalent to 0·2 of a gram. Each carat is divided into one hundred points, so that a diamond of two and three-quarter carats is written 2·75 ct. To weigh loose stones requires only an accurate balance of which many types are available, but the weighing of mounted stones presents difficulties. The Leveridge gauge takes the stone's measurements by means of calipers at one end, while the figures are shown on a dial at the other end. Elaborate tables giving the relative weights of every kind of cut are supplied with the instrument enabling any jewel to be weighed accurately to within 5%.

The valuation process

In practice, diamond merchants refer to their price lists for each grade and size of diamond in which they have to deal and the amateur is hopelessly ill-equipped to discuss prices with them. In *theory* the price lists will reflect differentials which have been worked out according to the following or some similar set of calculations.

First of all, a value for a 1-carat stone of ideal cut, clarity and colour is assumed at, say $10,000. Now the clarity of the stone to be valued is rated on the Scan. D.N. scale at V.S.I. because of a small clouded area, detected with the aid of a loupe, which reduces the value by 30% to $7,000. The colour rating indicated by the reflectance spectrophotometer corresponds to Wesselton or White in other systems which might reduce the value by another 50%, bringing it to $3,500.

Now the cut is assessed and found to be of the old-fashioned Brilliant type where the facets, although right in number, are set at the wrong angles, so allowing much of the light to escape through the back of the stone. It is estimated that the loss of weight involved in recutting it to ideal shape would be 30%. There would then be applied the Indian basis of valuation, first quoted by Tavernier, or some variant of it which rules that the value per carat of a stone does not remain constant as the weight increases or decreases – rather, the value is an exponential function of the weight. This is broadly a recognition of the fact that the rarity of diamonds increases with their size. The weight (W) of the diamond to be valued is squared and multiplied by the basic price of a diamond of identical quality weighing 1 carat (C). The value of any stone therefore is W^2C. In this case the weight of the diamond left after recutting is 70 points or

0·7 ct, and the value of a 1-carat stone of identical quality is $3,500. So the value of the stone is:

$$0·7 \times 0·7 \times \$3,500 = \$1715$$

less the costing of the recutting operation.

Uses and discoveries

Whatever the original uses of diamonds may have been they very soon became symbolic of wealth, power and rank. The expeditions of Alexander the Great to the East in the 4th century B.C. brought first-hand knowledge of diamonds to Europe, after which many Roman Emperors formed collections of diamonds and other jewels. Caligula's wife Lollia Pauline was smothered (according to Pliny) with emeralds and pearls, whose great value she was ready to prove on request by producing the receipts. In the 1st and 2nd centuries A.D., Romans wore diamond rings for superstitious reasons but, with the decline of their Empire, the history of diamonds becomes obscure. Paris was a centre of goldsmiths in the 7th century, when three jewellers were actually canonised, but for a long time the only jewellery workshops were attached to the monasteries producing pieces for the priests to wear.

The earliest surviving European piece set with diamonds (still uncut) is the Crown of St. Stephen amongst the Hungarian Crown Jewels, and can be dated to 1078. In the 12th and 13th centuries a number of secular jewellers were established, while in the 14th century many references are found to presents of diamonds, rubies, sapphires and pearls, although diamonds were probably still the least highly regarded. The fact that women rather than men were now receiving diamond jewellery as presents suggests that advances in cutting and polishing techniques had already been made.

There were evidently enough jewels being imported to England in 1283 for a law to be passed restricting the wearing of jewels to people of noble birth – similar laws being passed soon after in France and Spain. Judging by contemporary portraits, the pearl seems to have remained the most frequent ornament until the 17th century. Henry VIII seems to have preferred rubies for his collar and rings, although his buttons were diamonds. His contemporary François I of France wore a collar of large table-cut diamonds and some uncut octahedra. Elizabeth I of England wore some diamonds, although portraits of her invariably show her clothes profusely ornamented with pearls.

The diamond was gradually superseding the pearl in the course of the 17th century. Although in the England of Oliver Cromwell the wearing of any jewellery was in official disfavour, at the Restoration of the Monarchy in 1660 the growing popularity of diamonds was again evident. The circumstances favouring diamonds were firstly the flourishing European trade with India which was bringing more and more diamonds into circulation, and secondly the invention by Vincenzio Perruzzi in Venice in around 1650 of the early form of the Brilliant Cut. This step was important because by almost correct faceting it showed as no other cut had yet the diamond's great brilliance and fire.

It was, too, an age of uninhibited flamboyance typified by Louis XIV of France who wore, for instance, a dress with 171 diamond buttons, as well as diamond sprays and a diamond-hilted sword to go with it, while *décolleté* dresses encouraged women to wear diamond necklaces and pendants, which were seen at their very best in flickering candlelight. By the early part of the 18th century diamonds were established as the most sought-after jewels in the world.

Brazil

It is likely that the price of diamonds was stable and possibly on a rising trend throughout Europe at the time the Brazilian deposits were discovered in 1725. Some crystals had been found by the gold miners in the alluvial gravels in the Minas Geraes region of Brazil and sent to Amsterdam to be cut. The results showed the stones to be as fine as anything India had ever produced and prices began to drop sharply. For a time the Indian merchants managed to halt the slide by putting it about that the new stones were but poor quality Indian stones shipped to Brazil, but the tables were turned on them by the Portuguese, who soon shipped the Brazilian stones to India and sold them as Indian.

These deposits were worked by some 40,000 black slaves who dug the gravel by hand-spade and carried it to special areas where it was tipped into washing compartments. White overseers sitting on high chairs and holding long whips supervised this part of the operation, and any slave finding a stone over $17\frac{1}{2}$ carats was rewarded with his freedom. Very few are believed to have secured their freedom in this way.

For 150 years Brazil was the largest supplier of diamonds in the world, but the deposits were intensively worked, and in spite of subsequent discoveries the production of Brazil is relatively small today.

South Africa

The first diamond found in South Africa was the $21\frac{1}{4}$ carat Eureka diamond, as it afterwards came to be known. The sparkling pebble was found by a fifteen-year-old boy, Erasmus Jacobs, on his parents' farm in Cape Colony just south of the Orange River. It was eventually identified as a diamond and exhibited at the Paris Exibition of 1867. But the big find which triggered the first world-wide rush was an $83\frac{1}{2}$ carat stone found by a Griqua shepherd-boy and bought from him by Schalk van Neekirk, a Boer farmer and trader, for a horse, ten oxen, a

Washing for diamonds at Mandango, Brazil, *c.* 1760.

wagon and five hundred sheep. The stone, now known as the Star of South Africa, was sold at Christies in 1974 for $450,000.

By 1870, some ten thousand claims were being worked along the banks of the Vaal River and on neighbouring farms. A bizarre assortment of adventurers poured into South Africa from all over the world. Crooks and deserters as well as honest men lived together in the diggers' camps, where conditions were

101

chaotic with much fighting and stealing. One by one the great pipe mines were discovered – Jagersfontein, Dutoitspan, Bultfontein, De Beers, Kimberley, Koffiefontein, Wesselton and Premier in 1902 – each discovery precipitating another frantic rush to peg claims.

The story of the early days of the South African diamond-mining industry, which bristles with violence, intrigue and treachery, has often been told. The two figures that dominate the early years are Cecil Rhodes and Barney Barnato (né Barnett Isaacs). Rhodes arrived from England in 1870 and, having failed to buy a claim at the De Beers' diggings, made money hiring out a pump to diggers whose claims were flooded. The profits from this venture were used to buy other claims and join in partnership with diggers who did not want to sell completely. By 1880 Rhodes had built up, by organising amalgamations and further buying, an important stake in the De Beers mine and he formed the De Beers Mining Company Ltd.

Barnato's successful coup had been to buy up a large number of claims in the Kimberley mine when the diggers, having reached the stratum known as 'hard blue ground', believed they had struck the barren bedrock and lost interest in their claims. He sank shafts into the rock and found it still to be rich in

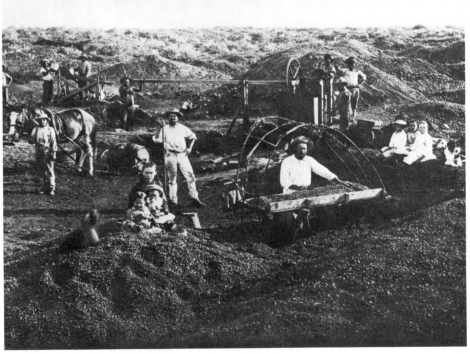

Working at a sorting table near Kimberley in the 1880s. It was unusual to find women and children living in the very harsh conditions.

102

The Kimberley Mines in 1877, now the largest man-made hole in the world. The picture shows the different levels to which claims have been worked.

diamonds at this level. In 1887, as the largest shareholder in the Kimberley mine, he began a bitter battle with Rhodes to acquire the only other large shareholding in Kimberley, held by a French mining company. The shares of the mining companies soared in 1888 during the financial battle, although sales of diamonds themselves were at the time declining sharply, with the price at one time dropping to $1.96 per rough carat. Rhodes and Barnato eventually sank their differences and finished up as shareholders in a new company, De Beers Consolidated Mines Ltd., which controlled the majority of the mines in the Kimberley area.

The other important pipe mines to be discovered later were in South West Africa, Finsch 1961, Congo (Zaire), Angola, Ghana, Sierra Leone, Tanzania, Botswana and Lesotho. But it was the Premier which produced in 1905 the largest diamond ever found, the Cullinan weighing 3106 carats. It was cut into 105 stones, of which the two largest are still the largest cut diamonds in the world, and can be seen in the British Crown Jewels at the Tower of London.

Most of the African diamonds of gem quality discovered today come from the 140-mile strip of coastal sands running from Luderitz to the mouth of the Orange River in S.W. African or Namibian territory. The first finds were made in 1908, and a large part of the area eventually passed into and has remained under the control of De Beers.

103

U.S.S.R

The news that diamond pipe deposits had been discovered in the U.S.S.R. in 1954 equal in size to those of South Africa was originally greeted with some scepticism in the West. It was known that systematic prospecting had been going on since 1938, mainly in a vast tract of Siberia geologically similar to the diamond-bearing structures of India and Africa.

Since 1954 about twenty pipes have been discovered, of which the largest is the Mir (Peace) pipe in Yakutskaya. In this area, the ground is permanently frozen to a depth of around 1000 feet which makes the extraction not only arduous, but extremely expensive. Yet, in spite of these conditions, so important are diamonds to Soviet industry that about a quarter of the world's total annual production of 40 million carats is now accounted for by the U.S.S.R. Around 20% of their output is of gem quality and these are mostly sent to London for sale although some diamond jewellery has recently gone on sale in Moscow.

Synthetics and simulants

Synthetic diamonds are those which have been made by scientists in an attempt to reproduce the exact composition of a natural diamond, while simulants are those made in other materials to resemble natural diamonds. Many simulants such as marcasite, rock-crystal and paste were first manufactured in the 18th century, to which have been added in the present several excellent and very misleading varieties. The properties of simulants can be tested in a number of ways, one of which will invariably identify them for what they are.

Paste, the commonest simulant, tends to have abraded edges to the facets while its refractive index, which can be tested in a refractive liquid, is much lower than that of a diamond. Diamonair (Yttrium Aluminium Garnet) which first appeared in 1969 also has a low refractive index, 1·83 compared with 2·42 for diamond, and a higher specific gravity although its 'fire' is strong enough to imitate a diamond. Strontium Titanate, first introduced in 1953, is too soft to be polished as highly as a diamond, yet its refractive index is almost the same and its dispersion at five times that of a diamond gives a quite spectacular 'fire' which can at first be most deceptive. Many other simulants such as zircon, synthetic rutile and synthetic spinel frequently appear, yet they cannot mislead anyone who can use the appropriate testing equipment.

Attempts to synthesize diamonds have been made for centuries. The first synthetic diamonds were made in 1880 by James Hannay, a Glasgow chemist, by a process which caused the carbon from paraffin to re-crystallise as diamond. The crystals he produced were accepted as diamonds then by the Royal Society of London, but he was unable to repeat the process.

104

Although several nations including Sweden, U.S.S.R. and U.S.A. claim to have been first to develop a repeatable process, it was General Electric of U.S.A. that was the first to announce its success in 1955. General Electric's process – basically a repetition of the heating and squeezing operations that produced natural diamonds – is no longer a secret. Although the process is used primarily to produce industrial diamonds, a variation of it has proved capable of producing gem-quality diamonds of over 1 carat, using synthetic industrial diamond grit as feedstock. The Gemological Institute of America has subjected these stones to X-ray diffraction tests and detected, perhaps with relief, different characteristics in the synthetic stones although these are hardly of the kind to interest a non-scientist. The colourless or yellow stones proved to be electro-conductive where their natural counterparts were not, and they also tended to have higher fluorescence and phosphorescence. It was also claimed that the nitrogen impurities in synthetic and natural diamond were differently distributed, while the synthetic stones generally were found to be of a more regular structure and to exhibit minutely different surface characteristics.

It should be emphasised that these are differences, not disadvantages. There is no question that the synthetic diamond is a real diamond in the full scientific sense and these minutely different characteristics may just as reasonably be held to add to as detract from its appeal as a gem.

In the present G.E. process of making diamonds, the costs of production do not rise proportionately with the size of the diamond. To produce 1-carat weight of perhaps 50,000 tiny diamond particles might take an hour or so whereas to produce a single 1-carat stone of gem quality would take five days. This is because the rate of crystal growth in the modification of the industrial process used for larger stones is only 2–3 milligrams an hour.

Industrial quality diamonds are now produced synthetically in at least six countries by three different routes and the market price of the material has, broadly speaking, halved since the process was discovered. At present it is cheaper to dig gem diamonds from the earth than to produce them synthetically, yet it would be surprising if scientists now working to discover a means of accelerating the synthetic process were not at some future date successful. It is possible that natural gem diamonds, if they could still be distinguished from synthetic, might, albeit irrationally, command a premium over the synthetic material (as has been the case with synthetic rubies and emeralds) but this would be small consolation to holders of natural diamonds if the market price of synthetic fell, say, to $100 for a flawless 1-carat stone.

The history of prices

The earliest price lists for diamonds are to be found in Buddhabhartha's *Ratnapariksa* and Varahamihira's *Brhatsamhita* written during the 6th century

A.D. From these, it is clear that prices in those days bore no relation to production costs. A 1-tandula stone, equivalent to $\frac{1}{2}$ carat, of fine octahedral form, was according to Buddhabhartha worth 1,000 silver *rupakas* which was enough to pay a day's wages to 30,000 labourers, while both authors valued a 20-tandula stone (i.e. 10 carats) at 200,000 *rupakas.*

Most attempts to relate the prices in antiquity to present-day values fail because no integration into a common economic background is possible. For example, in 6th-century India the silver/gold exchange rate was stable at 16:1 and it can be calculated that a 10-carat stone would have cost 1500 oz tr of gold. Taking the price of gold at $250 an ounce, this suggests that to buy the stone would have cost the equivalent of around $800,000 in today's money and on that basis long-term holders of diamonds have not fared too well.

Tavernier explains, however, that until the discovery of new deposits in the 16th century, stones weighing more than 10 or 12 carats were almost unknown. Yet even taking account of the extreme rarity of such stones, the prices seem intrinsically improbable. It is known from Buddhabhartha that the slightest deviation from the ideal octahedral shape or the presence of any internal or external flaw was considered serious. The dealing prices may therefore have been as low as between 5% and 15% of the prices quoted in these documents.

There will probably never be an acceptable valuation of diamonds in antiquity, and the absolute level of prices matters less than their volatility. The early rulers of India, according to Varahamihira's *Ratnacastras*, fixed the price of diamonds through production control and stockpiling, although it is not clear whether any part of their stocks was ever released. This control over prices continued to be exercised until the mines were exhausted in the 18th century. For instance, in 1621 when rich new deposits discovered in Golconda exerted severe pressure on prices, the Ruler closed all the mines in 1622, which had the effect of trebling prices along the Coromandel Coast. Mining was resumed in 1623, but for the next three years the Ruler stockpiled all production. Although the power to control prices was well understood, to judge by the violent swings in price during the 17th century, it must have been exercised fairly erratically.

A rather wild attempt was recently made to plot the course of diamond values, starting with the valuation of a 1-carat diamond made in the 12th century by the Arab Teifaschius. He reckoned it at 2 *dinars*, equivalent to 12 dollars. By 1600 the value, so it was claimed, had reached 50 dollars. The Thirty Years War in the 17th century caused it to collapse to between 16 and 24 dollars. The discovery of Brazilian deposits brought it down to 2 dollars and in the mid-19th century prices were said to vary between 25 and 40 dollars. Because no specifications of the stones in question are nor could be given, the exercise does not carry much weight except to the extent that it supports the view expressed in other accounts that prices have been volatile over the very long-term.

David Jefferies, a London jeweller, wrote a treatise in 1750 in which he advised the purchase of diamonds for investment. He is one of a large band of writers who, because they stand to profit when their advice is taken, have to be considered as a special group. He was writing within living memory of the time when the price of rough diamonds, thanks to the discovery of the Brazilian deposits, had dropped from 100 to 25 gold francs per carat in the space of a year, although the drop in finished diamonds had not been so severe.

The Portuguese who then controlled Brazil, had not been wise in handling their Brazilian windfall. Over-exploitation through a high tax on each negro slave employed, and a freight tax based on value, soon caused illicit digging and smuggling to flourish as it does even to this day. In 1735 the Portuguese Government leased the rights to exploit the Brazilian deposits to a private Dutch partnership for a fixed percentage of sales value, but with a restriction on the number of slaves that might be employed. This was the first European attempt to regulate production and was reasonably successful in stabilizing prices. But by the early part of the 19th century, Brazilian rough prices were down to 45 gold francs a carat on the Amsterdam market, although they rose gradually again until 1870, partly due to increased demand and partly to the decline in Brazilian production.

The early years of South African production coincided with an unprecedented growth in demand for finished diamonds throughout Europe, and especially in the U.S.A. South Africa produced 7 million carats in the first seven years to 1877, more than Brazil had produced in the previous 150 years. Considering this great influx, the price of rough diamonds remained fairly stable, falling to a new low of just under two dollars a carat in 1877.

But Cecil Rhodes was displeased by the low prices the free market again set for diamonds in 1888 and was anxious to prevent this happening again by regulating the price himself. This he was able to do by bringing more and more mines into the De Beers organisation and so reducing the opportunities for producers to cut prices when demand turned weak. He was reasonably successful and rough prices fluctuated between $2 and $4 per carat until 1915, when war-time demand for industrial qualities sent the crude average over $4 for the first time at $5.10.

Pent-up demand for gem stones when the war was over sent the average to $9.80 in 1919 and $11.40 in 1920. Then followed a sharp drop to around $6.00; a level that was successfully held until the economic crisis of 1929. This was a major achievement by the four largest producers, who had entered into a cartel agreement at the beginning of 1926 only to find that in that year massive alluvial deposits were discovered at Lichtenburg, 120 miles east of Johannesburg and along the Atlantic coast of Little Namaqualand, which raised total South African production by over 60% in two years.

By this time diamond sales were heavily dependent on U.S. buying, and the decline of U.S. diamond imports by over 80% between 1929 and 1932 was more than the producers' agreement could withstand, and prices fell from $8.00 in 1929 to $3.50 in 1932. The Diamond Corporation was set up in 1930 to carry out long-term marketing, so relieving members of the need to stockpile their own production as well as to buy up outside production when it threatened to upset market prices. The Diamond Producers Association set up in 1933, with the Union of South Africa itself as a partner, organised the control of production as it has done ever since.

Although industrial quality diamond demand and gem quality demand are related to the extent that high industrial activity may signify prosperity, which may in turn stimulate gem quality demand, the price per rough carat can never be more than a fairly crude indicator of the state of the market, since it ignores the composition of sales. De Beers have now ceased to divulge the breakdown of their sales, so fuelling doubts about the real level of gem demand.

Diamonds were discovered at Lichtenburg in the Western Transvaal in 1926. The area was proclaimed public digging and the pegging of claims was carefully organised with several thousand people taking part in a single rush. The picture shows the 'off' at Vaalbosputte, a diamond field in the Lichtenburg district.

The market now

The Central Selling Organisation, which is part of De Beers, is a group of marketing companies through which all the main diamond producers now sell their production on a cooperative basis. The C.S.O. handles about 80% of all rough gem diamonds sold throughout the world, and nearly all of these pass through London.

When the rough diamonds arrive in London, they are sorted into about 2,000 grades of clarity, colour, weight and shape, and are offered at fixed prices to some 300 dealers, known as the direct buyers, ten times a year. At these sales, which are called 'sights', a dealer is offered parcels of diamonds, which will include what he is known to want but may also include some that he does not want and will have to sell on the open market for rough diamonds. The price of a box may be up to $2,000,000, and each one is offered on a take it or leave it basis, no bargaining being allowed. It has been widely accepted that stability in the price of gem diamonds is beneficial to everyone associated with the diamond industry whether as miner, cutter, polisher or retail jeweller.

Since gem diamonds, leaving aside investment considerations for the moment, are purely a luxury, demand for them can contract sharply during an economic recession. In such circumstances, the policy of the C.S.O. is to stabilise the prices of those grades for which demand has fallen by offering fewer of those stones for sale. The artificial shortages so created are maintained until the prices of the grades affected resume their earlier levels. Although this manipulation of the market has been and remains most effective, it has resulted from time to time in the need to stockpile large quantities of stones. These stocks are financed by the cash and near-cash resources of the De Beers group which currently amount to approximately $1000 million. When demand returns to its earlier level, the stockpiled stones are released for sale.

Economic recessions affect industrial as well as gem demand, although a decline in industrial demand makes less impact on the revenue of a balanced producer because although 75–80% of world production is of industrial quality, its value per carat is a fraction of the value of gem quality stones.

The marketing practices of the C.S.O. may offer protection and stability to people involved in the trade at all levels from miners to retailers, yet no such benefits are enjoyed by the public who ultimately buy the diamonds. The 300 or so direct buyers who attend the sights (the closed market) resell at a profit the stones they do not want to other dealers in the open market for rough stones. These may change hands several times before arriving at one of the great cutting and polishing centres of the world, such as Tel Aviv or Antwerp. They may go elsewhere to be mounted before finishing up in the windows of the fifty thousand retail jewellery shops around the world. A parcel bought at a sight may have risen by 500–1000% by the time it is offered as finished jewellery, the largest mark-up, frequently 200%, being made by the retailer on the price he pays the wholesaler. So if the retailer's mark-up were 200% on a diamond ring that cost him $800, this would bring the price tag (ignoring tax) to $2,400. But this would not necessarily mean that a customer who bought the ring could expect to sell it back to a similar jeweller for $800, since the second jeweller might value the piece on a break-up basis, that is stripping out the cost of the mounting and valuing the loose stones only.

There are three basic ways in which a retailer will value a piece of jewellery and of course he will want to know the reason for the valuation before he mentions any figures. The value will be high for insurance (replacement cost basis), low for Capital Transfer Tax or Probate and very low if he is being asked to buy the piece. Anyone contemplating diamonds for investment, therefore, should confine himself to loose stones or at least to mounted stones where the design and fabrication element is under 5% of the total cost, for that part of his outlay will almost certainly be lost when the time comes to sell. So many people trying to sell jewellery have heard a dealer justify a miserably low offer by claiming that there is no longer any demand for this design or that setting and that the stones will have to be completely remounted.

The shrewd way to buy loose stones or any other commodity is obviously to get as close as possible to the producer or wholesaler. It is not at all difficult to discover the name of one of the select international group of 300 dealers who attend the sights in London, and anyone of them might be prepared to handle an order from a private investor if it were large enough. But having bought a parcel, there is no means of knowing what the dealer himself paid for it nor if it contained part of the dealer's old stock that he had found hard to shift.

Apart from these uncertainties, only a deep knowledge of cutting techniques would enable the buyer to assess the final weights and shapes of the cut stones that could be obtained from the little heap of glassy pebbles for which he may just have paid perhaps $200,000. There are some trustworthy and knowledgeable dealers with whom it would be safe to deal, yet it would be surprising if there were not also less scrupulous operators about, and any such transaction must necessarily involve risks.

Although the manipulation of the market in diamonds is, among other things, intended to reassure buyers of its long term stability, such reassurance is paradoxically impossible because the stability is itself artificial. At the producing end, prices are held firm by matching supply to current demand, while at the consuming end demand is stimulated by world-wide advertising campaigns which seek to establish an image of diamond as a symbol of love and conjugal felicity. The diamond-producers also justify the price-stabilisation policy as the only one that gives the miners security in their jobs. But for this policy, prices for diamonds, they claim, might fall to a point at which mining would become uprofitable, black miners would have to leave their well-paid underground jobs and their commodious hostels and be forced to return to their families in the homelands.

The present stability certainly maximises the revenue of the producer countries, and is naturally favoured by their governments. What else could explain the harmonious cooperation of such disparate political régimes as those of U.S.S.R., South Africa and the newly independent African states?

The outlook for demand

Industrial diamonds compete with tungsten and many other hard materials which can fulfil similar cutting and abrading functions, while gem diamonds compete more vaguely with a whole range of luxury goods such as emeralds, fur-coats, expensive cars and so forth. To assess the likely future course of demand, it may be relevant to consider the reasons why diamonds were worn in antiquity, and why they are still worn today.

The conscious self-adornment of man dates back many thousands of years and its original functions were probably either sexual, intimidating or amuletic. The attention-seeking or sexual role of jewellery is especially obvious in the case of the polished diamond, whose optical effects are closely similar, at least in the way they are described – flashing, sparkling and so on – to the attracting activities of the human eye. Because diamonds were considered beautiful and were also rare, they soon rose in value. This caused them to lose this role, or at least to subordinate it to its new role as a symbol of power, wealth or status.

The primary sexual role now seems largely lost or at least transformed in most people's minds into a role symbolic of love. The convention of giving diamond rings at times of emotional importance seems well established. In Sweden where fewer young people go through the motions of a marriage ceremony before living together, the sale of diamond engagement rings is actually rising.

The future demand for diamonds as a symbol of wealth may be less certain. Diamonds over say 2 or 3 carats are inevitably associated in people's minds with money. For the time being there seems to be a general trend away from formality in dress as well as a growing distaste for the display of wealth. Perhaps for this reason there is also a tendency on the part of rich people, that is owners or potential owners of big diamonds, to keep a lower profile than formerly. If then the opportunities to wear diamonds are taken less and less frequently, so the attraction of owning them and the inclination to buy them must be correspondingly diminished.

In the course of the last ten years, the C.S.O. has raised its average selling prices by around 200% while dealers generally claim that top-quality 1-carat diamonds have risen in value by 500–1000%. What they mean is that the stones in question are now being offered for sale at prices 500–1000% higher than ten years ago, which is not quite the same thing as having risen in value by that amount since the sizeable gap between the prices at which the retailer will buy and sell diamonds is not taken into account.

111

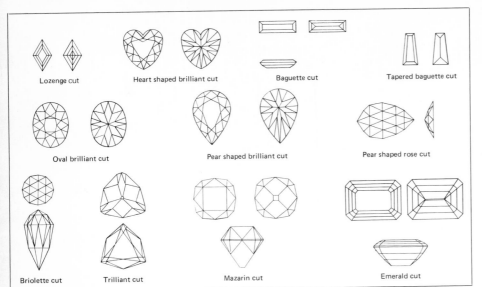

Lozenge cut

Heart shaped brilliant cut

Baguette cut

Tapered baguette cut

Oval brilliant cut

Pear shaped brilliant cut

Pear shaped rose cut

Briolette cut

Trilliant cut

Mazarin cut

Emerald cut

(*Left*) Diamond Cuts.

(*Opposite*) A selection of polished diamonds.

KEY

1 Hungary, 20 *korona*
2 Austria, 1 *ducat*
3 Austria, 4 *ducats*
4 Austria, 1 *ducat*
5 France, 10 *francs*
6 Great Britain, 1 sovereign
7 USA, $20, 'Double Eagle' (Liberty)
8 Austria, 8 *gulden*
9 Austria, 20 *kronen*
10 Mexico, 20 *pesos*
11 Switzerland, 10 *francs* (Half-Vreneli)
12 Italy, 20 *lire*
13 Mexico, 5 *pesos*
14 Mexico, 50 *pesos*
15 France, 20 *francs* 'Napoleon'
16 USA, $10, 'Eagle'
17 Mexico, 2 *pesos*
18 USA, $5, 'Half Eagle'
19 Belgium, 20 *francs*
20 Great Britain, £1
21 Germany, 20 *marks*
22 Austria, 100 *kronen*
23 Great Britain, half sovereign
24 Switzerland, 100 *francs*
25 Austria, 20 *kronen*
26 South Africa, 2 rand
27 Hungary, 20 *kronen*
28 Denmark, 20 *kroner*
29 Netherlands, 10 *guilders*
30 250 gram bar
31 10 gram bar
32 20 gram bar

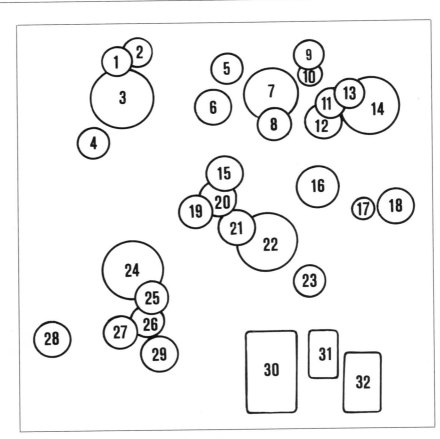

Key to the selection of bullion coins and bars shown opposite.

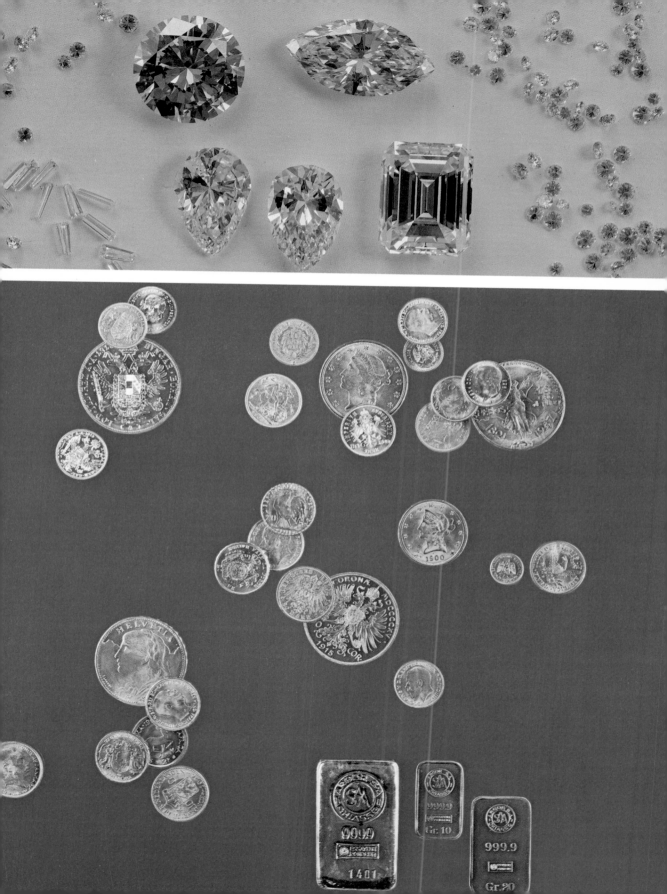

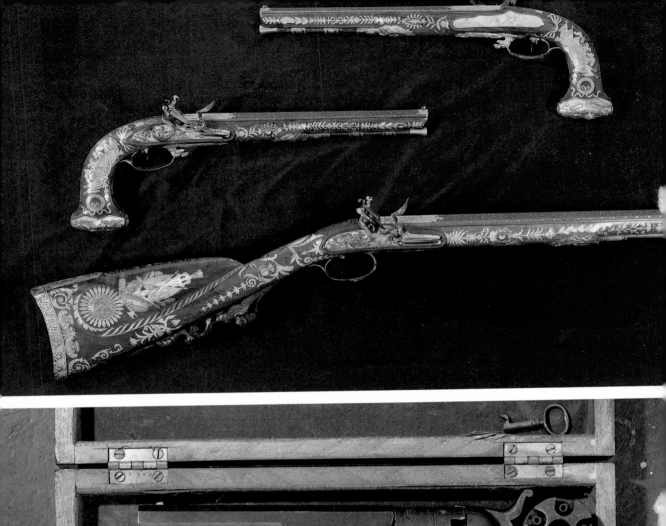

The leading English and American auction-houses now handle a much larger volume of jewellery. Between them they hold weekly sales of pieces estimated to be worth less than $100, monthly sales of pieces estimated at over $100 and occasional sales in London, Geneva, New York etc. of more important pieces. Although these sales seldom include loose stones, they provide a much more realistic market-place for anyone wishing to buy or sell mounted stones.

An inherently worrying aspect of diamonds is that the world's stock of diamonds is continually growing. This places them in a special investment class. They share with some other commodities which are not normally regarded as long-term investments the element of production costs in their final price, whereas no such costs are involved in the market price of investments whose existing stock is fixed. For example, if no further paintings turn up that can be

---

A Magnificent Garniture of French Empire Flintlock Fire-arms—by Boutet, Versailles.
The Rifle with octagonal sighted barrel spangled with gold stars and gilt and the breech and muzzle, the former decorated with a festoon of flowers and foliage and with gold-lined vent and pan, engraved with the serial number 55, and retaining its original blue-grey matted finish, the lock engraved with swans and the steel with wyverns, with safety-catch and graceful swan-neck cock, the figured walnut full stock carved around the tang, which is engraved with a term figure and two fishing scenes in miniature, and set with full silver furniture of the highest quality, the trigger-guard decorated with a figure of Diana and a Medusa mask with a globe above and a trophy of the arts beneath, the butt-plate with a palm tree, a trophy of classical arms and another Medusa mask, the ramrod pipes formed as fasces, the rearmost with central medallion of a wolf caught in a trap supported on either side by a putto holding a torch and a Napoleonic eagle beneath, the side-plate depicting a boar hunt with mounted figures in classical dress, inlaid throughout the wood with pierced silver engraved with running foliage involving trophies of arms and serpents, decorated behind the trigger-guard with a winged caryatid finely carved in ebony, with set trigger and original silver-tipped ramrod. Barrel 27¼ins.
The Pistols with multi-grooved rifled octagonal barrels en suite with the Rifle, engraved with the serial number 56, the tang of each engraved with a parrot, the locks with harpies and sphinxes, the figured walnut full stocks set with cast and chased silver furniture, the trigger-guards decorated with a figure of Zeus and supported by amorini, the finials with a stand of flags, a Napoleonic eagle above, the pommels with symbolic devices including those of Justice, Wisdom and Strength, the cap formed as a classical head, with silver ramrod pipes, the rearmost decorated with a male profile and the ordeal of Mucius Scaevola, and the side-plate with an allegorical scene, perhaps representing the triumph of Science over Ignorance, the wood inlaid throughout with pierced silver engraved with foliage, involving trophies and laurel wreaths, each pistol with set trigger and original silver-tipped ramrod. 17ins overall. The Rifle and Pistols each signed on the lock and in script beneath the barrel.

A Colt Paterson Pocket Model Percussion Revolver. Serial No. 346. 4½ins barrel. With much of the original blued finish, in its original mahogany case lined with red velvet with extra cylinder and original flask, combination tool and cleaning rod. 8½ins overall. c.1840. The barrel is engraved Patent Arms M'g Co. Paterson. N-J. Colts Pt. The cylinders engraved with centaurs in combat.

reliably attributed to Rembrandt, then the world stock of Rembrandts is known and fixed and any increase or decrease in the market price of his pictures is a result of changed demand, there being no production costs to affect them.

But costs of extracting diamonds have risen by at least 200% in the last ten years, so that the prices charged by the C.S.O. merely reflect higher costs and do not include any rise in price due to pure demand. Of course, the costs of extracting diamonds are not likely to fall and, even if they did, the C.S.O. would not presumably allow diamond prices to drop as a result, so diamond-buyers need not be unduly worried on this score. The threat from cheaper production of synthetic diamonds is certainly more potent and only if people irrationally insisted on preferring to buy the more expensive of two identical stones could the price of natural diamonds remain unaffected.

At the retail level, prices over the period have risen far more steeply. It is impossible to say whether buyers at the retail stage have instigated the higher prices through genuine demand, or retail jewellers have simply found they could sell diamonds at higher and higher prices to a consistently ill-informed public. Not only can an unscrupulous jeweller usually count on a customer's total ignorance but also, because purchases tend to be made on emotional occasions, on the customer's financial guard being down. In 1560 the jewellers of Nuremberg and Augsburg recorded their fear that they and their cities might suffer all manner of inconvenience and disadvantage at the hands of the emperors, kings, electors, princes and others to whom their stones were sold as soon as the extent of their profits became known.

It is vital for everyone involved in the trade that prices should be seen to be rising, firstly because the rise tends to corroborate the 'diamonds for investment' argument, and secondly because if prices fell, nervous selling by investment-type holders might begin to undermine the whole precarious price-structure of diamonds. Yet, in a curious way, it seems to suit both the trade and the public that the real stability of the diamond market has never been tested. The trade continues to make its sizeable profits, while the public prefers not to ask itself awkward questions about the financial justification of buying diamonds. Possibly they think subconsciously that because people who have owned diamonds in the past have tended to be rich, they may, by a process of sympathetic magic, become rich by owning diamonds themselves, or perhaps the motive is a modern counterpart of the diamond's ancient amuletic function – to ward off the evils of inflation.

Of all the stones sold by the C.S.O. only 5%, when cut, would yield stones of 1-carat or more, while of these only 10% would fall within the colour/clarity grades that are claimed to have shown any significant appreciation in value. Probably less than $\frac{1}{2}$% of all gem quality diamonds sold, therefore, would be appropriate for investment on present evidence. It might be ten or even twenty years before an investor could expect to see his money back, thanks to the great gulf that separates jewellers' buying and selling prices, and only then if demand for diamonds had remained consistently strong might the investment begin to show real capital growth.

Apart from jewellers, there are only two kinds of people who can justify buying diamonds for financial reasons. They are firstly people who think they may one day have to make a run for another country – in other words, they buy diamonds, as many Italians have recently in fear of a Communist victory, as a highly portable asset rather than for their investment attractions. The second kind are very rich, very astute individuals who must know at least as much as the dealers from whom they buy. Most retail jewellers know very little about diamonds and many of their salesmen even less. These salesmen are often working on generous commissions and therefore have every incentive to make extravagant claims for the pieces they have to sell. Once a diamond is encased, it becomes difficult to make more than a rough assessment of its quality particularly since the setting itself may be designed to hide a flaw.

The average buyer will not usually have the faintest idea what he has got until he tries to sell it. It is then that the nasty surprises tend to begin. Many jewellers will simply refuse to make an offer at all. A jeweller has, after all, his regular supplier who offers him credit whereas the private seller will certainly want cash and so the only commercially sensible offer he could make might be as low as 20% of the original retail price – an offer which, unless the seller were in desperate straits, he would be most unlikely to accept anyway.

In America the jewellery business is not officially regulated and it is hard to get knowledgeable and impartial advice. The highly respected Gemological Institute of America is concerned only with the scientific appraisal of gemstones and will not be drawn into any discussion of their commercial value.

There are several 'laboratories' in America and England of doubtful scientific standing, attached to diamond investment organisations, which issue certificates purporting to give the buyer of any diamond its precise colour and clarity grading. C.I.B.J.O. is currently recognising a chain of Laboratories of Precious Stones in a number of countries which will scientifically grade stones to a common international standard. Its success can not yet be measured but its establishment at least acknowledges the need to introduce some order and perhaps even a little safety into the present diamond jungle.

A senior official of the G.I.A. summed up the whole 'diamonds for investment' issue as 'all so ridiculous'. It undoubtedly creates much ill-feeling among investors who have been gullible enough to buy and find themselves unable to sell without a serious loss. It can only be bad for the jewellery industry whose legitimate function – to sell people objects of aesthetic or emotional value – is increasingly abused by unscrupulous dealers who implicitly and often explicitly offer a guarantee of capital appreciation.

Over the last ten years, interest has grown in pieces of jewellery designed or executed by certain famous makers. Experts are beginning to be able to attribute unsigned pieces to particular makers and such attributions can do for

115

their price the same as an expert's attribution can do for the price of a picture. The work of two great Italian 19th-century jewellers Castellani and Giuliano is very much in demand today. They invariably signed their pieces which are of outstanding quality and therefore very hard to fake.

Similarly, demand for certain early pieces from the great 'houses' such as Tiffany, Cartier and Chaumet has grown considerably, as collectors have begun to appreciate their design and workmanship. Although the material used in these pieces may not be anything but good quality mêlée and the break-up value often quite low, the artistry and craftsmanship can lift the saleroom value to five or ten times that of a clumsy or unattractive piece of the same break-up value. If research in this field continues at its present rate and more publications appear, it is likely that rising prices will follow the newly-generated interest.

The fashion for fancy-coloured diamonds – pink, cinnamon, canary and so on – has always been fickle. Certainly the Japanese, who were important buyers of coloured diamonds before the 1973 recession, were taking losses on those investments when they realised them in 1977. Investment in diamonds remains a very hazardous business and honest, responsible dealers will usually dissuade customers from buying them for that purpose alone.

It has been possible to make money out of diamonds in the past but to have done so would have required the help of an unusually reliable diamond merchant as well as an extensive knowledge of the market. Anyone in the U.S.A. still determined to brave the dangers of diamond investment will have to persuade the G.I.A. to recommend some reputable dealers, while those in England will find this service offered by the London Chamber of Commerce.

Book list

ANDERSON, B. W. *Gem Testing* 8th ed. text ed. Butterworths

LIDDICOAT, RICHARD T. JR. *Handbook of Gemstone Identification.* 10th ed. (Illus.) 1975, Gemological

WEBSTER, ROBERT. *Gems: Their Sources, Descriptions, and Identification* 3rd ed. (Illus.) 1975 (pub. by Archon), Shoe String

WEINSTEIN, MICHAEL. *World of Jewel Stones* (Illus.) 1958, Sheridan

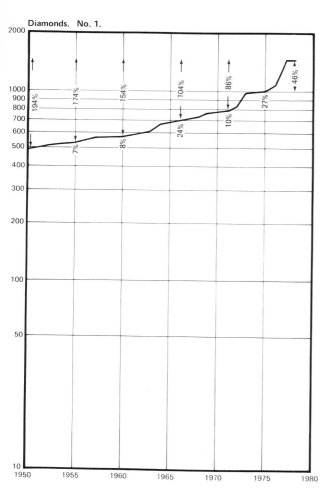

Diamonds. No. 1.

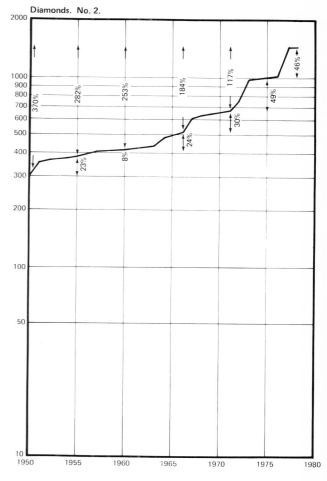

Diamonds. No. 2.

INDEX NO. 1.

Overall price increases applying to all sizes and qualities announced by the Central Selling Organisation, ignoring temporary surcharges and excluding increases made to compensate for devaluations of the pound and the dollar.

INDEX NO. 2.

Overall price increases applying to all sizes and qualities announced by the Central Selling Organisation (ignoring temporary surcharges).

The differences between these price increases and the much greater 'value' increases often claimed for diamonds can be accounted for by the extra costs borne and the extra profits taken by the cutting, polishing, wholesale and retail trades.

Note: The C.S.O. announced a 30% overall increase in August 1978, not included in the above graphs, which may be presumed to have comprised roughly a 10% straightforward price increase and a 20% increase to compensate for the effective devaluation over the previous eight months of the dollar against certain major currencies.

English Silver

The great age of English silver is usually reckoned to have run from 1660 to 1830. The first date, 1660, because that year marked not only the Restoration of the Monarchy but also the restoration of a prosperity which made possible a minor local Renaissance of arts and sciences. The richer classes were able to make good their losses in the recent Civil War in building or rebuilding their great houses and equipping them, amongst other things, with large quantities of silver plate. The period ends at 1830 because by that date machinery had taken over so much of the silversmith's work that the age of the craftsman in silver was to a great extent over.

Owning silver plate had been popular in England since the Middle Ages for two particular reasons. The first was that it provided a satisfactory way of

A Charles II caudle cup and cover, London 1682.

advertising wealth and the second was that it was readily convertible into cash. Almost too convertible really, for the continuous melting of fine silver right up to the Restoration resulted in the loss of probably more than 95% of all the silver plate made up to that date. Even towards the end of the 19th century, the collecting of silver for any but the most practical reasons was most unusual. Many owners were conscious of the form and decoration of their silver but only to the extent that they wanted it to be up-to-date, and this amounted to another good reason why it should go into the melting-pot and be refashioned according to the latest style.

Until the Renaissance made itself felt in the design of English silver around 1530, many pieces were influenced by the Perpendicular style of architecture. Only about four hundred pieces of medieval English silver have survived and, of these, the majority are of a ceremonial rather than domestic type. This preponderance of ceremonial silver does not reflect the original proportion since the more humble pieces would presumably have been the first to be sacrificed in times of financial crisis. Much of the early plain silverware certainly went into the melting-pot as a kind of part exchange for the new Renaissance models. The idea of keeping the older pieces for their aesthetic value seems to have commended itself to no one.

The most serious losses of silver plate were at times of political upheaval such as the Wars of the Roses, the Reformation and the Civil War when vast quantities were requisitioned. Furthermore the recurring financial crises of English kings could not in those days be solved by the printing-press and bullion was frequently the only remedy. From the ransom paid for Richard I in 1194 to the handover by twelve Oxford colleges of all their silver to Charles I in 1642 the sacrifice of fine silver either for personal or national reasons must have been almost continuous.

It was ironically Charles I's piratical approach to money that brought about the birth of the modern banking system. It had been the custom of many London merchants to deposit their money in the Royal Mint at the Tower of London. When the King threatened in 1640 to seize these deposits, the merchants turned to the goldsmiths of Lombard Street who already had facilities for the safe-keeping of precious metals. The goldsmiths took in the deposits on which they paid interest at 5% and lent notes at up to 8% which bore the promise to redeem them for gold or silver on demand. These were the fore-runners of the Bank of England which was to be established some fifty years later.

Evidence from wills makes clear that great quantities of silver were owned by rich people. Sir John Fastolf who died in 1459 left 1175 lbs troy of domestic plate and another 110 lbs in his chapel. Similar quantities were left by the 13th Earl of Oxford in 1509. The domestic part of these collections would have consisted mainly of the great Salts which occupied a highly symbolic position on the table of the medieval Great Hall 'set on your right side where your sovereign shall sit'*, standing cups, standing dishes, beakers, tankards and mazers which were drinking cups of maple wood mounted with silver. Ewers and basins were of great importance at mealtimes until forks came into circulation in the second half of the 17th century. Rose water from the ewers would be poured over the diners' hands before, during and after the meal. The rest of the collections would have been made up of plates, spoons and smaller salts, sometimes called trencher salts because one was to go with each trencher or plate.

It was certainly during the Civil War, when the demand for coin to pay the soldiers on both sides was so great, that important collections such as these, if they had survived that long, must have been melted. The result today is that pre-Restoration silver is rare and expensive. Even spoons, which were probably the most common pieces in a household of moderate means and seem to have survived in fairly good numbers, have been a favourite subject for collectors for so long that they are increasingly hard to buy. Apart from the variation in the shape and angle of the bowl, the main interest lies in the great variety of finials which might be an acorn, a lion sejant, a woodwose or wild man, or the familiar apostle which was for long a favourite christening present.

English silver reflects not only the style and mood of its period, it chronicles the introduction of new customs, new food, new drinks and spices from the outside world. Until the 17th century, drinking vessels were made to hold beer or wine. There had been standing cups for ordinary drinking but since no sets or even pairs have survived and because they were from their decoration clearly of great importance, they would have been used only by the head of the family. Two-handled cups and covers had been passed from hand to hand as loving cups. Tankards appeared probably from Germany or Scandinavia in the late 16th century with their characteristic drum shape with hinged cover and thumbpiece. These were followed in the early 17th century by the taller flagons either cylindrical or bellied but usually with scroll handles. Punch bowls, which were enlarged versions of the two-handled cup and cover, were made in the 17th century with capacities of up to three gallons in which were tried the various concoctions then recommended for disguising or improving the taste of the rough wines then available.

Since the middle of the 16th century, the wine-drinker's basic equipment had included a sugar-box and spoon but the punch-drinker of the 17th century needed as well as the bowl, a silver saucepan and ladle, lemon-strainer, orange-strainer, nutmeg-grater, spice-box, and of course wine cups or goblets. Between five and ten inches high, these wine cups and goblets were made in considerable numbers during the first half of the 17th century although the introduction of lead glass in the second half caused a decline in production. One- or two-handled wine tasters with shallow bowls, almost vertical sides and a raised centre, had been in use in the wine trade since the 14th century. They had been designed to enable the wine merchant more easily to judge the colour and

*Wynkyn de Worde's *Boke of Kervinge* 1508.

clarity of wine but were now found useful as domestic drinking vessels.

Candlesticks were quite familiar objects in rich medieval households although not a single one dated earlier than 1600 has survived. Judging from the surviving illustrations of those offered as prizes in the State Lottery of 1567, the form did not change much until the Restoration. It was only then that the functional greasepan, which had separated the stem and the base, was transformed into ornamental mouldings and candlesticks began to look more elegant. Wall-candlesticks or sconces usually fitted with a reflector plate had been used since the time of Henry VIII but now became very popular although, being often of rather flimsy construction, only a very few have survived.

Forks had been seen by English travellers in Italy during the 16th century. The first known English silver table fork, a two-pronged type, is no earlier than 1632 and even thereafter their introduction was only gradual. As late as 1652, their use 'by some of our spruce gallants taken up of late' was plainly a matter for ridicule and it was not until the 18th century that they were produced in the same quantities as spoons.

There arrived in Europe in the mid-17th century the three drinks – coffee, tea and chocolate – which were to transform the habits of the whole continent. Coffee seems to have arrived in England first from Turkey and was on sale in a coffee-house in 1651. The earliest surviving coffee-pot dates from 1681 and is of the straight-sided tapering cylindrical form with a straight spout and S-scroll handle – the form which was to remain more or less standard for coffee-pots ever since.

Tapering cylindrical coffee-pot. Maker William Fawdery, 1709.

When chocolate – jocalette – arrived from the West Indies in 1657, it was often served in the coffee-houses that had sprung up all over London. The silversmiths who were called upon to produce an elegant container for the new drink not unnaturally made them more or less to the same design as the coffee-pots, except that many were provided with a hole in the lid through which was fitted a stirring-rod that could be swizzled to bring the liquid to a uniform consistency before pouring.

Tea was first on sale in 1658 and by 1670 it could be bought either in leaf or as a drink throughout London. At that date, it was drunk without milk or sugar and was enjoyed primarily for its medicinal qualities. The original teapots were of red and brown stoneware, exported from Kiangsu in China with the tea itself. The form they took, although plainly derived from Chinese ewers and wine-pots, appears to have been designed specifically for tea. Some of the earliest to have arrived in England were mounted in silver, but by 1675 a small melon-shaped silver pot had been made which, in spite of endless variations, has remained the standard form ever since.

Salt was highly valued in medieval times for many reasons. It was not only the vital preservative for meat and fish, it was, apart from herbs, the only powerful flavouring available as well as being supposed to possess mystical and amuletic powers. Until the arrival of spices in much greater quantities in the second half of the 17th century, particularly pepper and mustard from the East Indies, the monotony of the English diet even in royal circles must have been deplorable.

Since the colonisation of the West Indies early in the century, imports of sugar had grown to 800 tons by 1660 and 8000 tons by the end of the century. The first caster for sugar was made in 1676 with straight sides and fairly coarse piercing at the top. Soon afterwards, companions were made to hold pepper and mustard although sets of more than three are known. The pepper was coarsely ground and cast through the pierced cover but the mustard caster was left blind or unpierced and taken in powder form by means of a small scoop. It was around 1740 that mustard in paste form came to be preferred and the familiar pots and spoons began to be made.

At the beginning of the 18th century, the caster began to be made in the curvaceous baluster form with the cover delicately pierced with arabesques and scrolls. The baluster is named from the flower of the wild pomegranate and has been probably the most influential shape in all silver work. In various degrees of distortion, it can be seen in candlesticks, cups and tankards.

The glass bottles known as cruets which had been in domestic and ecclesiastical use since the Middle Ages, were now more often silver-mounted and a pair for oil and vinegar were grouped with the casters in a cruet-stand although more elaborate examples are known.

An important architectural change in the great houses that had been built at the end of the 17th century, had been the replacement of the Great Hall by a dining-room. Candelabra began to be made in greater quantities for the table and sideboard. The great épergnes that came into vogue at the turn of the century took the place of honour on the table previously occupied by the salt.

Designed to save (épargner) the trouble of passing things at the table, they were made in very different sizes. A gilt one made for George I and mentioned in a royal inventory of 1725 included 'one Table Basket and cover, one foote, four Salt boxes, four small Salts, four Branches, six Casters, four Sauceboats' weighing 783 ozs all told. Tureens modelled on the oval shape of the French earthenware *terrines*, usually with four legs and two handles and a lid, became a familiar sight as well as sauce-boats, entrée dishes and saucepans. For fish, pierced oval plates known as *mazarines* fitted into a dish were introduced about 1720 as well as special fish-slices for serving.

For wine, small vase-shaped wine-coolers to hold a single bottle were introduced at the end of the 17th century. Wine fountains had been known in the Middle Ages but were evidently not really more than ornaments for the table. At the beginning of the 18th century, they began to be produced for practical use in the shape of an urn with a tap at the front and two or four handles. Silver wine-bottles which also date from this period were made in the form of the pilgrim bottle – a flask with two flattened sides, a long neck and a chain handle.

Wine cisterns began to be made, sometimes of enormous size, in which to cool bottles of wine. The largest known was bought by the Empress Catherine II of Russia and weighed 8,000 ounces. A replica in the Victoria and Albert Museum shows it to be an astonishing piece supported on four chained leopards. Coasters for decanters, wine labels and wine funnels were produced continuously throughout the 18th century although, as the quality of wine improved in the eighties, the volume of production rose.

In the second half of the 17th century, very large tankards for beer had been made with a row of pegs fitted down the inside at intervals of a pint. This arrangement is thought to explain the origin of the expression 'to take down a peg' – the right to drink successive pints depending on the outcome of some game of chance or skill. During the 18th century, the tankards tended to be made smaller to hold either a quart or a pint, and mugs a pint or a half.

Silver-handled knives began to be made about 1700 although few have survived. Spoons became more egg-shaped and the reinforcement between the handle and the stem became a favourite design known at the rat-tail. Forks began to be made to match the spoons both in design and number. Bone-marrow was rated a delicacy in the 18th century and marrow scoops like thin elongated spoons, now more often used for pickles and so on, have survived in considerable numbers.

Hall-marks

An Ordnance of 1238 required that the standard purity of English silver plate should be the same as for the English coinage. The following Troy scale (from

Troyes in France) which was then used for weighing silver is still in use today, except that the Troy pound was abolished to avoid confusion with pounds of another scale in the 19th century.

24 grains = 1 pennyweight (dwt)
20 pennyweights = 1 ounce
12 ounces = 1 pound

The purity of the English coinage was 11 ounces and 2 pennyweights of pure silver in every pound, the balance being made up almost invariably of copper. This was referred to as the sterling standard, the name coming from the silver penny coins then in circulation which were struck with a little star and known as starlings. The purity of all English silver plate from then on became the same as the coinage at 92·5%.

In 1300, the first hall-marking was introduced which has provided buyers of English silver with a safe-guard ever since. The Statute then required that each piece of silver plate should be punched by 'gardiens of the craft' with the mark of a leopard's head before leaving the goldsmith's workshop so guaranteeing that it was sterling standard. In 1363, every goldsmith was required to register a mark by which his work could be distinguished. Until the end of the 17th century, some symbol or a rebus of the craftsman's name would often be used. Unfortunately, records of individual craftsmen's marks before 1697 have not survived so that apart from a few cases where other evidence can be adduced, the names of the makers are not known before 1697 when they were required to re-register their marks as the first two letters of their surnames.

The date-letter, which enables each piece of silver to be precisely dated, has been in continuous use in London since 1478. The Goldsmiths' Company has used a cycle of twenty letters, one for each year with i and j treated as one, u and v also as one, and with w, x, y and z omitted. The goldsmiths' original purpose may have been to protect themselves against falsely struck hall-marks or at least to be able to identify which warden was responsible during the year in which the error was made. One cycle could be distinguished from another by changing the style of the letter – Roman capital, Lombardic, small Roman, Court hand, small Italic etc. – or the shape of the shield in which it was placed.

The next development in London hall-marking was the appearance in 1544 of the lion passant guardant (which in heraldic terms means the lion is walking with its face turned towards you) which has remained, apart from one short period, the standard mark for all English silver up to the present day. It has been suggested that the device was introduced as the Goldsmiths' Company's own guarantee of the sterling standard but must also have been recognised as an official mark since it had to be changed when the higher Britannia standard was introduced in 1697.

The interlude, which lasted until 1720, occurred because the demand for silver plate that arose in the prosperity of Restoration England was too great for the amount of silver bullion available. Large quantities of plate had been melted down to mint coin during the Civil War and the process was now being reversed. The shortage of coin accelerated the development of the credit system being run by the goldsmith bankers. After the successive debasements of the coinage by Henry VIII, to the point where its silver content was only 25%, the sterling standard had been restored in 1560 on the advice of Sir Thomas Gresham (now famous for his 'Law' that bad money drove out good). The common standard for coin and plate had existed as a matter of convenience for the Masters of the Mint who were able to convert bullion and plate into coin without having to refine it first to another standard. But silversmiths too were free to melt coin and work it into plate.

With the shortage of silver bullion the 'wicked and pernicious crime of clipping' coins – in the words of the New Sterling Act of 1697 – had become more serious, some coins circulating at only 80% of their original weight. The solution the Act put into force was to raise the required standard of purity of silver plate from 11 ounces 2 dwts of silver per 1 pound Troy to 11 ounces 10 dwts or from 92·5 to 95·8%. The measure was intended to involve the silversmith in the costly and laborious process of refining the metal from the coins anew and so dissuade him from doing it at all. It apparently had the desired effect, although it is not clear why a small addition of pure silver could not have been made to the melted coins to bring the overall standard of purity up to the required 95·8%.

As soon as the Act came into force, the hall-marking system that had until then been in operation was suspended and four new marks had to be made on each piece. The first was to be the first two letters of the surname of the silversmith, the second was to be the figure of a woman 'commonly called Britannia', the third a lion's head erased (i.e. with a jagged neck-line) in place of the earlier leopard's head and lion passant guardant. The fourth was to be the variable mark used by the Warden of the Goldsmiths' Company to identify the year in which the piece was made. A further Act of 1700 established different marking arrangements for the provincial and Irish assay offices.

By 1719 silver stocks had been replenished, to some extent by capture from the Spaniards, and an Act of that year allowed the higher standard to become optional, at the same time imposing a duty of 6 pence an ounce on all silver plate. Much protesting was heard from silversmiths who had had to pay the higher price for their raw material for the last twenty-two years but the duty was lifted in 1758 and re-imposed at a different rate in 1784 after which it remained in force until the licensing system replaced it in 1890.

Silver plate made from 1784 to 1890 was punched with a further mark of the sovereign's head in profile to prove that the duty had been paid. In the case of plate destined for export, the duty could be reclaimed and small pieces weighing under 10 dwts which would be disfigured by hall-marking were exempt altogether. From the moment the Act became law, there were

125

silversmiths who were prepared to dodge the duty or a large part of it by sending a small piece to be assayed and then incorporating the part bearing the hall-marks into a much heavier piece on which the duty would have been considerable. An Act of 1738 which made imprisonment the penalty for forging or transposing marks was actually replaced in 1757 by one imposing the death penalty but this was reduced in 1772 to fourteen years transportation and again in 1798 to seven.

The evolution of English styles

All the styles in which English silver has been made came originally from abroad. Although this holds good for both form and decoration, the English silversmith managed to adapt foreign themes and motifs in such a way that his work is nearly always unmistakably English. The few pieces that survive from the two centuries before the Norman Conquest show many influences, Classical and Celtic, Sassanian and Coptic, Scandinavian and German. After the Conquest, the Norman influence at first made English silverware almost indistinguishable from that of N.W. Europe but from the end of the 12th century until around 1525 the Perpendicular architectural and Gothic styles were dominant. The earliest Renaissance influences on silver design were the pattern books from Germany, the Netherlands and Italy. These suggested designs for the various forms of plate as well as the ornamental details with which they might be improved. Biblical and mythological scenes often occupied a central position while the borders might be engraved with arabesques, strapwork, scrolled foliage enlivened with birds, animals and so on. But although the Renaissance style was quickly assimilated in England, the overlap with the Gothic style lasted for a decade or more.

During Elizabeth I's reign, the more highly ornamented silver was, the more it was admired. The designs for it were still arriving mainly from Germany and the Netherlands but so too now were craftsmen. Frequent complaints began to be heard at the Court of the Goldsmiths' Company that foreign workers were settling in London much to the disadvantage of the local silversmiths. They brought with them the repoussé technique by which thin silver plate could be decorated by embossing, that is punching from the back, and chasing or punching from the front.

Towards the end of the 16th century, the fashion for exuberant decoration had begun to wane and a taste for rather plainer domestic silver began to develop. William Harrison wrote in 1587 that it was not uncommon to find furnishings and plate 'worth five hundred or a thousand pounds to be deemed by estimation' and he notes that 'a silver salt, a bowl for wine, (if not a whole nest) and a dozen of spoons to furnish up the suit' was the least a man of property would possess.

126

At the beginning of the 17th century, the silversmiths' new customers, the prosperous middle class, were ordering domestic plate still with fairly restrained decoration, while at Court the more extravagant ornament was still preferred. Both styles were still inspired by Continental pattern books but now more frequently Dutch than German. The Dutch influence was further strengthened when Charles I employed Christiaan van Vianen, the outstanding member of a great family of Dutch silversmiths. The embossed acanthus leaf decoration which is the most characteristic decoration of the Charles II period is undoubtedly of Dutch origin. Much 17th century silver was worked from quite thin plate so that the embossing was not only decorative but also done to strengthen the object itself. The profusion of flora and fauna – tulips, irises, poppies, carnations, lions, stags, horses, unicorns, bears, turkeys, peacocks etc.

Circular salver, the broad rim repoussé-chased with naturalistic flowers and animals. 1669.

– which now appeared on silver plate was the counterpart of the intense interest in botany and biology already being expressed in painting and inlaid furniture.

The Revocation of the Edict of Nantes in 1685, which threatened the further persecution of the Huguenots in France, resulted in the exodus of perhaps as many as a quarter of a million Protestants, many of them highly-skilled workmen or merchants including some well-established silversmiths. Their influence on the design and workmanship of English silver can hardly be overestimated. Although their arrival and competition were bitterly resented at the time, there is no doubt that the standard of their contribution and its effect on the native craftsmen was of the highest value. The great English names of the period were Anthony Nelme, Benjamin Pyne, Francis Garthorne and Thomas Jenkins, but many Huguenots came to be as well or even better known – Pierre Harache, Pierre Platel, David Willaume, Simon Le Sage, Paul de Lamerie, Augustine Courtauld, David Tanqueray, Lewis Mettayer, Isaac Liger and Simon Pantin. These men were not from Paris but from the provinces where the rich townspeople had wanted their silver ornamented but not gaudy and extravagant as it was at the Court of Louis XIV.

The Huguenot contribution to decoration then was to re-introduce order where motifs of flowers and leaves had begun to straggle uncontrollably all over a surface. They returned to a formality of decoration that was received with admiration and even relief by their new patrons. They were meticulous craftsmen and their attention to detail soon had to be emulated by their English rivals. Powerful as their influence was, other styles too were produced during the 1680–1720 period, mostly revivals and variations on 16th and earlier 17th century styles.

The quantity of silver in circulation at this period must have been very considerable indeed for in 1695, the Grand Jury of Middlesex petitioned Parliament to act to prevent the frequent and common use of silver basins, tankards, bowls, cups and tumblers in public houses and taverns which had occasioned many burglaries and murders. An Act forbidding publicans to use any plate whatsoever except spoons was passed soon afterwards.

At the beginning of the 18th century the only two important styles were Queen Anne for the more basic domestic pieces and the much grander Louis XIV style for important pieces ordered by royal or noble households. The chief characteristics of the Queen Anne style which continued until about 1720 was the absence of applied ornament and hence a reliance upon fine proportions and accurate execution. Coats of arms, which were engraved on almost every large piece of silver of this period, assumed a greater prominence and were often set in elaborate ornamental frames or cartouches. During the third decade of the 18th century, the two styles seemed to merge in preparation for the birth of English Rococo about 1730. Areas previously left plain began to be ornamented with elaborate designs of lines, curves and scrolls. The origin or cause of the rococo style, which was dominant in English silver from 1730–70, was a

128

reaction against the heavy symmetry of the Baroque. The word rococo which was not coined until the beginning of the 19th century and then in mockery of the finical affected style of *rocaille*, described, in the case of silver, a form of decorative extravaganza consisting of shells, scrolls, flowers, leaves and so on.

The leaders of the movement in England were Paul de Lamerie, Paul Crespin and Charles Kandler. Their work which shows an unequalled virtuosity and that of their lesser followers was widely admired although by no means to the

Pair of sauce-boats. Maker Eliza Godfrey, 1755.

Inkstand in the rococo style. Maker Paul de Lamerie, 1744.

exclusion of the traditional Queen Anne style which continued to be produced. In 1770 the taste for rococo began to pall and although some later examples can be found, the switch to the neo-classical style was relatively abrupt. The revival of interest in Classical art was already long-established by 1770. Excavations at Herculaneum and Pompeii had been going on for several decades and a spate of publications on those and other classical ruins had aroused great interest over the last twenty years.

Robert Adam had already published many of his drawings of Diocletian's palace at Split and his designs for the interiors of Syon House and Osterley Park near London and other great houses were causing a radical change in artistic and architectural fashion. William Kent had given birth to the idea that an architect should design not only a house but its contents and Adam followed his example.

In England, the Classical revival made itself felt first in architecture, then in interior decoration and lastly in silver plate. Adam styles were dominant from 1770 to 1790 – the classical urn was adopted for various kinds of vessel and the classical column was the natural choice for the candlestick and candelabrum. For Robert Adam, Classicism meant lightness, unity and grace. In decoration, this was best achieved by bright-cut engraving rather than soldering on cast ornaments. Whereas the old style of engraving had consisted of deep narrow

Soup tureen. Makers Andrew Fogelberg and Stephen Gilbert, 1792.

incisions the new bright-cut technique made shallow curved grooves in the silver of varying steepness which produced a more brilliant and sparkling effect.

One reason for the great impact of Adam's designs was that the invention of Sheffield plate in 1742 had vastly increased the size of the market for household objects with a silver content. Silver-working had, for centuries, been a labour-intensive trade even though, even before 1600, the practice of casting and die-stamping for borders, handles, brackets etc. had been quite general. The earliest candlesticks, for instance, had been hammered up from sheet and hand-chased until the introduction of casting by the Huguenots in about 1705 which was quickly taken up. But with the development in Sheffield and Birmingham of die-stamping, much of the personal workmanship involved in silvermaking disappeared.

It was discovered in 1742 that a thin sheet of silver could be fused to a thick sheet of copper and then passed through a rolling mill which would produce a sheet of any gauge. During the 1760s other machinery was developed which would carry out stamping, embossing and piercing operations. The metal of candlesticks for example, whether of Sheffield plate or silver, could be made so thin that they needed to be 'loaded' or filled with pitch or resin for strength, and the feet weighted to give them stability. Smaller rolling-mills could turn out ribbons of silver with a pattern along one edge – gadrooned, fluted, reeded, beaded etc.

By 1770 Matthew Boulton had a warehouse in London where silversmiths could come and buy all the ready-cast handles, legs and small pieces they wanted. In many cases, all that was needed was a bit of work with the soldering iron and the finished pieces could be taken along to Goldsmiths' Hall to be assayed, hall-marked and marked with the maker's name. The great mechanical advances could only be usefully applied to the production of objects of fairly simple construction and outline, and the designs of the Classical Revival were better suited than the asymmetrical Rococo for such processes.

The production of machine-made silver and plated wares from Sheffield and Birmingham became so vast during the 1770s that the supremacy of London in this field was broken. But the machine only came to dominate the production of such articles as spoons, forks, salt cellars, casters, candlesticks, teapots and so on. Any elaborate or commissioned pieces were still hand-made in the traditional ways. Nevertheless, English silver dating from before say 1740 is particularly valued because there followed the first phase of a takeover by machinery which, although capable of producing work of very fine quality, marked the end of the period during which a piece of silver very often actually was the work and design of the maker whose mark it bore.

At the turn of the century, the direction of the Classical revival which had so far been principally Graeco-Roman began to change. Egyptian motifs such as the lotus and the sphinx were often seen on increasingly ornate pieces. Great ceremonial silverware was produced celebrating British victories in the Napoleonic Wars. The firm of silversmiths, Rundell & Bridge, which had procured orders from George III during the first decade of the 19th century, now grew to employ a workforce of a thousand and, by commissioning artists and sculptors to design silver, they popularised a great variety of styles including revivals of Gothic, Rococo and Baroque ornament. Paul Storr, who was active 1792–1838 and is often hailed as one of the great silversmiths of all time, was for many years no more and no less than works manager of Rundell & Bridge and presided over a colossal and varied production.

Candelabrum centrepiece. Maker Paul Storr, 1813. Weight 464 oz.

Market trends

The bumpiest ride silver dealers and investors ever had was when the market rocketed and collapsed all within the space of two years from 1967–9. There were several unconnected reasons that helped to create an unreal market first in England and almost immediately after in U.S.A.

The price of silver bar had made a post-war recovery from 20 cents an ounce in 1945 to 58 cents in 1950 after which it traded in the 56–68 cents range for the next eleven years until October 1961. The price then fluctuated between 80 cents and 92 cents until April 1967 when currency fears began to affect silver as well as gold. By November 1967, at the height of the sterling crisis, silver had doubled to $1.80 and was to peak in June the following year at $2.20. It is possible that the unprecedented rise in the bullion price of silver caused many people who heard that 'silver was rocketing' to believe that silver plate either had risen or would soon rise at a similar rate. It was after all not so long before that bidding for silver plate at auction in the U.K. had taken place in terms of shillings or pounds per ounce and prices for the more hideous Victorian centrepieces used to be estimated on the basis of 'melt plus 10 or 20%'. The devaluation of the pound in November 1967 from $2.80 to $2.40 naturally made silverware bought in England more attractive to foreign buyers, although this advantage had been largely discounted before the event.

Throughout the 1960s, silver prices had been creeping up – particularly for the more popular investment pieces such as candlesticks, salvers and coffee-pots. In 1966 a pair of good quality George II standard candlesticks by Cafe or a maker of similar stature, of which large quantities have survived, were fetching $1,600–2,400. By the time of the sterling devaluation, they were up to $3,600–4,400 and were still rising fast through the dollar crisis and the suspension of the Gold Pool operations in March 1968 (see Gold, p. 170).

Since it was illegal for U.K. citizens at this date to hold gold, a natural alternative was silver bar even though its price-relationship with gold had been unstable for a long time. The strength of the metal price of silver throughout 1967/8 owed a good deal to speculation and hoarding by people who would have bought gold had it been legal to do so.

Two other kinds of buyer had been fuelling the market for silver plate. Firstly, high tax payers in the U.K. had been investing in silver with borrowed money and legitimately claiming tax relief on the interest they paid. This concession was removed by the 1969 Budget which made interest paid on only a narrow range of borrowings eligible for tax relief. The second kind of buyer was getting through a well-worn loophole in the Estate Duty legislation, which enabled individuals or trustees to switch money from conventional investments into objects that could be classed under the 1930 Finance Act as of national, scientific, historic or artistic interest and on which complete relief from Estate Duty could be claimed provided the heirs did not sell them for just three years.

133

This was one of the loop-holes that had led to the jibe that Death Duty was a voluntary tax and the 1969 Finance Act closed it by making the proceeds of a disposal taxable whenever that might occur.

If these measures cannot be said to have precipitated the collapse in values, they certainly happened to coincide with it. The George II candlesticks reached $6,000–7,000 in Spring 1969 and by the end of the year they were back to $1,600–2,400. Investors who brought such material into auction-houses for appraisal at the end of 1969, gaped in disbelief that a sector of the 'art market' could have lost 70% of its value in such a short time. By the end of the summer many dealers, who had watched interest rates rising and their stock gathering dust, slashed prices to such a low level that a few buyers were enticed back into the market. Quite a number of dealers went out of business at this time although the whole episode is now seen in retrospect by the trade as a painful but important lesson. Even now the George II candlesticks have only climbed back to $3,000–4,000 although pieces of the Regency and Victorian periods are generally way ahead of the high points they reached in 1969.

There is perhaps thirty or forty times more pre-1800 English silver than pre-1800 American silver in circulation today. This tends to make the American

Late neoclassical candlesticks. Maker John Schofield, 1790.

silver of this date very expensive. The best American silversmiths, such as Paul Revere and Myer Myers, made pieces that stand comparison with the best English silver yet they can command large premiums over their English counterparts. In 1969 a Paul Revere sauce-boat was sold at auction for $53,000, at a time when others of similar quality by English makers were fetching no more than $1,000. By the middle of the 19th century, the output of American silver had become colossal, although the majority of it is not very good and therefore quite uninteresting to the collector.

Throughout the 19th century every well-off American family would present a daughter on her marriage with a pair of candelabra, a set of flatware of which three thousand different patterns were on the market by 1900, and a tea-set. Many of the large and clumsy American tea-sets of 1820–30 are now appearing in salerooms and fetching less than the price of new ones.

There are not many American collectors of American silver, firstly because there is so little of fine quality to collect (much of the best is already in captivity in museums); secondly because it is so vulnerable to theft; thirdly because even affluent collectors find it increasingly hard to get anyone to clean it and lastly because there is a very large quantity of faked American silver around made in the early decades of this century of which collectors are understandably nervous.

The American silversmiths marked their silver from the 17th to the middle of the 19th century by stamping each piece with a monogram or full surname and occasionally with a symbol too. The only assay office ever to function in the U.S.A. was in Baltimore from 1814 to 1830 although some hall-marks were applied to pieces made in New York and elsewhere from the late 18th to the early 19th century. The faked American pieces are sometimes worked from scratch but are more often English pieces with the hall-marks erased and supplied with the initials of the great American silversmiths. Quite often pieces by English silversmiths with the same initials as those of the highly-rated American names are used and in this case just the assay marks erased.

A certain amount of forging of hall-marks on English silver still goes on in England but it is not usually very deceptive because the punches used are mostly of poor quality. Even more clumsy hall-marks are quite often added to English silver in Italy. There are also one or two dealers who play around adding the coats of arms of distinguished people and even faking inscriptions to give historical weight to everyday pieces.

In America, it is legal to sell fakes at auction provided they are so described, whereas it is illegal to do so in England. Thanks to the great experience of sale-room experts and the vigilance of the Antique Plate Committee at Goldsmiths' Hall and of the Assay Office, it is very rare that a faked piece reaches the point of being auctioned in England and from that point of view collectors may buy in auction-rooms with complete confidence.

There are many more American collectors of English silver than of American silver and their tendency is to attach great importance to the big names such as Lamerie, Bateman, Storr etc. The major rise in the price of Regency silver, particularly by Paul Storr, during the late fifties and sixties can be largely accounted for by American buying when some important collections were formed and dispersed.

Pair of campana-shaped wine-coolers, London, 1810. Weight 200 ozs.

In England and America there has always rightly been a premium on the work of the Huguenot silversmiths over that of their English-born rivals and within the Huguenot field a premium on the work of Paul de Lamerie. It does not seem to worry collectors that he ran a workshop employing tens and perhaps as many as a hundred craftsmen nor that very little of the plate that bears his mark could possibly be by him. The justification for the premium lies in the fact that not a single poor quality piece ever left his workshop. But the estimation of silversmiths and their styles can only be a personal matter. Paul Storr's detractors are fond of remarking on the industrial scale of his operations and that even the few pieces he may have had a hand in making are inferior to those of his lesser known Swedish teacher, Andrew Fogelberg. Similarly, some connoisseurs rate Peter and Jonathan Bateman's work superior to that of their better known mother Hester.

The extreme rarity of medieval English silver makes it quite out of the question to collect and even the 1525–1660 period, except perhaps for collecting spoons, has to be more or less ruled out. Thereafter the volume of material is immense but it is important to remember that the price differentials for pieces of silver depend not only on the popularity of one style or maker

Sugar caster. Maker Christopher Canner, 1690.

against another but also on the extent to which the practicality of the piece has survived into the ways of modern life. For this reason, spoons and forks, candlesticks, coffee-pots and salvers are, broadly speaking, more highly valued ounce for ounce than toilet sets, épergnes, wine cisterns etc. The main exceptions to this rule are certain small pieces such as wine labels, vinaigrettes, nutmet-graters and snuff-boxes about which collectors have for long been enthusiastic.

The peak prices for certain categories of silver that were seen in 1969 seem to have coincided with a peak of interest among American collectors. No statistics are available but the impression is shared by several authorities that the Americans have rather lost interest in silver. Some older collectors have sold up and although many young people's interest extends to eating with silver spoons and forks, to collect other silver objects is often considered quite eccentric. One result of this is that most of the fine Continental silver and a good deal of the fine English silver sold in America goes straight back to Europe.

Of the large quantity of fine silver in circulation, the tendency is for it to return to its country of origin although these general flows are modified by the state of a country's currency and economy. For example, there is certainly a net outflow of silver from the U.K. and a net inflow to Germany, not only of German but also of much other Northern European silver. In England, so large a fraction of the silver sold at auction goes to dealers that its final destination is not known although the export business of a few dealers is believed to account for the bulk of their trade. The recently growing demand for Victorian silver has been fairly general although the more ornate and flamboyant pieces appeal to the less educated taste and tend to go to Italy, South America, the southern states of America and certain areas of north London.

In July 1977, two vast and elaborate Victorian centrepieces weighing 1100 and 1400 ounces made by Garrard in 1842 and 1860 were sold at Sotheby's for $64,000 and $84,000. Although the buyer was a London-based dealer, their subject matter which included camels, Arab figures, merchants and blackamoors suggested a final destination in the Middle East. The price of the larger piece was three times the price ever paid before at auction for a Victorian piece and represented $60 an ounce at a time when the silver bar price was $5. Only ten years ago auctioneers, shaking their heads in admiration over the workmanship and in despair at the lack of interest in such material, would have estimated them at melt value plus perhaps 75% equivalent to (silver was then $1.20 an ounce) about $2,300 and $2,900.

Immediately after World War II the trade was, as it had been before, a very insignificant force in the salerooms. Silver sales in England and America were still dominated by private collectors who were very gradually to disappear as the trade strengthened its hold. The ring is very active and effective at silver auctions in America and the U.K. The worst abuses are perpetrated in small salerooms where an inexperienced cataloguer may not have recognised the value of a piece and so failed to recommend a high enough reserve. In a recent New York auction, the seller of a rare Georgian piece lost over $30,000 through just such a mistake.

The world of fine silver is quite compact; there are not more than a dozen important dealers in the whole of America and not more than twice that number in the U.K. The New York and London rings, which have as a nucleus perhaps five or so members with other dealers joining in on an occasional basis, are not as a rule effective against the international competition for really outstanding pieces and their successes are consistently scored in the medium and lower price-ranges. It is well known that if a private buyer begins to bid at a silver auction, particularly in London, the ring may well run him up by 50% or more above the price at which the bidding would have stopped if it had been a trade-only affair. Many dealers have come to regard salerooms as their wholesale supplier and are unwilling to let members of the public buy freely in 'their' market.

138

Most private collectors therefore prefer to pay 10% commission to a dealer to bid on their behalf. Unfortunately, not even that tactic can give full protection since it has been observed that dealers who would never dream of bidding against each other in ordinary circumstances have been seen to do so where one is buying for a client on commission and, being keen to inflate the buying price and with it the commission he receives, makes an earlier arrangement with another dealer to keep the bidding alive up to his client's limit. It is quite plain that these pernicious activities entirely undermine the spirit of a public auction and it is equally plain that nothing effective can be done about it. If auctioneers try to prevent these abuses by pitching their reserves just below the true market level, the ring-members will cease bidding at their normal low level and the auctioneers will be saddled with an unacceptable number of unsold lots. Moreover, dealers are by a long way the auctioneer's best customers appearing as they do at every sale and buying not only good pieces but all the rubbish as well, such as recently chased-up tankards and erstwhile mugs converted into coffee-pots which most private collectors would not touch.

Since 1945, the ice has become much thinner in places for private collectors of silver although in both England and America there are still dealers of great knowledge and integrity whose names may be learnt from the leading auction-houses.

Principal public collections

U.K.	Bath	Holbourne of Menstrie Museum
	Birmingham	City Museum and Art Gallery
	Cardiff	National Museum of Wales
	Edinburgh	Royal Scottish Museum
	London	British Museum
		London Museum
		Tower of London
		Victoria and Albert Museum
		Wellington Museum, Apsley House
	Norwich	Castle Museum
	Oxford	Ashmolean Museum
U.S.A.	Albany, N.Y.	Albany Institute of History and Art
	Andover, Mass.	Addison Gallery of American Art Phillips Academy
	Baltimore, Maryland	Baltimore Museum of Art
	Boston, Mass.	Museum of Fine Arts
	Cambridge, Mass.	Fogg Art Museum (Harvard University)

139

U.S.A.	Chicago, Ill.	Art Institute of Chicago
	Cincinnati, Ohio	Cincinnati Art Museum
	Cleveland, Ohio	Cleveland Museum of Art
	Detroit, Mich.	Detroit Institute of Art
	Minneapolis, Min.	Minneapolis Institute of Arts
	New Haven, Conn.	Yale University Art Gallery
	Philadelphia, Pa.	Historical Society of Pennsylvania
		Philadelphia Museum of Art
	Providence, Rhode Island	Rhode Island School of Design
	St. Louis, Mo.	City Art Museum
	Wilmington, Del.	Winterthur Museum
	Worcester, Mass.	Worcester Art Museum

Book list

BANISTER, JUDITH. *English Silver Hallmarks* 1978, Wallace-Homestead

GRIMWADE, ARTHUR. *London Goldsmiths, 1697–1837* 1976 (pub. by Faber & Faber), Merrimack Book Service

HAYWARD, J. F. *Huguenot Silver in England 1688–1727* 1959 (pub. by Faber & Faber), Merrimack Book Service

JACKSON, CHARLES J. *Illustrated History of English Plate* 2 Volumes 1969 Reprint of 1911 ed, Dover

OMAN, CHARLES. *English Engraved Silver* (Illus.) 1979 (pub. by Faber & Faber), Merrimack Book Service

PHILLIPS, J. M. et al., ed. *Waldron Phoenix Belknap, Jr. Collection of Portraits and Silver* 1955, Harvard University Press

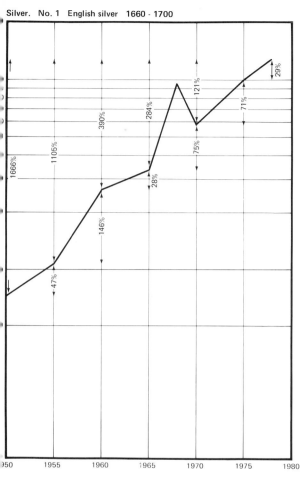

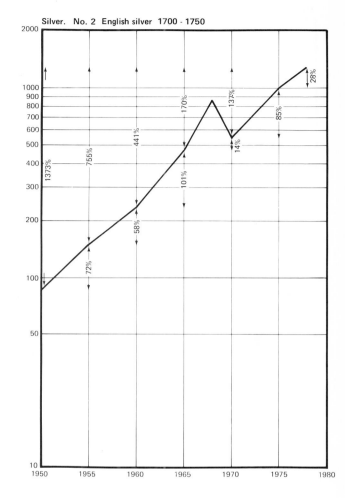

DEX NO. 1

Plain tapering cylindrical tankard on rim foot, with flat stepped over, bold scroll handle and corkscrew thumbpiece. Initials pricked near top of handle; coat-of-arms on front within foliate cartouche. Capacity about 2 pints. Height 7½in. Weight 29 ozs. Maker EG. 1685.

A Charles II Caudle Cup and Cover, engraved on either side with crossed plumes enclosing a coat-of-arms and crest below a chased girdle of stylized leafage, and lower part of the body chased with alternate palm and acanthus leaves, the domed over with similar alternating foliage below the finial, cast scroll handles. Height 6½in. Weight 22 oz. 10 dwt. London 1682.

Circular Salver on trumpet-shaped foot, the broad rim repoussé-chased with naturalistic fruits and foliage in relief. London 1661. Diameter 16in. Weight 37 ozs.

Cylindrical Sugar Caster, on narrow spreading foot with gadrooned border, the top rather coarsely pierced with trefoils and quatrefoils, the baluster-shaped finial with cut-card applied detail round the base, the cover secured by bayonet points. Maker Christopher Canner. Height 7in. Weight 8 oz. 15 dwts. 1690.

INDEX NO. 2.

1. Tapering cylindrical Coffee Pot with high-domed cover, on moulded base, the curved spout with hinged flap, set at right angles to the D-shaped wood handle, with plain handle sockets and the cover with vase-shaped finial. 1715. Maker William Fawdery. Height 10¼in. Weight 26 oz. 5 dwts.

2. Pair of plain octagonal cast baluster candlesticks. Maker James Gould. London 1728. Height 7in. Weight 28 ozs.

3. Waiter with Chippendale border on four cast scroll feet. Plain except for engraved armorials within a baroque cartouche. London 1735. Diameter 17in. Weight 70 ozs.

4. Inkstand in the rococo style with asymmetrical shell and scroll applied and chased decoration, on cast claw feet, the inkpot, pounce-pot and taperstick chased to match. Arms of Admiral George Anson. Maker Paul de Lamerie. 1744. Length 14½in. Weight 81½ ozs.

141

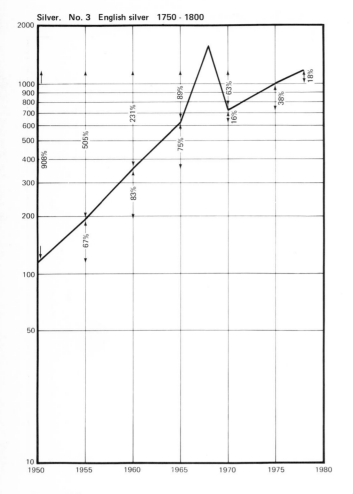

Silver. No. 3 English silver 1750 - 1800

908% 67% 505% 83% 231% 75% 89% 16% 63% 38% 18%

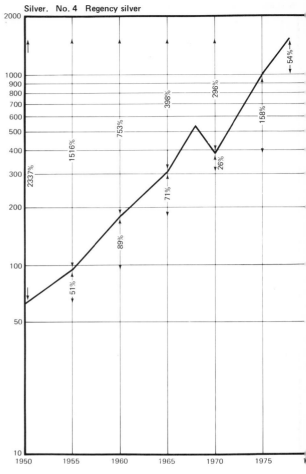

Silver. No. 4 Regency silver

2337% 1516% 51% 753% 89% 398% 71% 296% 26% 158% 54%

INDEX NO. 3.

1. Pair of sauce-boats with gadroon rims, leaf-capped double-scroll handles, on three lion mask and paw supports. Maker Eliza Godfrey. 1755. Length 8in. Weight 30 ozs.

2. Teapot, of shaped oval outline, on flat base, the sides decorated with bright-cut engraved festoons, with slightly domed cover engraved en suite, straight tapered spout, wood handle and knop to cover. On matching stand with four panel feet. Maker Solomon Hougham. 1799. Length 6½in. Weight 22 ozs.

3. Sweetmeat basket, with pierced swing handle, the sides pierced with pales, scrolls, husks, paterae and other neo-classical motifs, picked out with bright-cut engraving. With blue glass liner. Maker Hester Bateman. 1786. Height 6in. Weight 4 ozs. 15 dwt.

4. Pair of candelabra of neo-classical design, with tapering fluted stems rising from circular beaded bases, with beaded bands at the shoulders, fluted bell-shaped sconces with detachable circular beaded nozzles. Stamped and loaded sticks, cast branches. Maker John Scofield. 1790. Height 15in.

INDEX NO. 4.

1. Pair of Wine-coolers of campana shape, the bases of the bod half-fluted, with rising side handles decorated with reeding a springing from masks, the everted rims applied with gadro and leaf mounts on a similarly mounted stepped moulded fo With silver liners. 1810. Height 9½in. Weight 200 ozs.

2. Hot water Jug and Stand, of vase shape on a rim foot, with ov mounts at shoulder, a mask below the upper handle socket, shaped cover with bud finial, short high spout, the handle wood of twisted form. Fitted on triform lampstand with va shaped spirit-burner on paw feet. Maker Paul Storr. 18 Height 8½in. Weight 51 ozs.

3. Candelabrum-centrepiece of massive proportions, with lights rising from a chased central stem, supporting a dess basket in the centre, and rising from a triform base with li couchant supports, themselves resting on a pedestal suppor on anthemion feet. Maker Paul Storr. 1813. Height 24in. Wei 464 ozs.

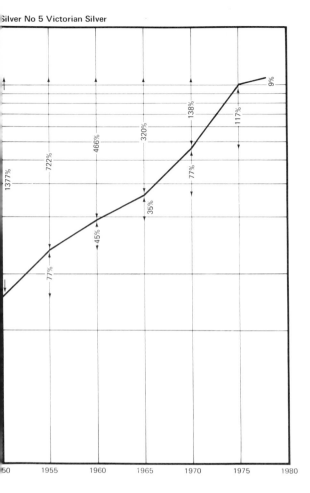

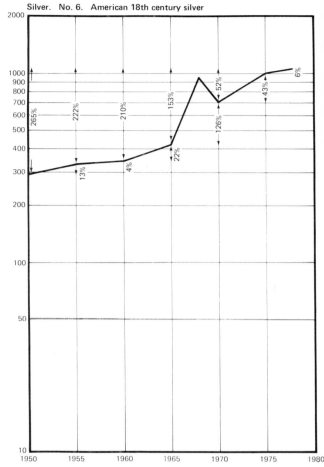

INDEX NO. 5.

hild's Christening Set, with mug cast and chased with scrolls
nd figures of children, on scroll supports, with elaborate cast
nd chased handle en suite; with matching knife, fork and
poon of decorative chased design. In fitted case. 1860. Weight
0 ozs.

our-piece tea and coffee service of compressed circular form,
anelled and chased in relief with scrolling foliage and
lowers, on cast scroll and foliate supports, double scroll silver
andles. Maker Barnard Bros. 1858. Weight 79 ozs.

'able Centre-piece, on shaped circular base with acanthus
croll feet, chased with vines, scrolls and with leaf-calyx
upporting a cut glass dish. 1872. Height 14in. Weight 25 ozs.

'air of Fish-carvers, with cast and chased silver handles, the
our-pronged fork engraved and pierced on the section below
he tines, the broad blade of the slice scimitar-shaped with one
dge curved for parting the fish, and elaborately decorated with
ngraving and piercing. Maker G. W. Adams. 1860. Weight 12
zs.

INDEX NO. 6.

1. Porringer of circular bellied form, with cast and pierced flat
   handle, plain narrow rim at lip. New York c. 1710. Diameter
   5½in. Weight 8 ozs.
2. Tapered cylindrical tankard on moulded foot, with rib around
   body above lower handle socket, scroll handle, fluted thumbpiece, stepped domed cover with wrythen knop. Providence,
   Rhode Island. c. 1735. Height 8½in. Weight 28 ozs.
3. Pair of plain oval sauce-boats, with slightly bellied bodies, on
   three scroll and shell feet with shell knuckles, leaf-capped
   flying scroll handles, beaded rims. Maker Paul Revere. c. 1790.
4. Plain circular bowl on stepped moulded foot. c. 1750. Diameter
   8in. Weight 18 ozs.

143

Fire-arms

From the 16th to the early 19th century fine fire-arms were produced in great quantities. Not only were they made by gunsmiths in the capitals and many of the provincial cities of Europe but also by gunsmiths permanently retained by many royal and noble households. These craftsmen were producing fire-arms not only to equip the elaborate hunting-parties that were a feature of European aristocratic life but also for their employers to give away – a pair of pistols or a set of hunting guns being a favourite form of present in those days.

Most of the great armouries of Europe simply grew of their own accord. Successive owners equipped themselves with the finest weapons that the technology and fashion of the time could offer without at any stage setting out to collect old fire-arms which were merely regarded as obsolete.

Fire-arms collecting really started when mechanical production and the interchangeability of parts pioneered by Colt in the 1830s seemed likely to mark the end of the era of fine craftsmanship. In the event, the highest standards have continued to be applied ever since the production of the finest fire-arms. During the 19th century, the Gothic Revival stimulated demand for arms and armour particularly. Suits of armour which had earlier been sold by weight, in much the same way as scrap metal, came to be sold at astonishing prices by the end of the century – prices which, in real terms, have not been equalled since. Some of this interest spun off on to fire-arms, but on the whole fire-arms collectors remained a small and fortunate group.

South German wheel-lock rifle, ebony stock carved and set with plaques of staghorn. Augsburg, c. 1600.

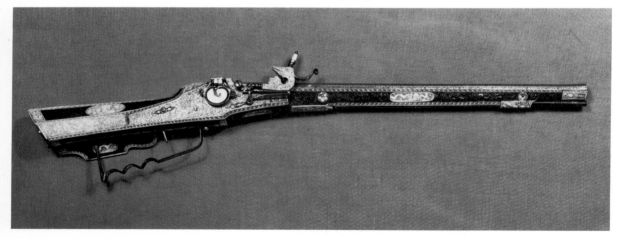

Fortunate because the political turmoil of Europe in the 19th and 20th centuries and the consequent impoverishment of many of its ruling families brought on the market many fine collections at a time when demand was very low. Some of these collections went straight to museums, while others were dispersed into private collections all over the world. This relative lack of interest in fire-arms persisted until around 1950 when prices began to move sharply upwards.

The earliest fire-arms

Many people in the West feel a strong but unexplained urge not only to credit the Chinese with a whole range of inventions that they never made, but often to date them many centuries before their actual invention elsewhere. Gunpowder and fire-arms may be cases in point. The Chinese were most ingenious at making fireworks, but it should not be assumed that they must have developed this knowledge to the point where they were able to construct a fire-arm.

In the present state of knowledge it seems that saltpetre, an essential ingredient of gunpowder, was known during the Sung dynasty (A.D. 960–1279). In 1044 mixtures containing saltpetre, sulphur and charcoal were known, although these were deflagrating and therefore suitable for incendiary rather than explosive devices. A manuscript of about 1232 describes the explosion of a bomb which may have contained something like modern gunpowder, and another account of about 1259 of an explosion which resulted in solid fragments being projected from a bamboo strongly suggests the existence of at least weak gunpowder. True gunpowder was known in the later part of the Yüan (Mongol) dynasty 1279–1368. It may have been a Chinese or Mongol invention, or knowledge of it may even have come from the West.

In the long history of incendiary compositions, there is no firm evidence of saltpetre before c. A.D. 1250. The substance used by the ancient Assyrians was liquid petroleum or naphtha from the oil wells of Iraq. The Greeks used liquid pitch for their fireships and incendiary arrows in the 5th century B.C. The Greek fire which struck terror into the Arabs at the siege of Constantinople in A.D. 674–78 contained a mysterious ingredient which was probably not saltpetre but a liquid rectified petroleum (the rudiments of distillation being known in Constantinople at that date) which was thickened to a jelly by dissolving it in a resinous substance. This was then apparently pumped by hand through a hole at the end of a tube to create a very effective flame-thrower.

The earliest Chinese cannons are dated 1356 which would make them, if genuine, ten or twenty years older than European cannons of similar size. Much of the Chinese documentary evidence on the subject is contradictory, while the picture is further confused by the time-honoured Chinese practice of putting early dates and reign-marks in places where they do not belong.

145

The earliest picture of a gun is dated 1326 and is in the manuscript of Walter de Milemete in Christ Church, Oxford. It shows a pear-shaped gun with a large arrow protruding from the muzzle standing apparently unattached, on a rickety four-legged table, and being fired by a man holding a red-hot iron to a touch-hole, presumably bored through the barrel to the chamber. The earliest known actual gun was excavated in the south of Sweden. It bears a close resemblance to the Milemete gun, and can be dated to the first half of the 14th century.

At the same period, smaller iron tubes closed at one end were being lashed to crude wooden stocks to form hand guns. At first these could only be fired by holding a lighted match or taper to the fine gunpowder in the touch-hole which inflamed and carried the fire down to the main charge in the chamber of the gun. Burst barrels must have been commonplace and the construction of most of these guns was such that the gunman can have been in only slightly less danger than his adversary.

The first improvement to this primitive weapon was the match-lock. It is the first appearance of the trigger principle which has not been significantly improved upon even today. It was a simple device consisting of a pair of jaws (the serpentine) holding, by means of a small thumb-screw, the lighted slow-match. The serpentine was linked to a pivoted lever and spring in such a way that when the lever was raised the serpentine swung in a circular motion, bringing the lighted match down on to the flash pan. This small receptacle, which in the earliest match-locks was welded to the side of the barrel, was filled with a priming of fine gunpowder and communicated with the charge in the barrel by means of a touch-hole bored through the side wall of the breach.

With various modifications, this system of ignition was in continuous military use in Europe from the end of the 15th century to the beginning of the 18th. Only a few fine European match-locks survive today. They were made in great quantities in Italy, mainly in Brescia and Milan, and also in Holland, but most had little obvious aesthetic appeal and would probably have been thrown away when they ceased to be serviceable.

The majority of those that do survive are copies made in various parts of Africa, India, the Middle and Far East, to which European explorers travelled with their originals. These are often even cruder than their European predecessors, but are sometimes found, particularly the Indian ones, with some distinctive and exotic decoration.

The 16th century

Although the match-lock persisted in military use in Europe so long, and in the East even until the 20th century, important mechanical and stylistic changes had occurred as early as the beginning of the 16th century.

The first drawing of a wheel-lock is by Leonardo da Vinci in the *Codex Atlanticus* now in Milan. It can be dated not later than 1505, although it is not clear whether the drawing is a design or a representation of an existing mechanism. Whichever it was, it soon became the standard form of lock throughout Germany (which in this context means present-day Germany, Austria and Bohemia) and Italy, and later throughout the rest of Europe.

With the wheel-lock, the lighted match and with it the inherent danger of premature discharge is dispensed with. The principle is similar to that used in a modern flint cigarette-lighter. A steel wheel with a serrated edge is wound up with a key against a powerful V spring. When the trigger is squeezed, the spring is released and the steel wheel rotates at speed while a piece of iron pyrites, held in the jaws of the 'dog', swings down simultaneously to contact the wheel, sending a shower of sparks into the priming pan.

The earliest wheel-lock fire-arms were often constructed in combination with another weapon such as a cross-bow, axe, sword, war-hammer etc. suggesting that the system of ignition was unreliable and so providing the gunman with a second weapon if the lock failed. In the 16th century, some Italian fire-arms were even made in which wheel-lock and match-lock mechanisms were set off simultaneously by a single trigger.

Although the process of gun manufacture varied from one country to another and according to the size of the town, it would have been unusual if a gun were constructed by one craftsman alone. Several trades were normally involved — the barrel-smith, the lock-maker, the gun-stocker, silversmith, engraver, etc. — and there exist a few 17th-century German wheel-lock rifles bearing stamps or signatures of five different craftsmen.

In the 16th century, Italy and Germany led the rest of Europe in mechanical and decorative invention. It was probably in Portugal that the snap-lock originated, this being the first of a generation of snaphaunce locks in which the spring-operated cock holding a piece of flint or pyrites strikes a spark from a piece of steel (rather than the rotating serrated wheel) pivoted vertically over the flash pan.

South German wheel-lock pistol. Nuremberg, 1593.

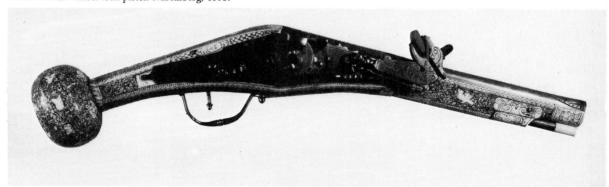

The chronology of improvements and modifications to the design of locks in different countries becomes confused at this period – not least because modern writers often use different names to describe the same lock. At all events, a sequence of modifications to the snap-lock culminated in the flint-lock not later than 1615, the credit for this important development usually being given to Marin le Bourgeois, a gunsmith at the court of Henri IV of France. It was this lock which, in general use throughout Europe by 1650, was unsurpassed until 1825.

The first reference to rifling is made in the rules for a shooting match organised by the Elector Augustus X of Saxony in 1563. Rifling, which was the spiral grooving on the inside of a barrel which imparted a rotatory movement to the bullet and so improved its line of flight, was to be allowed only if all competitors agreed. It was almost certainly a German invention and probably was adapted from the known ballistic principle by which the vanes on an arrow were set at a slight angle to the shaft to cause the arrow to rotate in its flight.

The very short stock known as a cheek stock was a feature of all German rifles and many smooth-bored fowling-pieces until the late 17th century. This did not reach to the shoulder and the full force of the recoil was therefore taken by the arms. These stocks were often very finely decorated, sometimes with erotic subjects or bawdy humour.

Another original German innovation was the ball butt which first appeared on holster pistols and was extensively copied elsewhere. These were not designed, as is generally supposed, to serve as cudgels if required but to help the gunman to be quicker and surer on the draw.

16th-century German gunsmiths also had to their credit the first breech-loading fire-arms, a superimposed loading system in which separate charges and bullets were placed in the barrel and separate touch-holes and locks arranged along the outside. They had even produced a serviceable revolver with a rotating cylinder of five chambers.

In England, until the last quarter of the sixteenth century, there seem to have been very few gunmakers at work and large numbers of wheel-lock pistols were

Italian match-lock arquebus, the walnut stock inlaid with engraved and green-tinted staghorn, *c.* 1560.

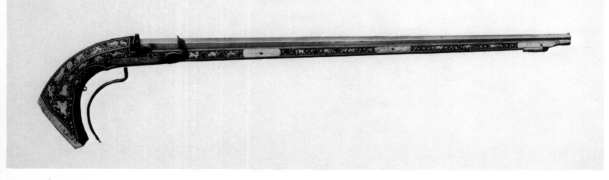

imported from Augsburg and Nürnberg and possibly Liège too. This ready availability of pistols had radically improved prospects for criminals and a statute of Henry VIII ordering that no one might carry a fire-arm less than one yard long suggests that pistols had become dangerously easy to hide. An inventory of Henry VIII's fire-arms at Greenwich in 1547 includes no fewer than ten breech-loaders. English gunsmiths were experimenting so extensively with this method of loading, they seem to have sensed it to be the right solution, although it was never fully viable until the invention of the metal cartridge case in the 19th century.

Although 16th-century English fire-arms did not on the whole compare favourably with either German or Italian work, by the beginning of the 17th century at least a few very fine English pieces had found their way all over the world. An outstanding example is in the Kremlin of a fine pair of pistols, perhaps by Stephen Russell, presented on behalf of James I by the English Ambassador to the Tsar Boris Godunov's son Feodor in 1604.

The 17th century

The 17th century saw Paris rise to dominate the whole of European gun-making. This came about because the French were able to combine technical mastery with a perfect elegance of form. Not only did gun-makers all over Europe imitate the French type of flint-lock, they even took to signing their names in French. It was Henri IV who allocated the ground floor rooms of the Palais du Louvre to an assortment of artists and craftsmen, including a gun-maker. Louis XIII owned seven arquebuses by the time he was ten, and by the time he died his collection had grown to 337.

During the first half of the century, decoration was quite restrained, but around 1660 there emerged the classic Louis XIV style, which was copied all over Europe. Barrels were richly damascened in gold fleur-de-lis, and lock-plates finely engraved with mythological and biblical subjects. But in the 1680s, there began a gradual intensification of measures against the Huguenots culminating in Louis XIV's revocation of the Edict of Nantes in 1685, as a result of which toleration of French Protestants was finally withdrawn. Thousands of families were driven into exile, including a number of fine gun-makers who settled in the Protestant countries of Northern Europe.

In 17th-century Germany, two different styles were evident. In the west, there was a demand for light fowling-pieces to be used for shooting flying birds for which a long shoulder stock was more convenient, while in the south and east demand was for wheel-lock hunting rifles as well as light rifles for shooting sitting birds. For this last purpose, the weapon known as the Tschinke became especially popular. Deriving its name from the Polish form of Teschen, a town on the old frontier between Germany and Bohemia, the rifle was produced in

149

considerable numbers. Many of the stocks were profusely inlaid with mother-of-pearl and engraved staghorn, and although sometimes quite coarsely finished, they are decorative and consistently popular with collectors. Meanwhile, in Munich, the Dukes of Bavaria were employing exceptional artists at the court workshop who produced some of the finest wheel-lock rifles ever made.

In Italy, the flint-lock was resisted for some time by the Brescian gun-makers who preferred the old snaphaunce. The Cominazzo family at Gardone near Brescia founded a dynasty of barrel-smiths whose fame spread with the barrels they exported all over Europe. The three most characteristic types of Brescian fire-arm of this period are the long holster pistol, the shorter belt pistol and the carbine, all of which were often mounted with flat inlaid panels of steel tracery, pierced and engraved with animals, birds, etc.

In England at the end of the reign of Queen Elizabeth I, there were thirty-seven gunsmiths carrying on business at the Minories adjoining the Tower of London, but James I unwisely granted a monopoly which resulted in the number dwindling to five by 1607. In 1637, six gun-makers first applied for a Charter and, eventually, in 1671 their successors acquired complete control of the trade, being incorporated as the Gunmakers' Company with the right to prove all hand guns – that is, to test the barrels for safety against a burst.

Pair of Italian holster pistols. Mark of Lazarino Cominazzo, 17th century.

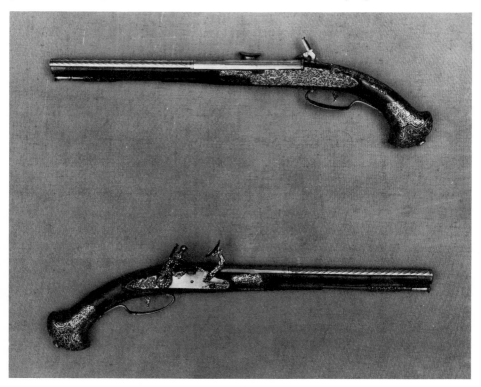

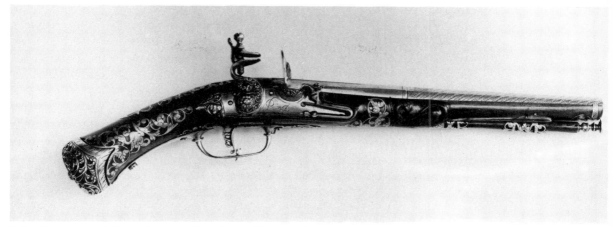

Italian flint-lock pistol, the stock inlaid with steel. Barrel by Bernardi Bazzone. Brescia, *c.* 1650.

During the English Civil War when the Royalist army was halted at Stafford, Prince Rupert, to prove his marksmanship, fired with a rifled horseman's pistol at the weathercock on a church sixty yards away. When the bullet struck the tail, his uncle Charles I said it must be a lucky chance, whereupon he immediately hit the target again with his second pistol. These remarkable pistols were made by Harman Barne, who was one of the first important gun-makers to work in England. After the execution of Charles I in 1649, he was often in trouble for his Royalist leanings until, at the Restoration, he was appointed Royal hand-gun maker at 16 pence a day.

It was Charles I's dwarf, Jeffrey Hudson, who fought one of the first known duels with pistols against Mr. Crofts, a member of the Queen's household. Mr. Crofts had accused the dwarf of having been defeated in a fight with a turkey. The dwarf duly issued a challenge but on reaching the ground found Mr. Crofts to have armed himself with a water-pistol. Hudson was incensed and demanded a duel on horseback with pistols. This was agreed to and he killed Crofts with his first shot, the bullet passing through his heart. Although this affair took place over a hundred years before pistols became the conventional duelling weapon, it emphasises how they eliminated the advantages of physical strength and agility which counted for so much in duels fought with rapier or small-sword. It might, of course, be argued that the introduction of pistols as the standard duelling weapons, far from levelling the odds, actually stacked them unfairly in favour of dwarfs generally.

By the 16th century, the clearing of forests and enclosure of the land had reduced the cover available for game-birds, which were now easier to kill in any case with flint-lock fowling-pieces than they had been with the crossbow. Early in the 17th century, game laws began to be introduced in England and France restricting the right to shoot game-birds to land-owners only.

151

ALTERNATIVE INVESTMENT

   In the late 17th century it had become fashionable to shoot birds on the wing.
Until then, birds had been caught either by a hawk, by a variety of traps and
snares or stalked and shot sitting with a gun. The hunter sometimes walked in
step with a stalking-horse, which allowed him to get close to the game which
could see only the horse. At other times, the stalking would be done in the
horizontal position. This strategy seems so unpromising today, it suggests
either that hunters in those days were more stealthy, or the game-birds less
jumpy. The new fashion resulted in a call in many parts of Europe for lighter
smooth-bore guns with reduced barrel-length and larger bore* to take more shot.

*The bore of a gun is a measure of the diameter or calibre of its barrel and is based on calculating
how many lead balls of the same diameter would weigh one pound. A 12-bore gun-barrel for
example, has a diameter such that twelve lead balls of the same diameter would weigh one pound.

Shooting with the help of a
stalking-horse. Johann
Elias Ridinger (1698–1767).
The purpose of the
elaborate harness was to
force down the horse's
head to fool the ducks that
it was grazing and that all
was well. The dog appears
to be joining in the ruse.

In Scotland, fine arms had been made since the 16th century but a minor industry established itself at Doune in Perthshire in the mid-17th century making
pistols in holster length and belt length, both provided with hooks for attaching
to the belt. Scottish pistols have several exclusive features. Firstly, their stocks
were made entirely of steel or gilt brass; secondly, they had an unusual form of
butt with a pricker for clearing the touch-hole. Thirdly, they were often
profusely and beautifully ornamented; and fourthly, they had no trigger
guard. Most of the early Scottish pistols are dated and stamped with the maker's
initials.

There has always been a strong demand for Scottish pistols, of which
curiously enough many more early ones have survived than of those made in
England. Some experts have rather implausibly explained this state of affairs as
resulting from the wooden stocks of English pistols having been eaten by
worms. But considering the population of Scotland between 1550–1750 was
never as much as a quarter of that of England, it seems likely that the greater
turbulence and bloodshed of Scottish life must have either called for or resulted
from a greater production of fire-arms in the first place. Even throughout the
18th century, Scotland remained largely unaffected by the changes in style
occurring elsewhere, and later generations of the Perthshire gun-makers,
Murdochs, Campbells and Christies, continued to produce fine pistols of the
same original design.

Spanish 17th-century guns and pistols were on the whole very decorative.
The barrels were of the finest quality, but were not appreciated outside Spain
until the 18th century. However at Ripoll in North Catalonia an arms industry
flourished large enough to provide work for eighty master gunsmiths and their
assistants. The pistols for which the town was famous often featured a small
version of the Spanish Miquelet lock, a gun butt or ovoid or spherical pommel.

An outstanding inventor of this century was Peter Kalthoff, a German from
Solingen, who worked successively in the Low Countries, England and
Denmark. While at the Danish Court, he made a wheel-lock repeating rifle

Spanish saddle-pistol.
Catalonia, 17th century.

which had a powder magazine in the butt and a bullet magazine running the length of the barrel. By an ingenious system of cogs and gears, the gun was loaded with powder and ball, primed and spanned by one double movement of a lever. Kalthoff was able to produce enough of these guns to arm the Danish foot-guards in the Scanian War of 1675–9.

While Denmark was considerably influenced by German fashion and Sweden by French fashion, the Russian Court workshop in the Kremlin was turning out very fine arms profusely decorated with abstract patterns showing a strong Persian influence. The Tsar Boris Godunov had already opened a small gun foundry at Tula in the 16th century and Peter the Great enlarged it into the State arms factory in 1705 whose production grew to 70,000 muskets a year by the end of the century.

The 18th century

In the late 17th century, there were some twenty Huguenot gun-makers settled in London, mostly in Soho, including Monlong and Gruché who had worked for Louis XIV. Partly as a result of their influence, the quality of English fowling-pieces and pistols rose impressively throughout the 18th century. In spite of the Huguenot presence and the arrival of German craftsmen with George I in 1714, however, a distinctly English style evolved which was more restrained than the extravagant rococo ornament which had become and was to remain until 1790 so popular on the Continent.

The blunderbuss at this time became a favourite weapon in England. These bell-mouthed carbines derived their name from the Dutch word *Donderbus* meaning thunder-gun, presumably because the shape of the muzzle amplified the noise of the discharge. They were produced continuously until the early 19th century mainly for defence against robbers and highwaymen. The purpose of the bell-mouth was to scatter the shot over a wider area. The effect of choking

154

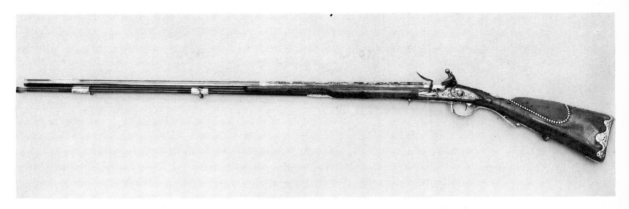

Single barrel fowling-piece. French, late 18th century.

a barrel, that is gradually reducing the diameter of the barrel towards the muzzle, to restrict the shot to a smaller area, had been known since the 17th century. The bell-mouth idea was perhaps an attempt to achieve the opposite effect. It was discovered much later that no such effect was achieved, but the bell-mouth appearance was maintained even though the barrels were made with the same bore throughout.

Large numbers of blunderbusses have survived and are extremely popular with collectors, the most sought-after being those with brass barrels and mounts, and those with spring bayonets hinged over or under the barrel which were released by pressing a catch in front of the trigger-guard.

From 1770 onwards, the fine proportions and unsurpassed workmanship of English duelling pistols won them an international reputation. The habit of duelling with pistols made specifically for the purpose seems to have begun because fashion dictated that swords should no longer be carried. Although infinite care was taken over the accuracy of these weapons, the duelling code rather perversely forbade the use of rifled barrels. Yet, in spite of this, the performance of the best over the conventional distance of about twenty yards was excellent.

A double-barrelled flint-lock pocket pistol by Joseph Egg, London, 1823.

155

Orders were received by London gun-makers from all over the world, including one by H. W. Mortimer in 1801 from the U.S. Government for presentation to the Bey of Tunis. It consisted of five fusees and five pairs of pistols all mounted with gold and set with diamonds, as well as some smaller models for the Bey's son. Mortimer's fee for this garniture was 5,000 guineas excluding the diamonds. At the other end of the scale, vast quantities of turn-off pistols, whose barrels unscrewed so that they could be loaded at the breech, were being made in Birmingham at this time. They were almost invariably of poor quality and were slightingly known as 'ironmongers' pistols'.

In Germany, the favourite fowling-piece had been the double-barrelled Wender gun which was designed with one barrel on top of the other and a swivel action to bring the second barrel into position. Pistols, although primarily for military purposes, were also used to give the *coup de grâce* in hunting but German noblemen were now tending to buy these in Paris or from Huguenot immigrants and the great centres of Augsburg and Nürnberg declined in importance. Germany had been slow to develop the flint-lock and when the wheel-lock eventually went out of favour the industry declined.

After Vienna was relieved from siege by the Turks in 1683, European gun-makers began to imitate the Damascus twist barrel which had been discovered on the captured weapons. The complicated process which was based on twisting lengths of steel like a rope gave greater flexibility and strength and was only superseded in the 19th century by the introduction of smooth-drawn steel. In the early 18th century, Vienna shooting became immensely popular. The Empress Amalia held weekly shooting contests in the garden for the ladies of the Court, with jewelled rings and gold snuff-boxes for prizes, while at Carlsbad some twenty gun-makers supplied the very grand tourist trade with luxury sporting guns.

In Italy, Brescia gradually lost its reputation for very fine arms and became a centre of large-scale military production. In 1696, several members of the great

A Flemish flint-lock pistol, 1720–30.

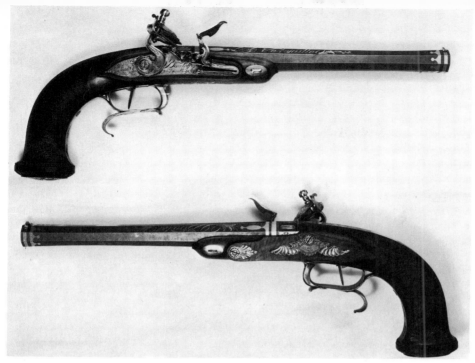

A pair of French flint-lock pistols, signed Boutet a Versailles, *c.* 1820.

Cominazzo family had been shot for political agitation, while others had emigrated with disastrous results for the local trade. In Florence, Lorenzoni, while working for the Medici, developed a magazine breech-loading system which improved upon the Kalthoff system and was made all over Northern Europe, particularly in England. In Naples, the last Royal arms factory was established in the mid-18th century by Charles III King of the Two Sicilies where, not surprisingly after two hundred years of Spanish domination, the finest pieces showed some Spanish influence.

In France, according to Diderot's *Encyclopédie des Sciences* of 1751, the gun-makers of Paris formed the largest community of craftsmen in the city. Throughout the 18th century, Paris dominated French gun-making, while St. Etienne developed as the centre of production for military arms, although later in the Napoleonic era the finest presentation arms were made at Versailles.

The greatest name in the history of French gun-making is Nicolas Noël Boutet who was appointed by Napoleon Artistic Director of the Manufacture de Versailles in 1792. In 1794 he established a workshop to specialise in 'armes de luxe'. His presentation arms, although they may not have been as practical as the best English arms, are widely regarded as the most beautiful ever made. He was the Fabergé of the fire-arms world, but although his work was very expensive in its time and also in constant demand, he was in almost permanent financial trouble. His achievement was not only to restyle the pistol fundamentally but also to apply to his arms the whole new ornamental style of the French Empire. This great man, the only gunsmith ever to describe himself as an artist, died in poverty in 1833.

157

American arms

In America the earliest rifles made were copies of the short-barrelled type originally brought over by Swiss and German settlers. They had thick straight butts, heavy trigger-guards, large calibre barrels and sliding patch-box covers. From these rather crude weapons, American gunsmiths developed the legendary Kentucky rifle. The immense popularity of these among U.S. collectors must have more than a little to do with the part they played in winning the American War of Independence.

At its best, the typical Kentucky rifle of the 1770s had a slender stock of maplewood with a curved or recessed brass heel-plate and a brass patch-box. It had a 42″-octagonal barrel and the whole weapon weighed no more than nine pounds. It had been developed very much with hunting and Indians in mind, and it was a happy accident for the Americans that it proved uniquely suitable for the sharp-shooting guerilla-type actions in which they often became engaged against the English, whose Brown Bess was clumsy and inaccurate by comparison. Some of the 1780–1820 Kentucky rifles are decorated with rococo scrollwork which, unlike the highly elaborate ornament on many European weapons, is applied on a refreshingly bold scale which seems more appropriate to the size of the weapon.

In 1807 the Reverend Alexander Forsyth had invented in Scotland the detonating or percussion principle by which a chemical compound would ignite under a blow and so take the place of the flint-lock mechanism. It was the most important event in the history of fire-arms since the discovery of gunpowder and over the next twenty years or so the system was adopted for nearly all fire-arms.

Flint-lock Kentucky rifle with octagonal rifled barrel and decorated with punchwork, the figured maple full stock with pierced and engraved brass furniture enriched with silver plaques. The barrel is signed J. Gumpf (of Lancaster, Pa.). Early 19th century.

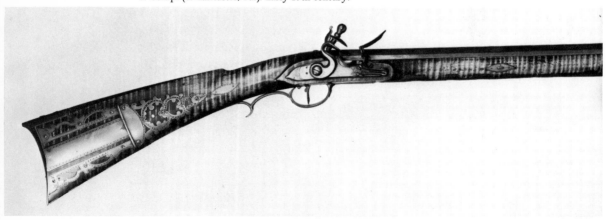

It was, of course, used in the great ranges of Deringers and Colts which for American collectors hold an almost mystical attraction. Henry Deringer Jnr. of Philadelphia was one of several German and English gunsmiths, mostly the sons of immigrants, who produced fine duelling pistols in the late 18th century. But his name is linked to the small pocket pistol that became so popular in the mid-19th century. Legends have grown up around saloon gunfights and the marksmanship of the men who packed the later Deringers. In reality, speed was usually a good deal more important than accuracy on these occasions and most Deringers, which could not be relied upon at anything over twelve paces, were at their best in use across a card-table.

Samuel Colt launched his first company in 1836 at the age of twenty-one. His first pocket revolvers, which were made at Paterson, New Jersey found a ready market in Texas which had just won its independence from Mexico. The Texas model and the 'Walker', named after Captain Walker of the Texas Rangers, were more accurate than most contemporary European revolvers which had a long heavy pull and hammers that usually obscured the line of sight. The original Colt Company failed in 1841 and arms dating from that period are extremely scarce and valuable. By 1845, America was at war with Mexico and Colt began in 1847, with the support of Government money, to manufacture at Whitneyville to meet the sudden demand. In 1851 he travelled to London to introduce his mass-production method, and in the following year opened a factory at Pimlico.

Forgeries

Some authorities take the view that alterations made during the active life of a fire-arm are acceptable, but that later improvements are not. An early flint-lock might in principle have undergone so many alterations as to be still in service today as a double-barrelled ejector sporting gun. Such an extreme problem of identity will not probably arise, yet such matters are vitally important for the investor.

A few collectors specialise in forgeries, while many more own some without realising it. The simplest definition of a forgery as it applies to fire-arms is the addition or replacement of any part, decoration, signature or date which is intended to deceive someone about its maker or original state. Or, in the case of a reconversion, to conceal the fact that the gun had once been converted.

Forgeries of differing qualities have been produced for hundreds of years. Barrels purporting to be by the famous Cominazzo family of Gardone in Italy were widely forged all over Europe in the 17th and 18th centuries, although the forgers used different designs and lettering which makes them possible to identify.

Isidro Soler, a famous Spanish gunsmith, complained in 1795 that Spanish

159

barrels were being extensively faked in Liège. Flattering as this may have been, it was extremely disturbing to the Spanish, whose genuine barrels were fetching up to £45 a piece in London at this date. The Liège guns were often signed 'London' and given fake proof marks. Many of the guns were miniature pocket pistols, mostly with steel stocks, often double-barrelled and signed 'Segalas', presumably after a not very distinguished gunsmith who had worked in London in the early part of the century.

William Greener, the Newcastle gun-maker, writing in 1830, complained of hundreds of Birmingham barrels which had failed their proofing, being repaired, swellings beaten down, proof marks forged and sold complete with a London gun-maker's name.

The Walter Scott fever in the early 19th century created a strong demand for early Scottish pistols. There are many wholly false brass ones in circulation, and many other genuine plain ones to which decoration has been added.

Fire-arms that have been re-stocked or supplied with a new lock are usually recognised quite easily. A replaced stock is often out of harmony by reason of proportion or shape with the rest of the gun, whereas a new lock will often be of a slightly different colour to the other steel parts. The most difficult kind of forgery to detect is when fine ornament has been added. Frédéric Spitzer had a workshop in Paris in the 19th century where a number of highly skilled craftsmen were employed to embellish plain old arms. When he died in 1920, the sale that took place after his death testifies to the brilliance of his work.

Barrels are often found to have been 'stretched'. When the faster-burning powder which was introduced early in the last century drove bullets to their maximum velocity in a shorter time, barrels did not need to be so long. There was no obvious reason to carry the extra weight around, and many barrels were cut down, only to be 'stretched' (have an extra section added) later by owners who realised that the original condition was more valuable. Similarly, many locks were converted from flint-lock to percussion and back again for the same reason.

Some extremely fine modern Japanese carved ivory is currently being added to the stocks of plain old wheel-locks. This is sometimes most difficult to recognise. A very fine 17th-century German wheel-lock, whose stock was carved with a glorious hunting scene, was recently offered to the curator of a London museum, who noticed only after careful examination that one of the huntsmen had suspiciously slanting oriental eyes.

There are plenty of upgraded Colts on the market, although it is unusual to come across a total fake. A Walker Whitneyville Dragoon, probably the most valuable of the entire Colt range, was brought to a London saleroom last year and found to include not a single original part. As the price of fire-arms rises, so inevitably does their forgery seem worthwhile to a growing band of practitioners.

The market now

In America, 80–90% of all fire-arms collectors are concerned with mechanically-produced American weapons which have virtually no aesthetic appeal. What they do have are powerful historical associations arising from the special parts they played in the wars with the British, Indians and Mexicans and these produce in American collectors a strong urge to own the guns that have helped to shape their history.

There are now nearly a thousand gun-shows a year in the U.S. The annual show at Columbus, Ohio, one of the largest, consists of 1500 eight-foot tables where dealers and collectors display their wares. Thousands of men mill about and all are members or guests of the Ohio Gun-Collectors Association. The crowd would be too great if all-comers were let in. For many people, the names of the guns on sale are highly evocative – Colt, Deringer, Remington, Harper's Ferry, Springfield, Pettengill, Henry, Winchester, Sharps, Spenser etc. Most prices are under $500 and these depend primarily on rarity and condition. What remains of the original condition of a fire-arm is often described on a percentage scale, as for instance: 90% blue on barrel, 70% blue on cylinder, 80% engraving on cylinder, 40% colour hardening on frame, 50% silver-plating on trigger-guard and back strap, 40% varnish on grips (if a civilian model). Matching serial numbers of the individual parts are important as is the general mechanical condition. Even though probably 90% of these weapons have disappeared for one reason or another, the survivors are so numerous that collectors are particularly keen on unusual specimens which can boast an extra screw or rivet in much the same way that stamp collectors show great interest in errors.

European demand for 19th-century American material is now so great that European dealers have been known to charter a plane and do a two- or three-week circuit of American shows. They can be seen plying up and down the aisles, heaping weapons into trolleys to ship home to eager collectors in Europe.

Each country in Europe, as well as the U.S.A., fixes a date after which a permit to own a gun is necessary and this is usually settled according to the availability of ammunition. In America, the owner of any fire-arm manufactured after 1898 requires a permit and this inconvenience tends to make post-1898 fire-arms inexpensive compared to similar ones of earlier date.

The minority of collectors of fire-arms in America, described as 'high art collectors', concentrate on fine weapons dating from before 1830. This is still the field that interests the majority of European collectors although as pre-1830 material becomes more rare and expensive, the proportion changes. During the latter part of the 19th century, collectors were mainly interested in a weapon's decorative appeal. Dealers ruined many fine arms by cannibalising elaborately decorated locks, stocks and barrels from different guns and fitting them all together to produce the kind of weapon for which collectors would pay a large sum. During this century, interest grew in constructional rarities and much research was undertaken into the subtleties of lock design etc, but in the last ten years decorative considerations have again become paramount.

For at least twenty years, connoisseurs have been understandably advising that it is too late to buy fire-arms yet prices have moved consistently higher. Fine German wheel-lock pistols that could be had for $40–60 in the early 1950s now cost $6–10,000. A moderate quality pair of mid-19th-century English percussion cap pistols that would have cost $20 in 1950 are now worth $2000. Prices have moved so fast that more and more people are being forced to collect junk. Now that a horribly crude 19th-century Levantine pistol can fetch $600–1000, it must be time to reflect that the same sum can still buy a very fine object indeed in other markets. Cased pairs of pistols have grown even more in value than long guns, partly because they are easier to handle and display and partly because they have become a form of international currency that can still be flown out of a country, without being X-rayed, in the hold of a plane.

Although no collector can be oblivious of the investment potential of the piece he buys, the market has been pushed up almost entirely without the help of pure investors. Furthermore, the market for the finest European arms has been supported by no more than a handful of American and Swiss collectors at least one of whom has reportedly stopped buying. At this rarefied level, the market is highly sensitive and when the famous Renwick collection came to be disposed in 1972, it was decided to spread the sales over four years to avoid disturbing price levels.

It is generally recognised that collectors get a greater lift from acquiring than having. Nowadays, many can only afford to acquire new pieces by trading something from their existing collections. The practice of trading has grown because many people have made such large capital gains and because they suppose (wrongly) that if the disposal of a fire-arm formed part of a swap, the gain would not be taxable – or at least that they stand a better chance of getting away with it than they would in the case of an outright sale.

Guns and pistols add up to just one corner of the vast and growing field of militaria. The only characteristics most fire-arms collectors seem to have in common are that they are male and began to collect as boys, the activity being a prolongation of a childhood interest rather than one to which they turned as adults. In the fire-arms world, it is not often possible to make a proper distinction between dealers and collectors. Most dealers usually have some pieces which are not for sale which identifies them also as collectors, while most people who collect are continually trying to fill gaps or trade up to better examples of the pieces they already possess. This means, in practice, that most pieces in their collections are for sale if they see the chance of securing a particularly desirable piece.

At auctions throughout the U.K. and U.S.A., about 80% of the lots go to dealers. Different rings operate wherever they can but as the market becomes increasingly international, their effectiveness is reduced.

Public collections

AUSTRIA	Graz	Landeszeughaus
	Vienna	Kunsthistorisches Museum
BELGIUM	Brussels	Porte de Hal Museum
	Liège	Musée d'Armes
CZECHOSLOVAKIA	Konopiste	State Castle
DENMARK	Copenhagen	Rosenborg Castle
		Tojhusmuseum
FRANCE	Paris	Musée de l'Armée
		Musée de la Chasse
		Musée des Arts Decoratifs
GERMANY	Berlin	Museum für Deutsche Geschichte
	Dresden	Historisches Museum
	Karlsruhe	Badisches Landesmuseum
	Munich	Bayerisches Nationalmuseum
ITALY	Florence	Stibbert Collection
	Naples	Museo di Capodimonte
	Rome	Odescalchi Collection
	Turin	Galleria del Piemonte
		Royal Armoury
	Venice	Doge's Palace
POLAND	Cracow	National Museum
SPAIN	Madrid	Army Museum
		Real Armeria
SWEDEN	Stockholm	Nordiska Museum
		Royal Armoury
SWITZERLAND	Basel	Historiches Museum
	Bern	Historisches Museum
	Geneva	Musée d'Art et d'Histoire
	Solothurn	Zeughaus
	Zurich	Schweizerisches Landesmuseum
U.K.	Edinburgh	National Museum of Antiquities
	Glasgow	Museum and Art Gallery
	London	Artillery Museum, Woolwich
		H.M. Armouries, Tower of London
		National Army Museum
		Victoria and Albert Museum
		Wallace Collection
	Windsor	Windsor Castle Armoury

U.S.A.	Cleveland	Museum of Art
	Los Angeles	County Museum
	New Haven	Winchester Museum
	New York	Lichfield Collection
		Metropolitan Museum
		U.S. Military Academy (West Point)
	Springfield	Armory Museum
	Washington	Smithsonian Institution
	Williamsburg	Powder Magazine
U.S.S.R.	Leningrad	Hermitage Museum
	Moscow	Kremlin
	Tula	Tula Museum

Book list

BALLIE-GROHMAN, WILLIAM A. *Sport in Art* (Pub. by Blom) Arno
GEORGE, JOHN N. *English Pistols and Revolvers* Saifer
LENK, TORSTEN. *Flintlock: Its Origin and Development* Saifer

Periodicals

American Rifleman (Washington, D.C.)
Gun Digest (Northfield, Illinois)
Gun Illustrated (Chicago, Illinois)
Gun Report (Aledo, Illinois)

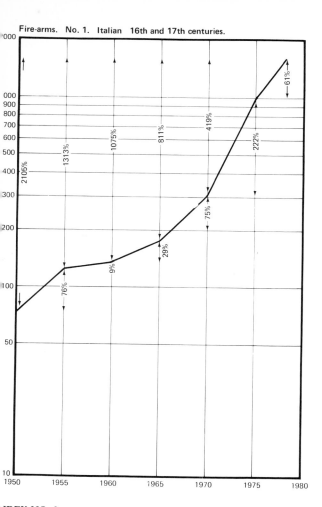

Fire-arms. No. 1. Italian 16th and 17th centuries.

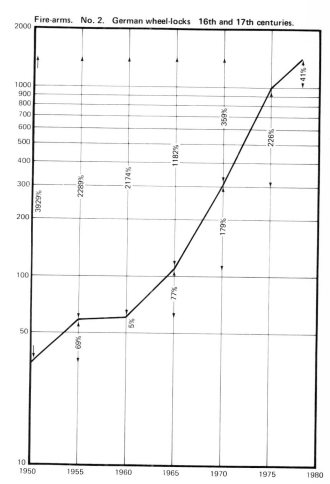

Fire-arms. No. 2. German wheel-locks 16th and 17th centuries.

INDEX NO. 1.

Italian match-lock arquebus, the walnut stock inlaid with engraved and green-tinted staghorn. *c.* 1560.
Pair of Italian holster pistols. Mark of Lazarino Cominazzo. 17th century.
Italian flintlock pistol, the stock inlaid with steel. Barrel by Bernardi Bazzone. Brescia. *c.* 1650.
Central Italian snaphaunce belt pistol by Giovanni Beretta of Brescia. Lightly carved walnut stock with chiselled steel mounts. Late 17th–early 18th century.

ALL IN FINE CONDITION

INDEX NO. 2.

1. Saxon wheel-lock sporting rifle with octagonal barrel dated 1683 and stamped with maker's mark HH, the lock dated 1682 and with pierced brass wheel-cover, the fruitwood full stock carved with foliage and studded with nails. From the Armoury of the Grand Dukes of Saxe-Weimar, Schloss Ettersburg.
2. Pair of Saxon wheel-lock pistols with chiselled locks and barrels, and stocks inlaid with scrolls inhabited by birds animals and masks. *c.* 1580. At one time in the Dresden Armouries.
3. A German wheel-lock pistol with octagonal breech engraved 'H. B. Storch' and brass poincon bearing 'Hubertus' over a stork. Large plain lock with internal cock spring and enclosed wheel; the wheel-cover and lock-plate inset with small ivory studs. The fullstock inlaid with engraved bone panels; the butt and large ball pommel intricately bone inlaid overall with spirals of tendrils and leaves, divided into sections by engraved bone strips. *c.* 1580.

ALL IN FINE CONDITION

165

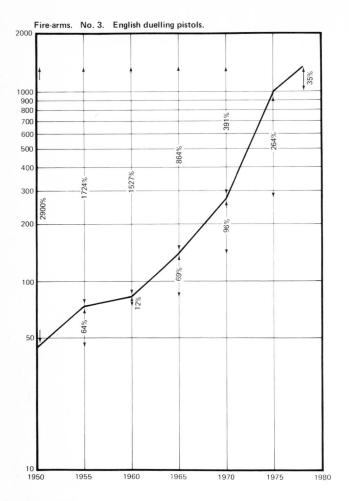

Fire-arms. No. 3. English duelling pistols.

2900% 64% 1724% 12% 1527% 69% 864% 96% 391% 264% 35%

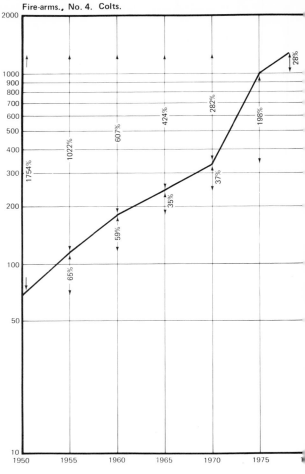

Fire-arms., No. 4. Colts.

1754% 65% 1022% 59% 607% 35% 424% 37% 282% 198% 28%

INDEX NO. 3.

1. Cased pair of early flintlock duelling pistols with long barrels of Spanish form, silver fore-sights and gold vents, the stocks with carved aprons and engraved steel furniture. Chequered flat-sided butts of early form. One ramrod tip is made of silver and unscrews to act as powder measure. Original oak case and fittings. By H. W. Mortimer, London. London proof marks, *c.* 1775–80.
2. Cased pair of flintlock duelling pistols with browned octagonal barrels, gold signatures, lines, fore-sights and vents, signed and engraved locks with rollers and gold-lined pans. Walnut half-stocks with finely engraved blued steel furniture, gold escutcheons, set triggers and original ramrods. In original case with accessories. By Durs Egg, London, *c.* 1800.
3. Cased pair of flintlock duelling pistols with octagonal twist barrels, patent recessed breach, platinum line, vent and maker's stamp, engraved locks with rainproof pans. Walnut half-stocks with engraved blued steel furniture and silver escutcheons. In original case with accessories and label. By Joseph Manton, Davies Street, Berkeley Square. *c.* 1815.
4. Cased pair of travelling pistols with octagonal barrels, platinum lines and vent, engraved locks and engraved steel furniture, full stocks and chequered butts. Original oak case with fittings and label. By Staudenmayer, London. Early 19th century.

ALL IN FINE CONDITION.

INDEX NO. 4.

1. Colt Baby Paterson with unsigned blued 4¼in. barrel, cylinder with stage hold-up scene. In original case with fittin 9¼in.
2. Cased Colt Paterson belt pistol, the barrel inscribed 'Pat Arms M'g Co. Paterson, N-J Colt's Pt.' the cylinder engra with centaurs in combat. In original velvet-lined case v fittings. 5½in. barrel. *c.* 1839.
3. Colt Whitneyville Walker Dragoon, dated 1847 on the right s of the barrel and stamped on the top 'Address Saml. Colt N York City', steel back-strap, brass square backed trigger-gu 9in. barrel.
4. Cased Presentation Navy Model, the barrel with Lon address and the cylinder with naval engagement scene, aln entirely covered with bold scrollwork engraving and v figured grips, plated trigger-guard and back-strap. Orig case with original fittings. London Proof marks.

ALL IN FINE CONDITION

Gold

Although gold coins were struck as early as the 7th century B.C., gold was far too scarce and valuable to serve as the principal currency of the ancient world. Golds coins did of course circulate quite generally but silver and copper coins were much more common. Until the 19th century, most countries were on a silver or bimetallic standard with gold valued usually at sixteen times silver. It was only the successive discoveries of the new gold fields of California in 1849 and later in the century those of Australia, Alaska and South Africa that produced enough of the metal for its general monetary function to be established.

A gold prospector's camp, Transvaal, *c.* 1880.

Between 1500 and 1850, only 150 million ounces of gold are estimated to have been mined whereas between 1850 and 1933 when gold lost its monetary role about 950 million ounces were mined. Of this 950 million, roughly 700 million was minted into coins – mostly British sovereigns and American dollars. As part of a set of moves to restore a stable currency after the inflationary period of the Napoleonic Wars, Great Britain had returned to payments on a gold basis in 1816. New gold sovereigns were minted and issued in 1817 weighing 0·2354 of an ounce giving a value of gold in sterling terms of £4-4-11½d a Troy ounce. The American five dollar piece or Half Eagle at the same date weighed 0·2813 Troy ounces giving an exchange rate of $4.18 to the £ sterling. The price of £4-4-11½d per Troy ounce had been set in 1717 when Sir Isaac Newton was Master of the Mint but the country had lost the habit of using gold coins during the 18th century through scarcity and a great increase in the note issue, and even after the minting of the new sovereigns in 1817 gold was not very extensively used in internal trade.

The price of $8.50 an ounce turned out to be comfortably above the production costs of the minefields discovered later in the century. From 1850 to 1933, price indexes were generally rising so that the profit-margins of gold producers, although still considerable, were gradually being squeezed. By the 1920s the effect was seen in a levelling off of world gold production. If it were not for the official support for the price of gold, the growth in production in the second half of the 19th century would certainly have resulted, as happened in the case of silver, in a substantial fall in its market price. During the Depression, when other commodity prices were apparently in free fall, gold, thanks to its official status, once again held its price. It was this sort of behaviour that fostered the illusion that gold possessed some special characteristic – some kind of intrinsic stability which insulated it from ordinary market forces.

Whereas the fixed price of gold had been a vital cornerstone of international trade in the 19th century, the pace of economic expansion in the 1920s meant that gold could no longer maintain its proportionate value. There had been a major redistribution of the world's gold which left most European countries with much lower gold stocks in relation to their liabilities, much of it having moved to America. The U.K. had returned to the gold standard in 1925 at the pre-war parity with the dollar which was to prove impossible to maintain. The purchasing power of sterling had been severely depressed and this misguided move was just part of an attempt to reproduce the highly efficient system of international economic arrangements that had existed before the war.

In summer 1931, following the near collapse of the German economy, heavy withdrawals of sterling from London began to deplete the Bank of England's reserves which, in any case, had not been adequately rebuilt after the First World War to maintain a safe ratio to its external commitments. Two large international loans were quickly used up and on September 21, Britain suspended the gold standard. In the ensuing six months, twenty-four more

168

countries went off the gold standard, increasingly protectionist policies were adopted and the international economic system already partially paralysed by disputes over war debts and reparations was only just kept from collapse by a series of improvisations.

Then in April 1933, the United States went off the gold standard. The continuation of severe depression in the U.S. had persuaded the U.S. Government to try this curious experiment in reflation. By the end of the year internal price levels were not rising as hoped and in January 1934 the U.S. returned to the gold standard, with the dollar devalued to 59·06% of its old parity. The new gold price of $35 an ounce was to remain fixed for thirty-seven years. The new price resulted in net industrial demand for gold in the U.S. being reduced to zero and a major expansion in world gold production which rose from 25 million ounces to nearly 40 million in 1939.

In 1944 the Bretton Woods conference which was held in U.S.A. to consider ways of rebuilding the world financial system as soon as the war should be over, restored gold to its former status as the ultimate reserve asset, the pivot and numéraire of the new world system of fixed exchange rates.

One of the aims of the International Monetary Fund which was established as a result of the conference was to make loans available to member countries to cushion temporary balance of payments difficulties. Under the new system, an ounce of gold was again to be worth $35 and the U.S. Government assumed a legal commitment in 1945 to maintain the convertibility of the dollar into gold on the demand of any foreign Central Bank. Such was the commercial and industrial strength of the U.S. at this date and so complete the disruption of European industry, that a U.S. balance of payments deficit in the future must have seemed inconceivable. Moreover the U.S. then held $20 billion worth of gold or 60% of the world's official reserves and no one scented danger in this open-ended undertaking.

By the late fifties, the U.S. balance of payments shifted from surplus into deficit partly because of the miraculous economic recovery of her former enemies, Japan, Germany, and Italy and partly because of massive military and foreign aid commitments throughout the world. The U.S. Treasury 'gold window' was doing a brisk one-way business as Britain, Belgium, France and the Netherlands cashed in their surplus dollars for gold. Germany, Italy and Japan refrained from trading their surplus dollars for gold, partly through gratitude for the aid that had made possible their economic recovery and partly through fear that if they did the U.S. Government might have to retaliate by cutting back its military commitments in Europe. Many of the Central Banks of South America and the Middle East were content for the time being to hold their dollars but they were convertible into gold on demand and any nervousness in the London market might trigger off conversions on a massive scale.

The flaw in the Bretton Woods system was that it was based upon uncertainty. For, if it were certain that the price of gold in dollar terms would

169

never rise above $35, what point would there be in anyone holding gold? Why not hold the dollars which could at least earn interest? Each time a bar passed out of the U.S. Treasury gold window, it might be considered an expression of disbelief that the dollar value of gold really was fixed for all time.

In 1954 the London Gold Market had reopened and quickly grown into a semi-official market in which the Bank of England intervened from time to time to maintain orderly conditions. In the late fifties, as the London market came to be regarded as the barometer of confidence in the gold-dollar parity, it became clear that there might well develop through private gold-buying a speculative attack on the dollar in London, the U.S. Treasury gold window being only open to Central Banks. So it was that the U.S. Treasury looked as though it might have to maintain confidence in the dollar-gold parity by having to sell to the Bank of England as much gold at $35 an ounce as the Bank of England needed to sell in the London market to keep the price down at $35. In other words the U.S. might now have to defend the dollar against private as well as official speculators.

In the autumn of 1960, the weekly Treasury reports of American losses through the gold window were making the front page of the *New York Times*. Misunderstandings over the control of the London gold price developed between the U.S. and the Bank of England and on October 20th 1960 the price shot up to $40. This triggered, as had been feared, a massive run on the dollar in foreign exchange markets and a stampede by foreign Central Banks to cash in their dollars at the gold window. A U.S. Treasury statement was issued supporting the Bank of England's sales of gold to stabilise the price in London even though this was ultimately at the expense of the U.S. gold stock.

Then in February 1961, Kennedy made his pledge that the dollar-gold price would remain immutable. The price settled back to $35 but the pledge was no more than a holding operation and negotiations between the leading Central Banks immediately began which were to result in the creation of the Gold Pool. This was an agreement whereby the Bank of England would sell gold on behalf of the eight leading Central Banks on the London market in sufficient quantities to keep the price at $35. The Bank was also to buy gold to replenish lost stocks if suitable opportunities occurred. The arrangement worked well enough in the early years, helped by unusually large offerings from the U.S.S.R. and South Africa to cope with poor harvests and balance of payments deficits respectively but in 1966 the situation reversed itself. Losses from the Gold Pool were running at levels up to $100 million a day in late 1967.

The question now was how much more official gold was to be diverted to the London gold market before it was acknowledged that the game was up. Several attempts were made to dam the flood, but with gold market speculation now focussing squarely on the dollar the crisis came in March 1968. On Monday 11th, Gold Pool losses were $118m, on Tuesday $103m, Wednesday $179m, and by lunchtime Thursday $220m. At 3.00 p.m. President Johnson discontinued Pool operations and it was agreed that the London gold market should remain closed for two weeks to allow time for a solution to be found. The Governors of the Gold Pool banks met in Washington on March 16th and settled for the long-canvassed proposal for a two-tier system. The Central Banks agreed to buy and sell gold among themselves at $35 but not to deal in the London market which would be left free to find its own level. The recent waves of speculation had been based on the expectation of a new official price for gold so that when gold markets reopened and there was no one on whom speculators could unload their holdings, prices opened at only $38. Later in the year $43 was reached but large stocks were overhanging the market and with increased offerings from South Africa in 1969 the price drifted back to $35.

Throughout the second half of the sixties there had been a clamour for the creation of some kind of new international money to supplement gold and reserve currencies. International liquidity was no longer adequate for the needs of a fast-growing world trade. Many saw the solution in raising the official price of gold which it was argued, by increasing reserves, would also provide greater stability to exchange rates in cases of temporary balance of payments difficulties or heavy movements of capital. The principal beneficiaries of such a scheme, and not unusually its most vociferous promoters, were those countries that either held or produced large quantities of gold.

Throughout the sixties the U.S. Treasury and the Federal Reserve Bank of New York had been phasing out gold settlements and substituted a range of credit facilities for settling payment imbalances, the Federal Reserve swap network, increases in IMF quotas and borrowings in the Eurodollar market as well as Special Drawing Rights on the IMF, with the result that gold became less important in Central Bank reserves. Many discussions had taken place on how to reform the Bretton Woods system by means of widened exchange bands, crawling pegs and so on, rather than destroy it.

But in January 1969 the crisis moved closer with the advent of the Nixon administration which embarked on a policy of benign neglect towards the dollar. The trade deficit rose from $3 billion in 1969 to $23 billion in fiscal 1971. Early in 1971 financial markets began to sense the impending dollar crisis. The main problem lay with the yen, the deutschmark and the Canadian dollar. For the week August 7–14th, the U.S. Treasury reported an outflow from dollars into gold and reserve assets of $3·7 billion and on August 15th Nixon closed the gold window and introduced a stiff economic package. The Smithsonian Agreement of December 1971 realigned world currencies with the dollar, devaluing it against other currencies by between 6% and 17% as well as raising the official price of gold to $38 an ounce.

A further crisis in 1973, occasioned by the refusal of the Nixon administration to defend the parities worked out in the Smithsonian Agreement, resulted in a further 10% devaluation of the dollar and was followed soon afterwards by a disastrous experiment in floating the dollar. That experiment was hastily ended in July 1973. The Nixon administration had chosen to rely on economic fundamentals to determine exchange rates. This was a serious misunderstanding of the role of the foreign exchange markets where, of the tens of billions of dollars of daily dealings, only a small fraction are concerned with foreign trade and long-term investment – the great majority being nervous short-term movements of capital to hedge against exchange-rate risks or to profit by interest-rate differentials.

The lesson of the Nixon era that money will not manage itself seems to have been well understood and the present system of managed floating made possible by the agreement of the ten leading Central Banks to intervene when necessary on a massive scale, may provide enough strength and flexibility for it to survive even greater currency scares.

The role of gold in the international monetary scene continues to be fiercely debated. The contemptuous reference by Keynes to it as a 'barbarous relic' must in many ways be valid. The entire world stock of gold above ground amounts to 163 billion ounces, while the world's known reserves that could be profitably mined at a price of $200 an ounce total about the same amount. The entire world stocks of gold above and below ground with a current value of $400 billion could be comfortably fitted into a single giant tanker yet its value is roughly equivalent to the value of all the shares of all the companies quoted on all the stock markets of Europe. Such an enormous value would not perhaps be so surprising if the metal was indispensable in certain roles that were basic for human survival. Although gold is technically and economically ideal in certain roles, none has been found for it that could not be played by other materials.

The continuing debate over the role of gold in the present international monetary system is of much more than academic interest to anyone forecasting the future value of gold. So far this century, the official role of gold has been gradually diminishing in importance yet it might also be held that this trend has been exactly parallelled in the growing inability of governments to control their economic fortunes. The arguments put forward by the so-called 'gold bugs' for revaluing gold and restoring it to its key role are, in outline:

1. Gold can not be printed, therefore it exerts a rigorous discipline over politicians. One of the only economic forecasts that can be made with complete conviction is that governments will tend to reflate their economies shortly before a general election, usually regardless of the suitability of the timing. In other words, they will buy popularity even at the expense of the well-being of the economy in order to be re-elected. Gold would hinder them from doing so. There are adequate but finite stocks of gold in the world which cannot be increased at the whim of politicians.

2. The universal acceptability of gold gives it a supreme advantage as a world currency. Wherever it is known, it is the archetypal store of value deeply implanted in the human consciousness and commanding complete confidence. It also possesses, incidentally, the other qualities needed for money that it is

portable, fungible, divisible and durable – although not even the most fervent gold bugs are pressing for the return to gold coinage.

3. The additions to the world stock of gold are steady and small enough to assure its continued scarcity.

4. It has remained valuable throughout every crisis in history, no matter what happened to other stores of value.

The 'Barbarous Relic' School argues that:

1. To increase the official value of gold would be monstrously unfair to countries possessing or producing little or no gold.

2. It is fundamentally ludicrous and uncivilised to devote so much skill, labour and resources to the extraction of a metal from deep in the earth, only to bury it again in other holes in the ground dug for the purpose beneath places such as Fort Knox and the Bank of England.

3. The use of gold as an integral part of the international monetary system hinders the acceptance of more sophisticated concepts of credit such as SDRs (Special Drawing Rights).

4. To raise the official value of gold would divert valuable resources into the search for and extraction of an utterly unproductive substance.

5. To raise the official price of gold to take account of the increase in value of other commodities in the meantime would not only be directly inflationary in itself but it would touch off another inflationary spiral which would result in the restoration of the gap between the present money price of gold and the money price of other commodities.

6. It unduly hinders the expansion of the monetary stock when economic conditions call for a stimulus.

Official U.S. policy commits itself squarely to the 'Barbarous Relic' camp and the U.S. Government is not only verbally committed to phasing out the international role of gold. The U.S. Treasury actually holds sales of gold, the first of 2 million ounces having been timed to coincide with the legalisation of gold-holding by American citizens in 1975.

It is nevertheless worth noting that for all the intellectual agreement about the redundancy of gold as an official instrument no major official monetary agency, with the exception of the IMF and the U.S. Treasury, has actually sold any of its gold. It must also be significant that the Italian and Portuguese financial crises of 1974 and 1975 were dealt with by raising loans against which those countries offered their holdings of gold as security.

The unwillingness of governments, particularly those in Europe, to relinquish their gold must ultimately arise from the fear that international cooperation may fail. The IMF may become unworkable and the value of SDRs doubtful. The U.S. recognises that Europeans have lived through greater currency turmoil than they and that European distrust of paper currency must to some extent be reflected in their feelings towards gold.

It seems likely that the arguments against an enhanced role for gold are too powerful to allow such a development, while the complete disappearance of gold from the system will probably be prevented by the psychological needs that its presence in the system gratifies. It is possible therefore that official monetary agencies, Central Banks and so on, will buy gold only if the price falls to a point at which a downward valuation of their reserves would become necessary. It was certainly agreed between the leading Central Banks in the summer of 1976 that it would be against their interests to see the price drop below $100 an ounce. There may well be a secretly agreed floor for the price in the future and there is no reason why that floor should not be raised. Otherwise the tendency will be for gold to seep gradually out of official channels and into the open market.

Official coins

The usual definition of a coin is that it must bear a face value and be officially minted for a sovereign country. From 1970–73 sales of such official gold coins were stable at around 50 tons a year. During these years, Austria accounted for the largest share of the market minting large quantities of her 'trade coins', the 4 Ducat and 100 Kroner. On the 1st January 1975 it became legal for U.S. citizens to acquire coins bearing a date earlier than 1960. There, and in the U.K., another country where private ownership of bullion was illegal, and in W. Germany where bullion was subject to V.A.T., very heavy buying of Krugerrands, the official South African gold coin, took the world consumption of official coins to 285 tons, more than five times its previous high.

During the first four months of 1975, 26 tons of gold coins were imported into the U.K. against a background of accelerating inflation. On April 18th the Chancellor in his budget speech prohibited further imports of gold coins for purchase by residents and the coins already in circulation for a time went to a substantial premium. By 1975, the Krugerrand had established itself as the leading medium for gold investment in the U.S. Priced at only 3% above its gold value, it captured much of the market from the Mexican Pesos which commanded an official premium of $7\frac{1}{2}\%$ and effectively pushed the Austrian Ducat right off the map. Also in 1975, the Soviet Union began to mint large quantities of its Chervonetz, a re-strike of a pre-Revolutionary coin but bearing a current date. In 1976, the Austrian Mint successfully launched the 1000 Schilling piece in addition to its standard 'trade coins'.

Bullion coins are those which are in abundant supply and are therefore reckoned to have very little numismatic interest, although the existence of several quite high premiums must indicate some such interest.

To buy a British sovereign at a 50% premium over its gold value is, in effect, to invest two-thirds of one's money in gold and one-third in whatever it is that creates the extra desirability of the coin over and above its intrinsic value. It

LEADING BULLION COINS				
Country	Denomination	Gross weight Troy ounces	Fineness	Fine weight Troy ounces
Austria	100 Schillings	0·7563	900/1000	0·6807
	4 Ducats	0·4489	986$\frac{1}{9}$/1000	0·4428
	100 Kronen	1·0891	900/1000	0·9802
Belgium	20 Francs	0·2074	900/1000	0·1866
France	20 Francs	0·2074	900/1000	0·1866
Italy	20 Lire	0·2074	900/1000	0·1866
Mexico	50 Pesos	1·3396	900/1000	1·2056
South Africa	Krugerrand	1·0909	916$\frac{2}{3}$/1000	1·000
Switzerland	20 Francs	0·2074	900/1000	0·1866
U.K.	Sovereign	0·2568	916$\frac{2}{3}$/1000	0·2354
U.S.A.	20 Dollars	1·075	900/1000	0·9675
U.S.S.R.	10 Roubles	0·2598	900/1000	0·2339

may be that the premium can be explained by the sovereign's historic associations or by the reassuring notion that some permanent value must exist in a coin that has been legal tender for 170 years and no doubt many other personal reasons peculiar to different owners. That premium may increase or decrease but at all events it will have nothing to do with the price of gold.

Anyone wishing to invest in gold should go for the bullion coin with the lowest premium which at the moment is, and seems likely to remain, the Krugerrand at 3–4%. The U.K. budget of 1975 completely insulated the domestic market so that it consisted only of coins already owned by residents of the U.K. who might sell and buy between themselves. That pool of domestic coins was to remain fixed in number and if dealers wished to acquire any new sovereigns minted by the Bank of England they must withdraw from the domestic pool and export an identical number of old sovereigns.

Under existing legislation, coins in the U.K. domestic market being fixed in number should at least theoretically be quoted at a premium over prices for the same coins in the international market which can be continually fed with supplies of gold from South Africa and U.S.S.R. When the clampdown on smuggling in India created a shortage, or at least restricted the quantity in circulation, the local price was seldom less than $60 an ounce above the international price. It must follow that since no greater premium now exists for Krugerrands in the U.K. then externally, there can be very little U.K. interest at present in gold for investment.

Bar hoarding, speculation and investment

Bar hoarding is defined as the physical acquisition of gold bars with the intention of keeping them at home in that form. Apart from carat jewellery, this is the conventional means of investing in gold throughout the Middle and Far East and South America. Speculation and investment in gold on the other hand denotes transactions in bullion after which the buyer does not take physical delivery but rather leaves his purchase in a bank. This is the usual form of bullion investment throughout Europe and North America. Apart from this distinction, the two activities are broadly motivated by similar circumstances in different corners of the world. In the West, hoarding used to be regarded as a rather disagreeable practice – the kind of thing misers and peasants went in for. It was better understood if practised in countries with a history of financial and political instability but, in recent years, many Western countries began to qualify for this description and took to hoarding although preferring to describe it as investment. In 1968/9, the French 'invested in' about 500 tons of gold during the student riots. When things settled down, they dishoarded about 50 tons a year from 1970–2 and thereafter began to buy again.

Since 1970 a wide variety of political events have affected people's propensity to hoard quite erratically in different parts of the world. For example, in 1971 the announcement of Nixon's plan to visit mainland China brought fears of political upheaval and encouraged hoarding in Taiwan and South Korea. At the same time South Vietnam began to hoard less. America had provided the money to make hoarding possible and the uncertainties of war had provided the motive, but now that American money had began to run down, the Vietnamese dishoarded continuously until they had no gold left in 1975.

Indonesia at this time was also a net dishoarder. In 1970 a high rate of inflation and fears over the weakness of the rupiah had sparked off hoarding but with the recovery of the economy this 'insurance' was no longer needed. Another form of accumulation was in Japan where gold stocks began to be built up in anticipation of the legalisation of gold imports in April 1973. When the important day arrived it was discovered, after an initial flurry of activity, that there was no real Japanese interest in gold and the price soon sank back.

In Europe, 1973 was a year of massive speculation and investment; the French were buyers of 100 tons followed by the Italians, West Germans and Swiss. American money via offshore funds and Latin American money helped to swell the total to nearly 497 tons. In 1974, with the gold price on average 60% higher than in 1973, an even larger amount – 547 tons – was invested in bullion. U.S. citizens were for the first time to be allowed to hold gold on January 1st 1975 and large stocks of gold were built up in Europe for shipment to America to be sold at a handsome profit on the great day when as many experts had forecast Americans would be queueing to swap their dollars into gold.

The American market too turned out to be a fiasco. At the time, the U.S.

economy was severely depressed and there had been official propaganda highlighting the risks of gold investment and the U.S. Treasury had offered 2 million ounces of its own for sale. In 1975 investor/speculator interest worldwide seems to have waned with purchases of only 164 tons. The American experience had been a major setback to the gold bugs and the market became even more nervous when the IMF announcement came in September that it proposed to auction 25 million ounces of its gold. The form and timing of these auctions was not clarified until April 1976 and in the meantime the price drifted back. The propensity to buy and sell gold seems to intensify in whichever direction the price moves. In 1976, bar hoarding amounted to 175 tons, a large increase of 45 tons in Indonesia, where the rupiah was again in trouble – as well as significant increases in Taiwan, 55 tons; South Korea 17·5; Thailand 13·0 (and Singapore 10, and Hong Kong 15), associated with other political tensions, but the figure for bullion for investment/speculation came out at a net sale of 86 tons.

Carat gold jewellery

In Europe and the U.S.A. gold jewellery, seen as an investment in gold, is a very poor bargain. The retail price is usually over 300% above the value of the gold the piece of jewellery contains, and pieces often sell for ten times their bullion value. In the so-called developing countries of the Middle East – in this case showing much more sophistication than the West – the mark-up on the bullion value of gold jewellery is usually no more than 20–30%. In the Middle East, a purchase of gold jewellery is regarded primarily as a form of investment while a buyer in the West may, in his ignorance, think of it similarly. The usage of gold jewellery is closely bound up with tradition in different parts of the world. In the West, the use of a gold wedding ring, a male signet ring and gold crosses in certain circles is firmly established. In Morocco, among certain classes, a bride is invariably given an 18-carat kaftan belt. In Turkey 22-carat jewellery and locally made coins are the basic form of savings.

In India very large quantities of gold are smuggled in (although there was a sharp drop when some of the leading smugglers were imprisoned during Mrs. Gandhi's State of Emergency; Mr. Desai has since let them out) in the form of 10 tola bars specially made in Europe for the Indian market. The position of gold in Indian culture might be compared to that of the sacred cow in Hinduism. Gold ornaments for a bride in India are a form of dowry. A bride is bought a set of necklaces, rings, ear-rings and bracelets. For centuries, under Hindu law, a woman had no rights over her husband's or her father's property – only her gold was her own. Even the poorest families try to buy at least one tola's worth of gold for a bride and a 4-tola boxful is most usual. If only one tola were bought for each wedding, the annual demand would be nearly 100 metric tons.

177

The demand for carat jewellery is known to be most responsive to changes in the price of gold and in the real income of consumers. After a steady world consumption of around a 1000 metric tons a year from 1970–72, the price jump in 1973 made all previous forecasts of gold price movements and carat jewellery consumption look absurd and any new ones impossible. Until 1973 much of the selling of gold in the developing countries had been associated with a crop failure or some other disaster. But in 1974 as the price edged towards $200, many small-time holders decided to realise their windfall gain and bought land, livestock or consumer goods.

In Europe, as the gold price soared, jewellery sales were badly hit; there was some switching to silver as well as to lighter articles and plated pieces. In India jewellery consumption halved to 67 tons – some brides were getting lighter pieces and others not getting the full set. In the U.S., through 1973/4, there was much publicity about the price of gold which it is thought must have alerted buyers to the poor deal they were getting by buying gold jewellery and this contributed to the 45 % drop between 1972 and 1974. The slide continued until the second half of 1975 when a striking improvement became evident led by the developing countries of the Middle East, India and the Far East. In 1976 the driving force in improved jewellery demand were the oil-rich nations of Iran and Arabia where the enormous wealth was percolating through to a larger slice of the population as well as to the large migrant labour forces engaged in the construction industries.

Meanwhile, a record wheat harvest and record inflation in Turkey in 1976 pushed up jewellery fabrication to 100 tons compared with just 3 tons in 1973, a remarkable figure when contrasted with a highest ever figure of 20 tons for the U.K. in 1973.

The trade in jewellery continues to be influenced by a strange assortment of crises, fears, harvests, inflation and traditions.

Medals, medallions and fake coins

The description 'fake' in this context is not used to throw doubt on the gold content of the coins to which it is applied. It is rather that they are facsimiles of official coins not struck by the nation of origin. Such facsimiles are produced in many parts of the Middle East, Italy and North Africa. These coins are very often used in jewellery, twenty or thirty linked 'sovereigns' forming a popular bracelet in the Middle East. During the last two years, fake coins have continued to sell well as people remained unaware of the availability and legality of buying official coins in a growing number of countries.

Private mints produce not only standard items such as St. Christophers, but medallions to commemorate important events and anniversaries. Quantities of gold used in these vary widely from year to year. All kinds of events are celebrated ranging from the World Cup soccer competition in 1970 to the 2500th anniversary of the Persian Empire. In 1973/4, medals and medallions practically disappeared under the impact of higher gold prices but demand is recovering with a very successful issue of Juan Carlos medals in 1976 as well as extensive faking of old Spanish coins.

Advertisements offering medals and medallions have, by law in most countries, to state the weight of gold they contain but not the value. A simple calculation will always reveal the premium (usually 100–400%) the buyer is being asked to pay for the artistic element and the fabrication cost. Although a medallion is a perfectly good medium for artistic expression, no modern artists working in it have yet, judged by saleroom evidence, had their work valued to the point where the price paid for the artistry and fabrication is ever fully recovered when the medallion is sold.

FABRICATION, SPECULATION AND INVESTMENT (Metric Tons)

	1970	1971	1972	1973	1974	1975	1976	1977
Purchased for Fabrication in developed countries	767	841	1015	745	710	704	823	890
Purchased for Fabrication in developing countries	611	549	332	111	21	253	536	510
TOTAL FABRICATION	1378	1390	1347	856	731	957	1359	1400
of which:								
Carat Jewellery	1063	1059	995	510	229	511	936	985
Electronics	91	88	107	127	92	64	72	75
Dentistry	63	69	71	73	61	64	70	80
Other Industrial and Decorative Uses	62	69	70	71	59	56	61	65
Medals, Medallions and Fake Coins	54	52	40	21	5	18	41	45
Official Coins	46	54	63	54	285	244	178	150
Net Private Bullion Purchases (Sales)*	(343)	(4)	(102)	546	519	164	89	210
NET PRIVATE PURCHASES	1035	1386	1245	1402	1250	1121	1448	1610

* excluding coins, but including 'identified bar hoarding'.
Reproduced by courtesy of Consolidated Gold Fields Ltd.

Electronics and miscellaneous uses

The versatility of gold is best seen in its industrial applications. One ounce of gold can be drawn into a fifty-mile length of wire and it can be rolled into a sheet three millionths of an inch thick. The high conductivity of gold makes it ideal for low current electrical and electronic uses where it is important that a weak electrical flow is not degraded by high resistance in the flow path. Gold was extensively used in semi-conductors and connectors in the early seventies, but efforts to economise in its use by substitution of alternative alloys, reducing the thickness of gold plating, increased recovery and recycling, have been very successful. It is now felt that the practical limits to such economies may have been reached and demand may move more in line with industrial growth.

Other industrial uses include the brazing of jet engine parts, space technology, certain chemical and medical equipment. Gold has decorative uses on pens and pencils, nibs, spectacle frames, ceramics and glass etc. Almost half of the gold under this heading is consumed in the U.S. Many of these applications are believed to be fairly insensitive to price changes in gold and are expected to move in line with general economic conditions.

The quantity of gold used in dentistry has remained very stable over recent years. The two main factors affecting its usage are insurance coverage of dental services and income growth. The fall-off in 1974 was due to the substitution of non-precious metal alloys and economising techniques. The U.S.A., Germany and Japan have continuously accounted for 70% of total world consumption in this category.

Outlook

The foregoing comments on markets for gold may have indicated the variousness and unpredictability of the factors which have borne directly on the price – the Russian harvest, Turkish inflation, Indian smuggling, the Chinese earthquake, American economy, Arabian oil and U.K. legislation, French student riots and so on. It is obvious that many of these factors are not accessible to predictive analysis. Even so, were it possible to construct an index of confidence in world monetary and political stability throughout history, that index would certainly have hit new lows more than once in the present century. Leaving aside the unpredictable, much work has been done on the responsiveness of demand for gold to changes in price and income. The conclusions are that gold has a price elasticity of -0.5 to -1.0 and an income elasticity of 0.8 to 1.5. That is as a result of, say, a 20% increase in the price of gold, demand will fall by ($-0.5 \times 20\%$ to $-1.0 \times 20\%$) between 10% and 20% and as a result of, say, a 20% increase in real income the demand for gold will rise by (0.8×20 to 1.5×20) between 16% and 30%.

There is, of course, no way of testing the response of jewellery buyers to a gold price of say $400. At such a price, elasticity would be very unlikely to have remained constant and the projections should be regarded as highly tentative. Paradoxically, gold is bought by many people when circumstances appear favourable and by others when they appear unfavourable. Indian farmers, for example, who since the Green Revolution have often had record yields, put their profits into gold whereas in Europe the attractions of gold apparently vary according to the degree of monetary chaos judged to be imminent. Two general patterns of gold-buying are noticeable – the poorer people of the world will often buy gold when they are able to as a form of insurance against the next crisis: for the richer, gold is the barometer of financial stability and the more grim the outlook the more gold they will buy.

Given that gold serves no really valuable purpose and that its price depends entirely upon confidence, it must be of the greatest significance that its price actually dived by almost half in the space of 18 months from December 1974 to June 1976. For over two hundred years, the price of gold had remained stable but when official stabilisation was withdrawn in 1968 it could only be succeeded by volatility or at least potential volatility. That collapse in the price came as a warning to many people that gold was no longer dependable as an investment vehicle. Gold may still have some semi-official status as part of a government's official reserves, but then governments hold strategic reserves or stockpiles of all kinds of commodities without attempting to control their market prices.

After the gold price collapsed in 1974 there was no reason, as far as most people could see, why it should not see-saw as wildly as any other commodity. In the event that view turned out to be too jittery and the central banking community to the relief of many effectively placed an unofficial floor under the price.

Two further questions on the outlook need to be considered. What will happen when mining costs rise above the present gold price? One answer is that the unprofitable mines will close down, gold will become more scarce and therefore more expensive. That forecast seems reasonable if real incomes will by then have risen fast enough to keep pace with the rising price of gold. But many such forecasts are based on and specifically refer to the behaviour of rational people. The only rational motive for buying gold is when it does a job more cheaply and more efficiently than any other metal, and the only area of demand where those considerations apply is in the relatively insignificant industrial sector, all other buying is irrational and to that extent unreliable. There is no reason whatever why gold for jewellery, which has before now lost ground to silver, should not remain subject to the vagaries of fashion as has been the case with garnets, pearls etc.

The other question that worries holders of gold is what will be the result of a black revolution in South Africa. The only reasonable guess is that the South

African mines, which have the most sophisticated equipment in the world, could not at first be run without white engineers. Assuming a complete cessation of work in such a catastrophe, the uncertainty over supplies could only drive the price of gold upwards. Whatever the colour of a future South African Government, the functioning of the gold-mining industry will continue to be indispensable to the economy and every effort including perhaps a deal with skilled white workers would presumably be made to maintain production.

Book list

ASHWORTH, WILLIAM. *A Short History of the International Economy Since 1850.* 3rd ed. text ed. 1976, Longman

EINZIG, PAUL. *The Destiny of Gold* 1972, St. Martin

NEVIN, EDWARD. *Introduction to Microeconomics.* Text ed. 1974, Verry

SOLOMON, ROBERT. *The International Monetary System: 1945–1976: An Insider's View* 1977, Harper & Row

Gold price. Annual range of monthly averages

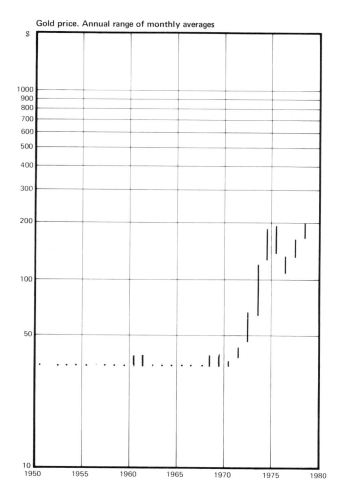

Modern prints

Modern prints are those that have been made since 1800 by either of the two processes that were by then long established – relief and intaglio – or by lithography, a third process which had just been invented. Only one further basic process, screen-printing, was introduced to Europe in the twentieth century and although the number of methods by which prints were made grew quickly after 1945, they were mostly combinations or modifications of the old processes.

The first primitive man to have walked bare-foot through water and on to a smooth dry rock would have probably understood the principle of relief printing. He would have seen that the parts of his feet that stuck out furthest – the heels, the toes and the balls of his feet – left marks on the rock surface. Relief printing then, which includes the processes known as wood-cut wood-engraving, linocut and metal cut, depends upon the artist-printer cutting away with a variety of chisels and gouges the parts of the matrix that are to leave no mark on the paper. The protruding parts are then inked and brought into contact with the paper on which they leave their reverse image. This process was in use in Europe by the late 14th century.

The second basic method was intaglio printing, which could be either direct or indirect. In the direct process, a copper plate was incised by hand with various tools to give the required image. Ink was then pressed with dabbers into the channels and cavities cut away by the engraver. The surface of the plate was then wiped clean, the whole plate was heated and laid against a sheet of dampened paper, then passed between two powerful rollers. In this way the ink was transferred from the parts the engraver had cut away to the paper. The kinds of print that result from variations of the direct process are drypoints, mezzotints and line engravings.

In the indirect process the artist covered the plate with a thin varnish which was resistant to acid. Then having blackened the plate so that the marks he was about to make would show up more easily, he began to draw with a sharp needle. When he had finished drawing, he covered the back and margins of the plate with wax and lowered the plate into an acid bath. The acid began to eat away the parts of the copperplate that the artist-printer had uncovered with his needle. He next removed the plate from the bath and the varnish from the plate, which could then be printed from in the same way as for the direct process. Among the best-known variations on the indirect method, usually known simply as etching, are the processes called soft-ground etching and acquatints.

The third basic process is lithography or planographic printing, so called because the line on the matrix is neither incised nor in relief but on the same level as the matrix with the ink held on the surface.

The lithographic process was discovered, apparently accidentally, by Alois Senefelder in Munich in 1792. He had been experimenting with sandstone as a matrix for intaglio and relief printing when suddenly, the legend goes, he needed to make a laundry list. Having no paper or pencil to hand he quickly wrote with a waxy crayon on the sandstone. Later, while trying to wash the stone clean, he noticed that the water would not stick to the places where he had written. He then coated the stone with oily ink to see what would happen and noticed that the ink stuck to the parts he had written on but not to the plain stone areas. Senefelder realised that the reaction was based on the natural antipathy of grease and water, but did not understand the chemical basis of his discovery. The fatty acids in the lithographic crayon consist of long molecular chains flanked by two groups of atoms with contrasting properties. One group attracts water and therefore sticks to the stone, which is covered with a thin film of water even when it appears dry. At the other end of the chain, another group of atoms rejects the water and is therefore directed away from the surface of the stone. These molecular bristles take on the oily ink while the rest of the stone rejects it.

The fourth basic process, silkscreen printing or serigraphy, was known in the Far East many centuries ago but only made its way to the United States and thence to Europe in the 1930s. It is really an elaboration of the stencil principle. A fabric screen with a fairly open weave is fixed to a wooden frame. The artist-printer than blanks out with glue or varnish the areas that are to appear blank on the finished print. The wooden frame and fabric screen is then placed over the paper, the ink is poured on and forced evenly through the meshes of the screen with a rubber scraper. This process can be repeated with different colours and with the silkscreen blanked out in different areas. Silkscreen printing differs from the other three processes in that no printing press is needed. For this reason it became very popular with artists in Europe and the United States since 1945.

Original prints

The improvements in printing technology and the proliferation of techniques used by artists and printers in the present century and particularly since 1945 have made it important to define the words Original Print. A wide range of prints is now being offered for sale at an equally wide range of prices and with differing degrees of originality. The tendency on the part of the inexpert buyer would be to suppose quite reasonably that a print described as original had

185

some close association with the artist. But how close? The 1960s saw a succession of attempts to settle this crucial issue. The first was at the 3rd International Congress of Artists in Vienna in 1960. This, briefly, is what they concluded:

1. The artist-printmaker has the right to fix the number of each edition of his graphic works in whichever technique: engraving, lithography etc.

2. For a print to be considered original, it must bear the signature of the artist, the total number printed and its own serial number within that edition. The artist may also indicate that he himself is the printer.

3. When the edition had been printed, the plates, stones, wood-blocks or other matrices used in the printing should be defaced or marked so as to show that the edition has been completed.

4. The above principles were to apply to prints which could be considered original provided that the artist made the original plate, cut the wood-block or whatever other material was used. Works not fulfilling these conditions were to be considered reproductions.

5. For reproductions, no regulations are possible. It is desirable that reproductions should be distinguished from original graphic work, particularly when they are of such high quality that the artist feels justified in signing them to acknowledge the work materially executed by the printer.

These conditions seemed too restrictive to the Print Council of America which, in 1961, offered a definition (since retracted) of an original print as a work of art, the general requirements of which were that:

1. The artist alone has created the master image in or upon the plate, stone, wood-block or other material for the purpose of creating the print.

2. The print is made from the said material by the artist or pursuant to his directions.

3. The finished print is approved by the artist.

In 1963 the U.K. National Committee of the International Association of Painters, Sculptors and Engravers issued some Notes in clarification of the Vienna proposals which suggested among other things that:

1. Original prints should include work done on matrices by an artist from his own design or interpreting the work of another artist.

2. Original prints may be produced in unlimited editions.

3. Trial proofs and artists' proofs should be marked accordingly.

Then in 1964 the French National Committee on Engraving ruled that if any mechanical or photo-mechanical process were used in the preparation of the matrix, the resulting print could not be considered original.

The New York State Legislature requires a high standard of disclosure in the labelling of fine prints. Both artist and printer are required to sign a statement which records the title, date, size of edition, number of proofs and the manner of numbering, the paper, and the medium and the printer.

186

As matters stand, no one seems entirely pleased with any definition of original print. The trouble began when people confused the temporal sense and the creative sense of the word original, and applied it inappropriately to a print in the first place. The sequence of events that takes place when an artist makes a print is comparable to the procedure involved in painting a conventional oil painting. In this case, the artist may use one means or another to convey the paint to the canvas – whether by brush, palette knife or bucket does not matter. The artist usually continues to convey the paint to the canvas in a series of movements which finish when he is well enough pleased with the result. At that stage he is unquestionably looking at an original painting. He may now, at least in principle, set about painting ninety-nine identical paintings, which would rightly be described as copies of the original painting.

An artist making a print might proceed in the following way. He might take a lithographic stone and make marks upon it with the tusche or special waxy crayon. He might then make a trial print, then make further marks on the stone and another trial print and so on until he is more or less satisfied with the result. The last trial print is traditionally marked in pencil 'O.K. to print', 'bon à tirer', or words to that effect. That last trial print is, in every sense, an original print, and it is the only one there will ever be.* The equipment used to produce it should be regarded as part of the 'batterie d'atelier' in the same way as was the brush, palette knife or bucket. Any further prints made can only be copies or reproductions of it and the use of the term 'original' to describe them is utterly misleading. For if any meaning is to be ascribed to the words 'O.K. to print', it can only be 'this is the print of which copies or reproductions are to be made'.

Original, when used temporally then, implies uniqueness. It makes sense therefore to speak of an original edition (primary in time) in relation to subsequent editions and it makes sense to speak of an original print in relation to those printed later which together form an edition (even though it may never be possible to identify the original) but it does not make sense to speak of an edition of original prints.

While it is well understood that many of the great print-makers, by varying the inking etc, used deliberately to produce quite different effects from a single matrix and the status of their work is more appropriately described as original, this holds true of extremely few print-makers working today.

The reason why many experts and dealers have been keen to retain the word 'original' has been the need to distinguish these prints from those which are copies, whether or not by the artist, of a work first executed in another medium. And another reason why the word 'original' is retained is because in its second sense it suggests that the innovatory or creative power of the artist is somehow present in the finished print, although everyone knows it has actually been produced by a machine, even though the machine-minder may have been the artist himself.

Print-publishers and dealers find people reluctant to pay a large sum for a

---

*Gabor Peterdi, the author of *Printmaking Methods Old and New*, 1959, holds that even if the graphic media allowed only single prints to be pulled, artists would still use them because they produce effects which are otherwise unobtainable.

print they know to be machine-made, and tend to emphasise the involvement of the artist at every stage. Before about 1880 artists always signed their prints in the plate, but since then publishers have found that collectors were reassured by the presence of the artist's hand-written signature which seemed psychologically to demechanise the print and raise its status to 'hand-approved' even if not 'hand-made'.

The only appropriate words to describe prints of many editions are as reproductions of an original print. The reason why they are not so described is because the word reproduction is charged with overtones of cheapness, inferiority, deception and so on. The English language is, however, quite equal to the task of describing accurately a print without the misleading use of the word 'original' and without in any way detracting from the creative effort of the artist or the aesthetic value of the result.

The early days of lithography

Although it was in Germany that lithography, as well as relief and intaglio printing, had originated, the first lithographs of artistic value were printed in England. George III granted Senefelder a patent for England and Wales in June 1801, and Philipp André, a German of Huguenot descent and a friend of Senefelder, became manager of the business established at 5 Buckingham Street, Fitzroy Square, London. André tried energetically to promote lithography as a graphic art and published in 1803 *Specimens of Polyautography* (as lithography was then known). The twelve specimens included work by Benjamin West, then President of the Royal Academy, Henry Fuseli, Konrad Gessner, Thomas Stothard and Richard Cooper. There was every reason to expect outstanding results from the new medium. It stood literally half-way between intaglio and relief and did not depend on other tools and materials to achieve its effect. All that was needed was to draw over the stone with a special pen or crayon which would attract the ink, while the other areas would repel it. It was therefore hoped that the spontaneous character of the drawing would not be lost and this promise, even in the early days, was to a great extent fulfilled.

However, after an enthusiastic start, the English public took little interest in the new art-form and in 1805 André returned to Germany. It seems probable that he had been unable to offset the losses on the publication of artists' work by commercial printing. His successor Georg Vollweiler was the first to use lithography to illustrate a book (an otherwise obscure publication on ancient frescoes discovered in a church at Stratford-upon-Avon) but he too returned to Germany in 1807.

So disappointing was the response from professional artists that Vollweiler's successor even sent a circular to amateurs in an attempt to arouse interest in the new medium. Lithography as an art-form in England was already in decline.

Georges Rouault
(1871–1958): engraving
Nous Croyant Rois from the
Miserere Suite.

Many artists were taking to water-colours, then a quite new medium, and the popularity of the older graphic arts, it seemed, was too firmly entrenched. It was not until 1819 when Rudolf Ackermann, the famous publisher and print-seller, who in the early days had shown some interest in buying the patent, brought out the first volume of his massive work, *The Repository of Art*, that interest in lithography was revived.

The early years in France were also difficult. In 1802 Peter Friedrich André, a brother of Philipp, was granted a patent for a new method of 'engraving and printing'. He published some pen drawings by Susemihl and Bergeret and also printed some music but the venture fared badly and he returned to Germany in 1805. Two Frenchmen, Gottfried Englemann and Charles de Lasteyrie had both been to Munich to study the lithographic process in 1814 and were responsible for its successful launching in Paris two years later. Each set up a press, Lasteyrie involving himself at first mainly with reproductive work but later

189

competing with Engelmann in persuading the leading artists of the day to work in the medium. Between them they secured Vernet, Régnault, Denon, Mongin, Ingres and Guérin.

In spite of the impressive results these artists achieved, lithography needed an artist of real stature to put it on the map and this task was performed by Théodore Géricault (1791–1824). He had broken away from the classical tradition of David and managed to convey for the first time in this medium a sense of power, life and dramatic movement in his figures which raised lithography from the status of a technique to the rank of an art-form.

The next artist of comparable stature to work in the medium was Eugène Delacroix (1798–1863) who applied himself to artistic lithography (as opposed to his caricatures) for the first time in 1823. He had been greatly influenced by Goya's graphic work and owned several prints by him. When Delacroix travelled to London and saw some of Shakespeare's plays as well as Goethe's *Faust*, he determined to illustrate them. One result was the set of seventeen lithographs for *Faust* which evidently impressed Goethe a good deal more than the play had Delacroix, although he conceded that it was capable of being particularly inspiring to an artist. He went on to illustrate *Macbeth, Hamlet* and several works by Sir Walter Scott and Byron. In all he executed about a hundred separate pieces and was the first painter to involve himself with the illustration of literary works which was to have a considerable effect on publishing for the rest of the century.

Eugène Delacroix (1798–1863): lithograph *Lion d'Atlas*.

190

In 1830 Charles Philipon founded a satirical weekly *La Caricature* whose special targets were Louis-Philippe d'Orléans, who had succeeded to the throne of France in July 1830, and his corrupt administration. Balzac wrote for it and Honoré Daumier (1808–79) used lithography in it as a political weapon with devastating effect. One particular drawing in which he portrayed the King as Rabelais' giant Gargantua devouring his subjects' money earned him, the publisher and the printer six months each in jail, and no doubt played a part in the eventual prohibition of political caricature in 1835. This meant the end of *La Caricature* and Daumier thereafter worked for *Le Charivari* satirising the bigotry and humbug he saw in much of French life.

Honoré Daumier (1808–1879): *Rue Transnonain le 15 avril 1834*, lithograph published in *La Caricature* after a case of police brutality.

A monumental project which in some ways amounts to a definitive account of the first forty years of French lithography was *Les Voyages Pittoresques et Romantiques dans l'Ancienne France*. Conceived by Baron Taylor and started in 1820 it developed into a forty-volume work which included lithographic contributions from most of the leading French artists of the day as well two important English artists, Thomas Shotter Boys (1803–79) and Richard Parkes Bonington (1801–28). But artists' lithography, which was never more than a small fraction of total lithographic work, shrank even further in the 1860s until the work of Daumier stood entirely alone. Daumier went blind in 1872 and it fell to Manet, prompted by the publisher Cadart, to rescue lithography from the mediocrity into which it had drifted. The revival when it came was powerful enough to establish lithography as the leader of the graphic arts, at least until screen-printing issued its serious challenge in the present century.

In Spain, Francisco de Goya (1746–1828) produced a body of graphic work which ranked him with Rembrandt as one of the two greatest graphic artists that had yet lived. The first of his famous sequences was *Caprices* (*Caprichos*), a set of eight etchings published in 1797 in which Goya viciously satirised 18th-century Spanish life and expressed a deep pessimism about mankind which was soon to be borne out by the events of the Peninsular War. These inspired him to etch his second great series, *Disasters of the War* (*Desastros de la Guerra*) which, taken as a whole, amount perhaps to the most impassioned denunciation of war ever made. The horror, brutality and honesty of his drawings contrast sharply with the romanticised view of the War taken by contemporary French artists such as Vernet, Raffet and Charlet.

His third series of etchings, the *Art of Bull-fighting* (*Tauromaquia*) was published in 1816. Originally intended to illustrate a treatise on bull-fighting by Moratìn, Goya extended it to include famous feats of the bull-ring some of which he himself had witnessed. The battle to the death between man and beast was a subject that appealed strongly to Goya's character and style. Having in earlier series recorded the great beastliness of man, he now conveyed the dignity and courage of a beast, and in these brilliant drawings he may well have been documenting a struggle about whose result he did not feel too deeply. The fourth and last series of etchings, the *Proverbs* (*Disparates*) show Goya's fantasies at their most extravagant, this time launching another desperate attack on the folly of the world.

Francisco de Goya (1746–1828): etching no. 18 from the Set of thirty-three known as *La Tauromaquia*.

192

It was perhaps Goya's deafness which came in 1792 that intensified his imagination and creative drive for, at the age of seventy-three and still at the height of his powers, he took up lithography. His first prints were *The Monk, Old Woman Spinning, Modern Duel, Inferno,* etc. They were rescued from obscurity by Loys Delteil, the great authority on Daumier, and reprinted in 1907, but the originals are now extremely rare and it is thought that Goya may have intended them for no one's eyes but his own. While in voluntary exile in Bordeaux, he lithographed the famous *Four Bulls of Bordeaux,* which were printed in an edition of one hundred and are still rated among the finest lithographs ever made.

In Germany, Wilhelm Reuter, the first of the German artist-lithographers, published in Berlin in 1804 *Polyautographic Drawings* by outstanding Berlin artists including himself. And in 1807 Johann Nepomuk Strixner was commissioned to copy and lithograph under the supervision of Senefelder himself Dürer's margin-drawings for the prayer-book of Emperor Maximilian I which had only ever been seen in the Royal Library. The drawings were faithfully reproduced and made available cheaply to the public. A succession of editions such as this ensured that Munich remained for long the centre of technical excellence in lithography. It was there that Johann Christian von Mannlich, the Director of the Bavarian Royal Art Gallery, produced great folios of the gallery's drawings and paintings. So fine were these prints that lithography had already, by 1810, reached its maturity and laid claim to the field previously dominated by copper- and wood-engraving.

Adolf von Menzel (1815–1905), the most influential figure amongst 19th-century German print-makers, produced his finest work in 1851 with *Experiments on Stone with Brush and Scraper.* A few other artists chose to work in the medium but in general, as Senefelder had foreseen, the process was principally used for commercial purposes. It is noticeable in Germany, as elsewhere, that the subjects of many of the publications, such as Joseph Alt's two hundred 'Views of the Danube', although unquestionably artists' lithography, appear to have been chosen with a special eye to the market for a sizeable edition. It may have been the very repeatability of the process that deterred many artists from working with it, at any rate while so much mediocre work was being produced.

Wood-cuts

The art of wood-cutting had descended during the 18th century to a very low point in quality and quantity throughout Europe. Wood-cutting was the ancient method by which the wood cut plank-wise was worked upon by the wood-cutter drawing the knife towards him, whereas in wood-engraving, which was perfected if not actually invented by Thomas Bewick (1753–1828), a

193

graver was used on the cross-grain section of boxwood which allowed very fine effects to be achieved without tearing up the fibre of the wood. Bewick developed the 'white line' technique of engraving. As far as possible he chose to make his engravings consist of white lines and achieved his effects by varying the width of the lines. His greatest works were published as the *General History of Quadrupeds, Aesop's Fables, History of British Birds* and many vignettes of great charm to illustrate other men's writings. Bewick raised the art to a height it had not enjoyed since Dürer. At one time he had eighteen apprentices working for him who, after his death, carried on the white line tradition and maintained the high prestige of the art during the first half of the 19th century.

But apart from William Blake (1757–1827), whose finest wood-engravings are the set of thirteen he made to illustrate Dr. Thornton's edition of Virgil's *Eclogues*, and some work by his two disciples Edward Calvert and Samuel Palmer, most wood-blocks at this time were drawn upon by the artist and sent to be worked by a professional engraver. Wood-engraving was a cheaper method of illustration than copper-plate and in the hands of the most able engravers almost as delicate. Gustave Doré in France illustrated 119 books including the works of Rabelais and Milton and kept a dozen or more engravers in full-time occupation. And in Germany where the medium was becoming increasingly popular at the expense of lithography Adolf von Menzel mostly used professional engravers.

Samuel Palmer (1805–81): wood-engraving *The Early Ploughman* (detail).

194

The revival in France

The much-needed revival of interest in the graphic arts during the last twenty years of the 19th century came about partly through the efforts of publishers, partly as a conscious resistance by artists to the growing threat of photography and partly from the feeling shared by most artists that much graphic work masquerading as art was a mockery of the name. Photography, which was first hailed as an art-form as early as 1855, was being used to reproduce with perfect accuracy not only faces but pictures too, and all at the expense of engraving.

The art of engraving as far as the French public was concerned was all but dead. A Parisian columnist, reporting a Salon exhibition in the 1880s, writes of overhearing someone tell his companions that he had actually seen a man in the gallery where the engravings were shown, whereupon they all trooped off to see what could be detaining him. A few of the more imaginative engravers in Paris realised that from then on engravings would have to be exclusively original and were quite glad to be free of the fidelity to detail that had been expected of them. They saw that the way forward consisted in offering free and personal interpretations.

By and large lithography had got bogged down in commercial work such as the printing of labels, music covers, maps and purely reproductive work. A lithographic colour process, patented by Engelmann, had considerably extended the range of uses to which lithography could be put, but artists on the whole chose, rather surprisingly, not to lithograph in colour and progress virtually stopped. In 1870 Odilon Redon wrote, 'I am amazed that artists have been unable to deepen or propagate this malleable and rich art, lithography, any further – an art which obeys the subtlest breath of sensitivity.'

The revival of etching which had been started by Charles Meryon (1821–68), one of the two greatest etchers of the 19th century, with his famous series *Eaux-fortes sur Paris*, was further strengthened by the painters of the Barbizon School such as Millet, Rousseau, Daubigny and Corot but even more so by the American James McNeill Whistler (1834–1903). The publisher Cadart founded the Société des Aquafortistes at his house in 1861 and the membership which included Daubigny, Legros, Bonvin, Manet and Jongkind ensured a high reputation for the business at least in the early days. But soon for every fine etching there appeared fifty mediocre and even Cadart's publications deteriorated in quality. The line-engravers were on the offensive, asserting that etching was too easy, the work of technicians rather than artists, that the effects were slick and the printers swamping the plates with ink to hide poor draughtsmanship.

Whistler, the other of the two greatest etchers of the century, had already completed the magnificent *Thames Set* of etchings when he was commissioned in 1880 by the Fine Art Society of London to do twelve etchings of Venice. He

James McNeill Whistler (1834–1903): etching *The Doorway*, from the first Venice Set.

returned the following year with forty fine plates in which the influence of the Impressionists is certainly evident. Yet most of the critics and most of the public, hobbled together by their ancient bond of vicious and irrational hostility in the face of the unfamiliar, excoriated these sensitive drawings as worthless sketches.

Although the beginnings of this renaissance in the Graphic Arts can be traced to well before 1890, it was about then that the great surge of creativity began in Paris with the painters who were then in their twenties. Collectors had by then

196

grown as tired of etchings as they had become earlier of the old-style popular engravings, while lithography and its vulgar brother chromolithography in particular had distinctly commercial associations. The whole business of print-making was taken by this generation of artists back into their own hands. Lithography was the medium most of them preferred and being primarily painters, some naturally wished to work in colour.

As early as 1862 Cadart had persuaded Manet, who had already done a

Edouard Manet (1832–83): lithograph *Le Gamin*.

197

number of etchings, to try his hand at lithography. The results showed him able to express himself more effectively on the stone than on the copper-plate. Other great artists – Corot, Fantin-Latour, Bresdin, Redon and Degas – were among the earliest to produce some of their finest work in one or more of the graphic art-forms.

Paul Gauguin (1848–1903): lithograph *Manao Tupapau*.

In China and Japan, coloured wood-cuts had for long been an important art-form, and it was the World Exhibition in Paris in 1867 that showed Western artists for the first time the effects that could be achieved by juxtaposing blocks of colour. As late as 1898 the critic of *Le Temps* was asserting that colour prints were only fit for advertisements. But artists thought differently. Jules Chéret had seen colour posters in London in 1866 and when he returned to Paris began to lithograph coloured pictorial posters for theatres, ballets and music-halls but it was a long time before the traditional letter-packed bills were superseded. Colour lithography came into its own through colour poster printing, but it was not until Henri de Toulouse-Lautrec (1864–1901) made his series *Elles* that it could claim to stand independently as an art-form. Toulouse-Lautrec's first poster was for the Moulin Rouge, and by the end of his short life he had made over 350 lithographs in which can plainly be seen the influence of the great Japanese wood-cutters Utamaro and Hokusai.

Henri de Toulouse-Lautrec (1864–1901): lithograph *Promenoir*.

The honour for restoring lithography to its appropriate status should probably be shared between Manet, Degas and Toulouse-Lautrec. But a case can be made for including a man who was not even an artist – the remarkable Ambroise Vollard, whose influence continued to be felt right up to 1939. Publisher, promoter, adviser and friend to a dazzling circle of artists including Vuillard, Denis, Roussel, Bonnard, Renoir, Cézanne, Degas, Sisley and many more, he persuaded them all to make lithographs for him and he published for

199

Pierre-Auguste Renoir (1841–1919): lithograph in colours *Le Chapeau Epinglé*.

the first time in 1896, in an edition of one hundred, twenty-four colour prints entitled *Album des Peintres-Graveurs*. The following year brought an edition with thirty-two prints but the issue planned for 1898 was never published. Cézanne, Renoir and Sisley, having no experience of colour lithography, executed their contributions in black only, then coloured a black and white print by hand leaving it to the master-printer Clot to colour the stones from which the edition was printed. Such subtle differences in the manner of production can affect prices very considerably, this group of lithographs printed from stones coloured by Clot being regarded by collectors as falling short of original in the fullest sense.

Vollard also persuaded Bonnard, Vuillard, Redon and Denis to illustrate various literary works with original graphics and later Rouault and Chagall to do the same. Other important Paris publications of the 1890s were *L'Estampe Originale* and *La Revue Blanche* to which the group of painters known as the Nabis contributed, including Vuillard, Denis, Redon, Valloton and Sérusier.

Repercussions in Germany

The inspiration provided by the French School was felt most strongly in Germany, where a group of painters dissatisfied with Post-Impressionism found themselves turning naturally to the wood-cut, etching and lithograph as they began to stress vigorous lines and strong colours in the search for a new means of expression. But the vital link between the French and German Schools was the Norwegian Edvard Munch (1863–1944) who achieved a complete

Edvard Munch (1863–1944): wood-cut *The Kiss*.

mastery over all the graphic techniques then in use. Although his first lithographs made in Paris – the *Young Model* in 1895 and the *Sick Girl* in 1896 – were deeply impressive, his full impact was not felt until the Expressionists adopted him as leader in 1905.

In the 1890s in Germany, the Etching Clubs had begun to make lithographs, while the art quarterly *Pan*, founded in 1895, to which some leading French artists already contributed, offered German artists a chance to have their work published. Julius Meier-Graefe's publication of Lautrec's *Mlle. Lender*, a half-length portrait in which the colours produce a rather shrill effect, had triggered the full range of reactions from outrage to rapture. This lead was quickly followed by many of Germany's progressive artists, especially Lovis Corinth, Max Liebermann, Max Slevogt and Käthe Kollwitz. But it was in a break away from this group that Ernst Ludwig Kirchner (1880–1938) founded the Expressionist School whose members were Schmidt-Rottluff, Heckel, Pechstein, Nolde and Mueller. All of these were strongly influenced by Munch and Gauguin and in particular by their wood-cuts.

Expressionist is perhaps one of the less revealing labels attached to an artistic movement. Its members were certainly pre-occupied with expressing the intensity of their feelings. But which artists have not been, one might wish to know? It was perhaps because this group renounced scientific perspective and detail in their representation of objects that they were able to convey their feelings in a new and arguably more expressive style. The Expressionist movement, which was also known as 'die Brücke', soon split up and each member had gone his own way by 1913.

A little earlier, in 1912, *Der Blaue Reiter*, an almanac, had been published in Munich with contributions from a group of artists including Kandinsky, Marc, Klee, Jawlensky and Münter. At first, some showed the influence of the Expressionist School but this was soon developed into Abstract Expressionism. Kandinsky, Russian by birth, illustrated with colour wood-cuts his poems *Klänge* and later in 1922 after he was appointed Professor at the Bauhaus, founded by the architect Gropius in Weimar, he began to make a number of lithographs.

Paul Klee made about 150 lithographs and etchings which form an important part of his whole *oeuvre*. The Hungarian Constructivist Laszlo Moholy-Nagy in 1922 set an early problem for the debaters of originality when he had a picture painted by telephone. He called a sign factory and placed his order with the representative who took it down using a square grid and a colour chart.

Germany was increasingly well served with print-publications during the early part of this century. Paul Cassirer started *Die Kriegszeit* in Berlin in 1914, and in 1916 *Bilderman* to which many leading artists contributed. Munich had *Das Zeit-Echo* and *Münchner Blätter Für Dichtung und Graphik*, while Weimar had *Das Kunstblatt* and the portfolios brought out by the Bauhaus.

In the 1920s there was a major boom in prints. Some publishers yielded to the demands of collectors and printed luxury and super-luxury editions, signed and unsigned, so establishing a four-tier price structure for a single work of art. But as the financial chaos of Germany intensified during the 1920s, so the enthusiasm of collectors waned and the flood of publications abated.

After 1945, the younger generation led by Paul Wunderlich, Horst Janssen, Ernst Fuchs and Horst Antes began to blaze new artistic trails supported by a number of enterprising galleries such as Editions Rothe in Heidelberg, Galerie Brusberg in Hanover, Galerie Der Spiegel in Cologne and Galerie Ketterer in Munich.

Further developments in France, America and England

By 1900, Impressionism and Post-Impressionism had been accepted by the Establishment. The new wave of artists beginning to rock the boat were Matisse, Picasso, Braque and Léger. Henri Matisse was slightly influenced by

Pablo Picasso (1881–1973): mixed method. *The Minotaur seated with three women and a man holding a glass.* From a set of eleven plates 'Le Minotaure' in the Vollard Suite.

203

the German Expressionists in his noisy (*klangartig*) use of colour in painting, but he never made a lithograph in colour. His first prints were made in 1906 and in time he became a master of the lithographic technique choosing dancers, odalisques, flowers and fruit as his subjects. After 1930 he tended to prefer etching and wood-engraving for his book illustrations.

The range and quality of Picasso's graphic work is barely credible. It was to him at least as important as his painting and began with a series of seventeen etchings in 1904/5 which included the famous *Repas Frugal* and *Salome*. He was developing Cubism at this time with Braque and Léger and his first Cubist prints, commissioned by Kahnweiler in 1910, were illustrations to Max Jacob's *Saint Matorel*. For the rest of his life, he continued to make prints using every known technique with occasional bursts of creative energy as, for example, in 1945 when he lithographed every day for four months with Mourlot, the great Parisian printer, and at Mougins in 1968 when he completed in that year alone over 300 etchings and aquatints. The graphic work of many other great artists, among them Vlaminck, Dufy, Utrillo and Rouault, maintained Paris at least until 1939 as the creative centre of that world. But it led the world too in the matter of technique. An Englishman, Stanley Hayter, founded the Atelier 17 in Paris in 1927 where, as well as producing fine prints of his own, he pioneered many important technical developments, the most valuable of which was the discovery of the way to print by the relief and intaglio methods from one plate simultaneously by using inks of different viscosities. With him were Anthony Gross and Joseph Hecht, who worked hard to reinstate engraving as a respectable graphic art after Seymour Haden's largely successful vilification of it in the last century.

Since 1945 two Paris publications, a periodical *Edition Verte* and *Derrière le Miroir* founded by the Galerie Maeght, have included much of the best work done by artists living in France. These gave the prolific Chagall a chance to publish many lithographs in colour on his return to Paris from America after the war. It is considered unfortunate that Chagall, Braque and Picasso should all have authorised publishers at this time to reproduce some of their paintings and engravings by photo-mechanical means which they then proceeded to number and sign as though they were 'original' prints. These, apart from the signature, bear no trace of the artist's participation and are valued accordingly by the market.

In America, lithography developed primarily as a commercial printing process, copying, for example, J. J. Audubon's engravings *The Birds of America*. During the 19th century, the firm of Currier and Ives produced a large number of lithographs of which a significant part can be classed as artistic, including Henry Walton's *Views of New York State*, George Catlin's portrayals of *American Indian Life*, and the picturesque landscapes of Gustav Grünewald. However, the first strong foreign influence was felt in America as early as 1910 when a few artists returning from Paris experimented in modern styles. Yet even then there was more interest and even speculation in the conventional collector's prints from England and in the etchings of local artists.

Then, surprisingly as early as the end of the twenties, the New Movement had been quite widely accepted. It had grown partly with the realisation that the modernity of American civilisation could provide aesthetically just as powerful an inspiration to the artist as older civilisations elsewhere. The Atelier 17 in Paris and the workshops modelled on it in America helped to win the battle for freedom of expression. But not only were there new styles and new subject-matter, there were the revived print-making techniques – new at least to the artists working in them for the first time. Lithography had made an impressive come-back and wood-engraving too was challenging the lead held by etching.

Then in 1938 Anthony Velonis perfected silkscreen printing as a medium for artists. This was not only a land-mark in the history of printing technology, but meant that artists now had the chance to use colour in an impressive range of new effects. A number of leading artists moved to New York from Europe during the thirties and the early part of the war. In 1942 Peggy Guggenheim, the wife of Max Ernst, opened her museum-gallery in New York and exhibited the work of the talented young generation of American artists including Jackson Pollock, Adolph Gottlieb, Robert Motherwell and Mark Rothko. The exchange of ideas between, as it were, the native and immigrant groups was immensely fruitful and established New York as the world capital of modern art. Stanley Hayter, who set up another *atelier* in New York after the war, recalled that in the early thirties modern prints were difficult to give away. The rate of change since then has been bewildering.

Since 1945 a quick sequence of movements followed, New Abstract Expressionism, Op Art, Pop Art etc. The most influential of these, at least as far as Europe was concerned, was Pop Art, whose ablest exponents are Andy Warhol (whose prints are executed after his designs by other artists), Robert Rauschenberg, Jasper Johns, Roy Lichtenstein, Claes Oldenburg, Jim Dine and Tom Wesselman all of whom have tended to use the lithographic or silkscreen processes.

In England, the first quarter of the 20th century saw a considerable volume of mediocre etching. Seymour Haden had done much to establish the fashion for collectors' prints. These were invariably printed in limited editions and commanded prices which attracted them to the more speculative collector. The artists were often highly-skilled etchers who were involved in this one art-form alone, and whose names are today mostly forgotten. There developed a school of fine wood-engravers including Eric Gill, Paul and John Nash, Blair Hughes-Stanton and others following the modern trend in painting. The Senefelder Club had been founded in 1909 and a number of artists, William Rothenstein, Brangwyn, Shannon, Conder, Wilson Steer and the Americans, Sargent and Pennell, had tried to popularise lithography in England, but their

Roy Lichtenstein: offset litho *Woman Crying*.

work compared unfavourably with that of French or German artists of that period, and their efforts were on the whole a failure.

In 1946, the Society of London Painter-Printers was founded and fifty artists became involved in lithography, many of their exhibitions being put on by the Redfern and Leicester Galleries, the best-known names emerging as Henry Moore, Graham Sutherland, Reg Butler, John Piper, Victor Pasmore, Alan Davie and Ceri Richards. The influence of American Pop Art exerted itself over an English group including Allen Jones, Eduardo Paolozzi, Peter Blake and Howard Hodgkin. Although there are now many outstanding British artists working in the various graphic media, the influence of American artists and techniques remains very strong.

Market trends in modern prints

The continuous reappraisal of artists and artistic movements means that changes in value are occurring all the time. There are no sectors of the modern print market that are losing ground at the moment although it is worth remembering that there have been some spectacular collapses in the past. The mezzotints by Richard Earlom, for example, after portraits by Reynolds which were eagerly bought at the turn of the century for prices in the $2–4,000 range, might now be worth a tenth or less. Over the last ten years or so, interest has slowly grown from a very low base in the *incunabula* of lithography. The interest has stemmed mainly from museums and in many cases for historical rather than aesthetic reasons since the artistic reputations of some of the earliest lithographers have not stood up too well.

Although the work of Tissot, Zorn and Meryon has always been popular with the older generation of print-collectors, Meryon and the French etchers of the Barbizon School including Théodore Rousseau, Corot, Millet and Daubigny have been rediscovered by a young generation. Prices rose strongly in 1974 and 1975 partly on German buying, and in the case of Millet moved further ahead in 1976 in response to a major exhibition of his work held at the Hayward Gallery in London.

The largest rise in value of any single group of prints is probably in the entire sequence of Romantic English etchers starting with Samuel Palmer and Calvert right up to Graham Sutherland and including D. Y. Cameron and James McBey and many others whose work had become very inexpensive during the 1930s.

There is a strong and growing tendency for each country to buy the work of its own artists yet in the case of the U.K., not only is there a general drain abroad of such fine prints by foreign artists as there were, but also of those by British artists. The British have never really understood or developed a taste for prints, regarding them with suspicion as some kind of reproduction. Of those British that have some knowledge of pictures and water-colours, probably less than 2% ever buy a print and, of those, at least half are Continental Europeans now living in England but who grew up with a long and firmly established print-making tradition.

In the U.S.A. the equivalent group is generally better attuned to prints although still relying heavily on European immigrant knowledge and taste. The Impressionist is the most international of all the schools of print-makers but with a particularly strong following in the U.S.A. where that market moved ahead very fast from 1968 to 1972/3 and then held steady until another strong surge in 1976. American collectors have for long covered the whole range of schools, but during the last five years started to pursue rather more keenly the work of American print-makers of the 1920s and 1930s, George Bellows, John Sloan etc., as well as the second-line names such as Edward Hopper.

The Japanese, who have always taken some interest in European prints particularly those of Picasso, Miró and Chagall and the more colourful Impressionists, are now throwing their net much wider to include William Blake and other early 19th-century English print-makers, the Pre-Raphaelites and the French Symbolists. Japanese interest continues to spread with a television company having recently launched a subsidiary to deal in prints and several large department stores in Tokyo now including a print gallery.

Although the world of prints has by now been pretty well explored, research can still produce interesting re-discoveries. This role is played mainly by the leading print-galleries such as Colnaghi's in London which recently put on an exhibition of artists of the Vienna Secession, the Austrian branch of the Art Nouveau movement. The exhibition threw new light on the work of Klimt, Kokoschka, Schiele and several lesser-known artists and helped to establish new prices for their work of that date. But it would be a mistake, in the light of this development, to snap up any Kokoschkas on the market since many of the arbiters of taste who are also to some extent the people who set present and future price-levels have pronounced that Kokoschka ran out of creative steam in 1923 with the result that only a small part of his *oeuvre* should be bought for investment.

The lithographs of Daumier were usually printed several thousand at a time and carry on the back whatever story the publication in which they appeared happened to print on that day. These have been in quite plentiful supply and, being of little interest to collectors, have remained quite inexpensive. While the prices of these at $20 to $50, depending on condition and subject, might seem superficially attractive, by far the better buy in the past, although far more expensive, has proved to be the same lithographs that were printed 'sur blanc', that is on plain white paper, and in very limited numbers.

Even the market in Picasso's graphic works is to some extent hazardous. The reason is that there are many people with much money and little knowledge who are anxious to own a Picasso print. A good deal of Picasso's later work, including much of his production at Mougins in the 1960s, when he was adding to the world stock of Picasso prints at the rate of three hundred a day, is just not very good or at least compares unfavourably with most of his earlier work. It is therefore necessary to be very selective with Picasso, yet so long as there are so many undiscerning buyers around prices for his lesser work will tend to remain artificially high. As a whole, the market for Picasso's graphics peaked in 1974 and has been rather volatile in the salerooms ever since, depending on which kind of dealers and collectors are present. Such are the factors that can influence print prices and they will be different in the case of each artist.

The contemporary print market

In 1955 the First International Print Biennale dedicated to international cooperation, held at Ljubljana in Yugoslavia, made a strong impact on artists in many countries. Interest began to accelerate in America particularly after 1958 when Tatyana Grossman, having founded Universal Limited Art Editions, invited leading artists to come to her workshop to make prints. This was the first time artists had been offered these facilities and many memorable works including Jasper Johns' *Ale Can* dated from this period.

Thereafter, the contemporary print market began to grow dangerously fast. Many highly reputable organisations such as the Tamarind workshop and the

Pablo Picasso: etching *Le Repas Frugal*, 1904.

Pratt Graphics Center had come into being, but so too had other gallery-publishers who were merely moonlighting in the print market. There began to develop during the sixties a hot-house atmosphere in which print-publishers were talking hard to keep the print market on the boil. 'Artists' who could draw no better than first-year art students were being sponsored and promoted by gallery owners with considerable success.

In a period of growing prosperity, culture was again becoming a hot

209

commodity. Large new buildings were going up and a new person called an Art Consultant was suddenly born whose job it was to cover the large bare walls with contemporary prints. There were slighting references to 'Bank Art', Bonwit Teller in New York opened a Print Boutique and Elizabeth Arden's salons, along with shops and offices all over America, were suddenly covered with prints.

In New York, particularly, where art is an important element in the commercial life of the city and where some degree of cultural involvement is experienced at more levels in society, the reaction to the flood of prints was characteristically bold and receptive. But too great expectations were built up and a lot of buyers had been drawn into the market who never understood why the prints by nonentities for which they might have paid $100–300 should suddenly be unsaleable, while work by Rauschenberg and Johns was holding its value.

In London the boom in prints came a little later. Editions Alecto placed an advertisement in *Studio International* announcing, 'We're going to do for prints what Henry Ford did for Detroit'. Certainly it seemed that the time had arrived, of which many people had dreamed, when the printing-press would supply great art cheaply to the whole world as it had done for literature. Everyone apparently, artists, publishers and collectors, were combining to make this dream a reality and prints were appearing on the walls of bed-sitters and in students' lodgings.

But the dream was short-lived. Although one or two publishers persevered with cheap unlimited editions (which even now are occasionally tried), financial pressures forced them all to resume the more commercial formula of expensive limited editions. It had turned out that the better-heeled collectors felt inexpensive prints, let alone those printed in unlimited numbers, lacked *cachet* and were happier to pay the higher price for the knowledge that only so many or preferably so few other people in the world would own such and such a print. It is now a canon of the art world, observed to great advantage by dealers, that collectors do not like their art too cheap.

From the earliest days, the market for abstract prints in the U.K. has been more or less moribund and no publishers of this material could survive without their overseas sales. Thinking about modern art is an exertion the British prefer to live without. This is partly borne out by the enormous following in the U.K. for Hockney with his strong whiff of modernism yet undemanding subject-matter consisting typically of such familiar objects as flowers, people, trees, furniture etc. The same explanation partly accounts for the popularity in the U.K. of other contemporary print-makers such as Patrick Caulfield and Jim Dine.

Among the contemporary artists whose prints are being marketed in the U.S.A. and U.K. there are certainly winners to be picked out but only a taste formed and refined by a great knowledge of modern art is likely to be any help

210

in making the right selections. It is equally certain that the majority will be worth less in real terms than they are being sold for today. After all, 19th-century artists whose prints are sold at auction nowadays are really the sole survivors of the process of selection and rejection that has left the work of the majority forgotten or destroyed.

As well as the International Print Biennale, which is held in a different country each time, there are two or three major Art Fairs held each year in different European cities. The annual sale held by Kornfeld & Klipstein in Berne is the world highlight of the print-sales, including the finest modern and contemporary material. In the U.K. Sotheby's, Christie's, and Phillips conduct print-sales between them at least every two weeks. In the U.S.A. New York is the centre of print-selling where again Sotheby Park-Bernet and Christie's dominate the field. Catalogue descriptions have to be very full since so much bidding takes place unseen. Some buyers are extremely discerning while others who have actually attended the sale will sometimes come up afterwards and ask to see the lots they have bought. Salerooms everywhere almost invariably end up by undercutting the dealers, particularly in the contemporary field and sometimes by well over 50%, yet the dealers in this field have neither the money nor the inclination to support their own markets.

Collectors are becoming increasingly fussy about condition. Dust, humidity, strong sunlight as well as strong artificial light can damage prints. Print-restorers can make miraculous repairs to worm-holes, cuts and tears, which can sometimes only be detected with a microscope. Light-staining which can turn paper brownish near the mount and time-staining on poor quality paper, particularly in the case of the Expressionists' prints where war-time paper often had to be used, can seriously affect the value of a print if, as often happens, these can not be removed.

There is more conscious investment in contemporary prints in the U.S.A. than in the U.K. and more buying by museums. American and British print-publishers' editions range from 20 to 500. The selling prices are often arrived at by multiplying by five the sum of the artist's fee and the printing cost, and although many galleries have expensive overheads there is always room for bargaining. The leading print-publishers hope to sell a large part of each edition to provincial and foreign galleries and to do so offer them substantial discounts.

Contemporary prints are now more and more often marketed through advertisements in periodicals. The editions range from bona fide original prints where the artist has been fully involved at every stage of the process to others which are no more than photographic reproductions. A careful reading of the small print will usually make clear which process has been used. It may also reveal that the advertised edition is limited to a specific number of prints in the U.S.A. or in the U.K. which of course leaves the publisher free to sell as many as he wishes elsewhere in the world, so making the implied rarity almost meaningless. No connoisseur, even in a mood of wild optimism, would forecast

211

a rise in value for the great majority of the prints marketed through periodicals although a few exceptions make too sweeping a condemnation impossible.

Certain factors have regularly affected the price of prints. Most established artists, particularly dead ones, have already had published a *catalogue raisonné* of their work but, where this has not yet happened, the first publication of a *catalogue raisonné* has always stirred up new interest in an artist's work which is usually followed by new price-levels. Major exhibitions in major public galleries of work by less well-known artists have also consistently made an impact on market prices. Most large galleries have a fixed programme of exhibitions for at least the next six months and a tentative programme for a further year beyond and are quite willing to disclose those plans.

It is also worth noting what acquisitions of contemporary prints are made by leading museums. Although all museums of Modern Art have cellars full of prints and pictures bought years ago when they seemed relevant or excellent and therefore a museum's acquisition of a print by no means guarantees that it will turn out to have been a wise buy, nevertheless the presence of an artist's work in a state or national collection adds an element of official approval which is often reflected at least for the time being in the market price for his work.

An Austrian financial journalist Willi Bongard has produced in his art newsletter, *art aktuell*, an analysis of the investment attractions of the world's one hundred greatest contemporary artists (many of whom are also print-makers) by taking the price of one of their minor works (usually a small drawing or graphic) and relating it to the number of points the artist has accumulated according to a formula which takes account of one-man shows, representation in thirty-nine leading museums throughout the world, inclusion in important group shows, treatment in fifty-four leading art books or magazines etc. The artists are then classified according to the resulting ratios into blue chips, glamour stocks, growth stocks. Although there are many flaws in the theory, it seems to be based on a superficially reasonable assumption that the future market price of a work of art will eventually reflect the current consensus of opinions of the arbiters of taste (i.e. museum curators and leading art critics but not gallery owners for whom objectivity is almost impossible), there being a time-lag between the recognition of the merit of an artist by the professionals and his recognition by the wider circle of collectors.

Yet art-history bristles with instances of professionals lagging far behind amateurs in their appreciation of new art-forms and styles. Even now, important galleries such as the Tate in London have such a bad reputation for petty political in-fighting and for having created a system whereby almost every adventurous idea is assured of a lingering death by bureaucratic strangulation that the choices made by such galleries are not likely to be blazing the new trails in the art-world. Taste in artistic circles, or art-snobbery as many would describe it, operates on different levels. Some influential commentators have reserved a special contempt for the postwar prints of Salvador Dali and

Chagall while the work of Russell Flint, Lowry and John Piper is regarded as quite beyond the pale. Others, believing their taste to be even more refined, will pour scorn on the work of Elizabeth Frink, Paolozzi and even Hockney. However distasteful these attitudes may seem, they have to be the concern of the investor for it is on precisely these that changes in value depend.

Book list

GILMOUR, PAT., ed. *Artists at Curwen* (Tate Gallery Art Service) (Illus.) 1977, Barron

HAYTER, STANLEY W. *About Prints* 1962, Oxford University Press

PETERDI, GABOR. *Printmaking* rev. ed. (Illus.) 1971, Macmillan

ZIGROSSER, CARL and GAEHDE, CHRISTA M. *Guide to the Collecting and Care of Original Prints* 1965, Crown

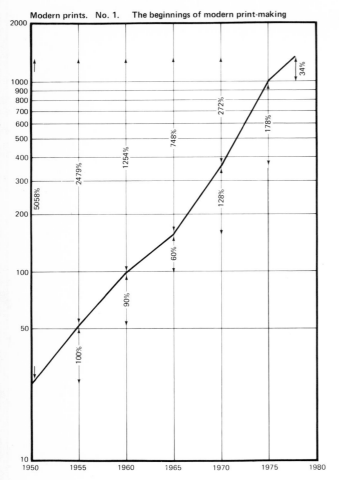

Modern prints. No. 1. The beginnings of modern print-making

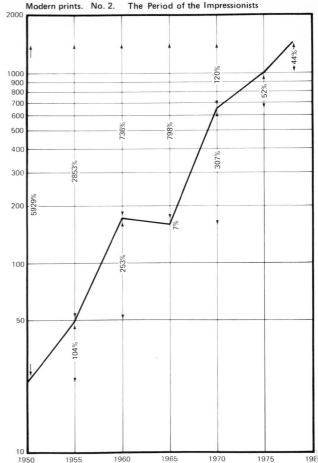

Modern prints. No. 2. The Period of the Impressionists

INDEX NO. 1. The Beginnings of Modern Print-making

1. Francisco José de Goya y Lucientes. The Disasters of War. Etchings with aquatint, title page, introduction and set of eighty plates. First Edition of 1863. Each c. 6 × 8".
2. Théodore Géricault. The English Farrier. Lithograph. 1821. 11 × 14".
3. Samuel Palmer. The Early Ploughman. Etching. 5¼ × 7¾".
4. Charles Meryon. La Morgue. 1855. Etching. 9 × 8¼".
5. James Whistler. Riva No. 1. Etching. 8 × 11½".

INDEX NO. 2 The Period of the Impressionists

1. Henri de Toulouse-Lautrec. 1895. Mademoiselle Lender e Buste. Lithograph in colours. Edition 100. 12¾ × 9½".
2. Pierre Bonnard. Place Le Soir. 1899. Lithograph in colour Edition 100. 10½ × 15".
3. Pierre-Auguste Renoir. Le Chapeau Epinglé. Lithograph colours. Edition 200. 12½ × 18".
4. Mary Cassatt. Maternal Caress. 1891. Aquatint in colou Edition 25. 14½ × 10½".
5. Camille Pissarro. La Charrue. Lithograph in colours. Editio about 35. 9 × 6".

214

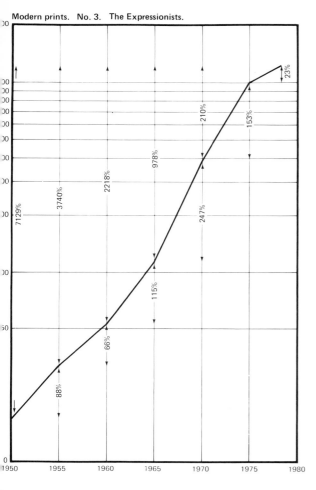

Modern prints. No. 3. The Expressionists.

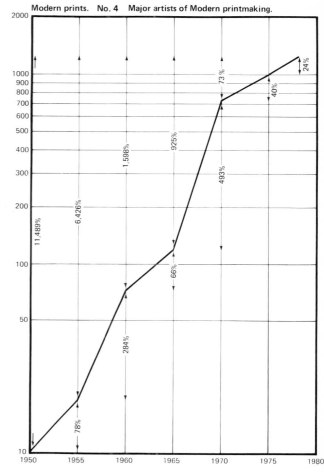

Modern prints. No. 4 Major artists of Modern printmaking.

INDEX NO. 3. The Expressionists.

Edvard Munch. Self-portrait. 1895. Lithograph. Edition not known. $18 \times 12\frac{3}{4}''$.

Emil Nolde. Double Portrait. 1937. Woodcut. Edition 150. $12\frac{1}{4} \times 8\frac{1}{4}''$.

Erich Heckel. White Horses. 1912. Woodcut in colours. Edition about 80. $12 \times 12\frac{1}{4}''$.

Max Beckmann. In the Tram. 1922. Etching and Drypoint. Edition about 30. $11\frac{1}{2} \times 17\frac{1}{4}''$.

Ernst-Ludwig Kirchner. Head of Ludwig Schames. 1918. Woodcut. Edition not known. $22\frac{1}{4} \times 10''$.

INDEX NO. 4. Major Artists of Modern Print-Making.

1. Paul Klee. The Loved One. 1923. Lithograph in colours. Edition 100. $10\frac{3}{4} \times 7\frac{1}{2}''$.
2. Pablo Picasso. Le Repas Frugal. 1904. Etching. From the edition of 250 after the steel-facing of the plate. $18\frac{1}{4} \times 15''$.
3. Georges Braque. La Théière Grise. 1947. Lithograph in colours. Edition 75. $14\frac{1}{4} \times 21\frac{1}{2}''$.
4. Marc Chagall. The Acrobat with the Violin. 1922. Etching and drypoint. Edition 150. $16\frac{1}{2} \times 12\frac{1}{2}''$.
5. Henri Matisse. Danseuse, one from the series Dix Danseuses. 1927. Lithograph. Edition 130. $18 \times 10\frac{3}{4}''$.

215

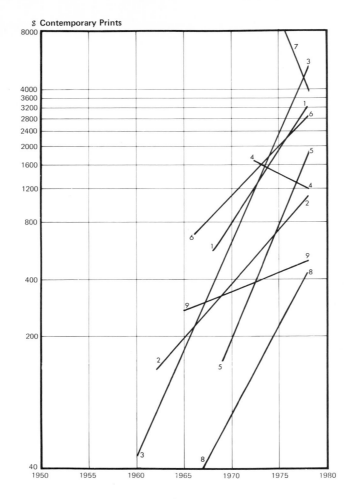

$ **Contemporary Prints**

INDEX NO. 5. Prints by some major contemporary print-makers

1. Ten from Leo Castelli. The complete set of ten prints and multiple objects, each numbered and signed, the set published by Leo Castelli, 1968, in an edition of 200 (plus 25 lettered sets). The collaborating artists were;
Lee Bontecou, Jasper Johns, Don Judd, Roy Lichtenstein, Robert Morris, Larry Poons, Robert Rauschenberg, James Rosenquist, Frank Stella and Andy Warhol.
2. Robert Rauschenberg. Stunt Man III. Lithograph printed in colours. Edition 36. Published 1962 by Universal Limited Art Editions.
3. Jasper Johns. Target. Lithograph. Edition 30. Published 1960 by ULAE.
4. Jasper Johns. Painting with a ball. Lithograph printed in grey and black. Edition 42. Published 1972–3 by ULAE.

5. David Hockney. Flowers and vase. Etching and aquati Edition 75. Published 1969 by the Petersburg Press.
6. David Hockney. Illustrations for fourteen poems of C. Cavafy, edition D. The complete portfolio comprising twel loose etchings with text. Edition 75. Published 1966 by Editio Alecto Ltd.
7. Andy Warhol. Mick Jagger. The complete suite of silkscreens printed in colours. Edition 250. Published 1975 Seabird Editions at $8500.
8. Andy Warhol. Liz. Silkscreen printed in colours. Edition 1(Published 1965 by Seabird Editions, at approximately $10.
9. Roy Lichtenstein. Shipboard girl. Offset lithograph printed colours. Unnumbered edition. Published 1965 by Caste Gallery.

Stamps

The word post is derived from the Latin *positus,* which was used to describe the positions along a road at which messengers and others were able to change horses. Messenger systems are no doubt as old as messages themselves but the earliest arrangements were usually made for the benefit of their organisers and it was not until the 15th and 16th centuries that public services were introduced to most European countries. These were on the whole expensive, slow, unreliable but, worse still, the messages themselves were open to scrutiny by the operators of the postal systems who all too often doubled as secret police.

Until a Scotsman, Rowland Hill, devised and introduced the Penny Post in 1840, most letters and packets had been carried not only on a cash-on-delivery basis but also, in a sense, on approval, in that the recipient might choose not to accept the letter and therefore not pay the postage due. In this way, the Post Office allowed the sender a form of credit and as a result the rights in the letter seemed to belong, at least until the debt was discharged, more to the Post Office than to the correspondent. The system of prepayment of postage was therefore felt to be an important step on the road to freedom and a symbol of the right to private communication.

The idea of prepaid postage seems to have been born in typically Scottish fashion. In 1836, Rowland Hill saw a Scots peasant girl being offered a letter by the postman. After a careful examination of the envelope, she declined to accept it saying the postage was too high. Talking to the girl afterwards, Hill discovered that a pre-arranged code enabled her to correspond with her lover in London by means of messages on the outside of the envelope and so avoid paying a penny for their correspondence – the letter inside being quite blank.

The world's first adhesive postage stamps which were issued on 6th May 1840 were the penny black and twopenny blue. The portrait of the young Queen Victoria, which was based on a medal by William Wyon struck to commemorate her entry into London, was received with great enthusiasm. Indeed, the general effect of dignity, strength and prettiness had much to do with the birth of stamp collecting. So attractive were the stamps that many people felt it disrespectful or for some indefinable reason hard to throw them away.

A German magazine of 1845 carried this news item. 'In England, which has a very insignificant yet regular postal service, the Post Office sells small square pieces of paper bearing the head of the Queen and these are stuck on the letter to be franked. In this simple manner the postage due is paid. To prevent a label being used twice the Post Office cancels the little piece of paper on the letter received with a black cross. The Queen's heads (sic) look very pretty and the English reveal their strange character by collecting these stamps.'

The stamps were printed by line-engraving on sheets made up of 240 stamps – twelve across and twenty down. As a precaution against forgery, the stamps were printed with two letters, the one in the lower left-hand corner from A to T to show from which horizontal row it came and in the lower right-hand corner from A to L to show from which vertical row it came. In this way the position of each stamp on the original sheet could be identified and the earliest form of stamp collecting was called 'plating' whereby people tried to reconstruct a complete sheet by sticking each used stamp according to its letters in its known position.

The glue, or cement as it was then known, was originally potato paste but later replaced by gum arabic when that became more freely available. In spite of dire warnings that the licking of stamps would spread cholera and many other diseases faster than ever nature could, the mucilage managed to survive and no more efficient method has yet been devised.

Two Italian covers of the 1850s showing, top, the purification cachet of the fever hospital 'Lazzaretto' and just visible the two vertical disinfection slits; and, bottom, a purification cachet of the Commissariato Di Sanita. Standard precautions at this date against the spread of cholera.

The problem of cancelling the stamps also received much attention in the early days. The standard means of cancellation was to stamp them with a red Maltese cross but many letter-writers took to coating the mint stamps with fish-glue before posting so that the recipient could wash off the glue and the cancellation together. Several bizarre solutions to this problem were offered including one from a Spaniard, Dr Mariano Pardo de Figuero, that stamps should be printed on two-layer paper between which there should be a small charge of gunpowder which would explode when the stamped was franked.

A perforating machine was invented in 1850 but stamps issued before then had to be cut from the sheet with scissors. This was often done very carelessly to the exasperation of modern collectors by Post Office clerks who scarcely imagined that one careless snip would later knock thousands off the value of a stamp. Imperforate stamps with full margins are thus highly desirable and far more rare and expensive than those without.

The Swiss canton of Zurich was the first postal authority after the British to issue stamps. The 4 and 6 Rappen of 1843 with their elaborate patterns looked rather like paper coins and encouraged the concept of stamps as another form of money. By 1854 the Swiss had come to feel that a female figure was a more appropriate symbol for a Republic and chose the seated figure of Helvetia for the 1854 issue. This fine and beautiful engraving shows the lady's hair unkempt and is consequently known as the Strubeli (tousle-haired) issue.

The first American stamps resulted from a characteristic pioneering spirit. In 1845 the law required the entire population of the U.S. to prepay postage in cash and only during office hours. These inconvenient arrangements were changed by the North American postmasters who, flouting the law, designed and issued their own highly individual adhesive 5 cent stamps sometimes bearing the portrait of the President. The stamps were universally popular and Congress, recognising their necessity, eventually gave them legislative approval. No American collection today seems complete without a specimen of these issues symbolising the victory of the will of the people over an obtuse government.

As early as 1854, when only twenty-four countries had so far issued stamps, the fourteen-year-old Edward Stanley Gibbons was given a room in his father's shop in Plymouth to develop his swapping and selling. He found people of all ages unaccountably drawn to these little bits of coloured paper. Most people could not expect to visit the faraway, sometimes exotic countries from which the stamps had travelled and collectors seemed to enjoy a vicarious sense of adventure, while even the cancellation itself seemed to confirm officially that the exciting journey had taken place. It was in this shop that Gibbons bought the famous sackful of triangular Cape of Good Hopes. Two sailors had won them in a raffle in South Africa and went off well pleased with the £5 Gibbons offered them and presumably never learnt that he had sold them for a total of over £500.

By 1862 the business of stamp collecting, or 'timbromania' as it was sometimes known, was becoming serious. The French magazine *Pittoresque*

219

remarked that although only 1400 stamps had been issued by about 100 states, provinces and colonies, some already cost a hundred times their face value. More important for its growth, stamp collecting seemed to go with high social status. It was known that the Austrian Emperor, the King of Italy, Pope Pius IX, Prince William of Prussia, the King of Portugal, Baron Rothschild and an assortment of maharajahs and millionaires were vying with each other to achieve completion. Stamp collecting which was regarded by many people, as it still is today, as a pursuit of unsurpassable silliness was defended on the grounds that it formed an interesting collection of heraldic, geographical and historical knowledge.

In 1865 Uruguay became the first country to issue unnecessary stamps by overstamping new values where those values already existed on earlier stamps. They also printed tête-bêche errors (where the whole of the design is inverted), inverted surcharges and even double and treble surcharges as bait for the collector. But apart from a few isolated cases, stamps remained until the 1880s by and large what they were intended to be – adhesive receipts for prepaid postage. Then in 1887, on the occasion of Queen Victoria's Golden Jubilee, the borders of British stamps received a more florid treatment than before and this was the first time a stamp had been used to express something apart from its primary use.

Tête-bêche error

In 1894, the Portuguese Post Office issued a set of thirteen stamps commemorating the five-hundreth anniversary of Henry the Navigator some of whose values, which went up to 1000 *reis*, were too high for postal use. The Portuguese had discovered and were openly exploiting the buying-power of collectors. The idea of selling people useless little scraps of paper at 1000 *reis* a time was just too tempting. The good news spread to postal authorities all over the world and many took advantage of the opportunity. In 1895 the Society for the Suppression of Speculative Stamps was founded in the U.S.A. but this attempt to retaliate was not successful for long. There were soon some dealers who would not join the boycott and any attempt to dictate to people what they should or should not collect was quite alien to the spirit of philately and certain to fail. The stamp trade still occasionally condemns this or that abuse but time has shown that a few of the condemned issues become as rare and desirable as more conventional issues.

Stamps have always been closely related to money and in many parts of the Middle East stamps are legal tender even today. They were widely used for

220

small change in South Africa during the gold rush of the 1880s. Before the First World War, many European countries with Post Offices inside the Turkish Empire issued their stamps at a discount on face value if they were bought in bulk. The Turks regarded any European stamp as money and so a kind of postage-currency grew up parallel with the ordinary coinage. Single stamps were useful for small change while whole sheets were dealt in and quoted as on a stock market. The prices varied according to the issuing Post Offices – the Austro-Hungarian Post Office offered the largest discounts and were therefore usually quoted well below par. The British, French and Russian made up the middle ground while the German sheets which had never been offered at a discount were the blue chips of the market. In many parts of Europe during both World Wars, stamps were used as currency when coin shortages developed.

The world's most valuable stamp, the British Guiana One Cent Black on Magenta, 1856. Catalogued at $600,000.

The Cape of Good Hope triangulars of which Edward Stanley Gibbons bought a sackful for $10 in 1863 enabling him to develop the now famous business.

221

Until about 1890, it was the fashion to collect globally but even before then, anything near completion had become an unattainable goal. So the sights were lowered and people aimed to complete a collection of one particular country or reign or more recently one particular theme. Thematic collecting of which many postal authorities and philatelic agencies are keenly aware and only too eager to take advantage, may consist of a theme such as space, air travel, fish or flowers or a purpose of issue collection such as the stamps commemorating the Red Cross centenary or the memorial issues for John F. Kennedy. Fashion in collecting can be quite capricious and to have bought successfully is often to have correctly anticipated a change in fashion.

Types of issue

DEFINITIVES: These are the stamps normally issued by countries and generally kept in use for long periods. The numbers issued are so large that they do not normally hold much interest for the collector, yet in the case of the U.K. where the Queen's head first issued in 1952 appears on a variety of single colour backgrounds, the water-mark was changed in 1955 and again in 1958 so making, as far as collectors are concerned, three different sets.

But as well as these, the stamps printed for booklets are printed in such a way as to have an inverted water-mark, while those produced in coils for use in machines have their water-mark sideways. Yet more variants are the sets printed in 1957 with graphite lines at the back for experimental electronic sorting and those that replaced them in 1959 with phosphor lines on the face.

PROVISIONALS: These are definitives which have been surcharged or overprinted to fill unexpected gaps in postal supplies or to cater for a change in a political or monetary situation. For example, in 1964 the Sultan of Zanzibar was deposed and overprinted stamps were issued for a short time until the new Republican series could be printed. Provisionals have almost by definition a short life and have therefore tended to prove good investments.

COMMEMORATIVES: All such issues are in a strictly postal sense unnecessary although it might be held to be in the public interest, for example to celebrate some important event such as the Abolition of Slavery by making a centenary issue. Many collectors convey their disapproval of such issues by describing them as speculative and it is true that many countries not only make issues so frequently as to be eventually counter-productive, they also abuse the spirit of philately by printing large numbers of such series with deliberate errors. Anniversaries are usually celebrated in round numbers such as 25, 50 and 100, admittedly for no very sound logical reason, yet many countries have used anniversaries as the flimsiest pretext for a speculative issue. One such example is the Sierra Leone series commemorating the 104th anniversary of the adhesive postage stamp although the centenary itself had been totally ignored.

MINIATURE SHEETS: These began in 1923 in Luxembourg where a small sheet was released bearing a 10 franc stamp in honour of a philatelic exhibition. Other souvenir issues quickly followed and, in 1937, Stanley Gibbons decided to exclude them from their catalogue because they were essentially non-postal. Before long, they became so important that their quasi-postal status has been recognised and their re-admission to the Gibbons catalogue was followed by rocketing prices.

CHARITY ISSUES: These began in England in 1890 to celebrate the Golden Jubilee of Penny Postage. A one shilling stamped pictorial envelope was sold, the cost of which was divided, a penny going to the Post Office and eleven pence to the Post Office workers and orphans. During the First World War, a spate of charity stamps was issued for the Red Cross and other causes which created intense interest at the time but this suddenly evaporated when the war was over with the result that many dealers were ruined. During the 1930s, several Sinking Fund issues were made in France but collectors got sick of paying Frs5 for a Frs1·50 stamp and eventually gave up buying. The French Post Office realised that collectors might yet 'give' for a specific cause and made several such successful issues including one for the Unemployed Intellectuals Fund.

LIMITED ISSUES: Some countries will offer a limited quantity of imperforate or miniature sheets, sometimes in altered colours, to dealers who will buy ten times the number of normal sets. The stamp trade is on the whole very contemptuous of such practices and these countries are to be avoided.

Many other minor kinds of issue which hold a special interest for many collectors have taken place such as:

POSTAGE DUE STAMPS in cases where the letter has been carried without prepayment and the recipient has to pay the Post Office the amount shown on the stamp.

TELEGRAPH STAMPS issued as receipts for prepayment of a telgraphic message.

LOCAL STAMPS which were valid for short distances e.g. the Oxford stamps issued in the 1870s and 80s which paid the carriage to and from anywhere within that city whereas GOVERNMENT STAMPS were good for unrestricted distances.

SPLIT STAMPS were those perforated down the middle and sometimes divisible into more than two parts to enable the user to cope with a variety of postage costs with a single stamp.

SPECIAL SERVICE ISSUES – registration stamps and special delivery stamps.

UNISSUED STAMPS, such as essays – that is stamps printed with a proposed design which were not adopted or not without some alteration. Also proofs and other trials showing variations in colour, gumming and so on.

Determinants of value

The most important factors affecting the value of a stamp are as follows:

COUNTRY OF ORIGIN: Each country has a status which depends to a great extent on its policy towards philatelists. All countries are happy to receive the golden eggs laid by the philatelic geese. Many countries which had pursued a sensible policy turned over the responsibility for issuing stamps to philatelic agencies whose object was to produce the greatest revenue for themselves and the issuing country. The rise of these commercial philatelic agencies gathered momentum in the 1960s when the addiction of thematic collectors was intensively exploited. Issues became too frequent, too large and included unacceptably high denominations. Many countries produced endless sets on every theme known to interest collectors from space to insects. A favourite idea was to 'honour' great international figures. Ecuador for instance issued a series including Churchill, Kennedy, Schweitzer, etc. with no conceivable postal use. Themes such as Churchill, Kennedy, Art and Sport are still usually good business. The Kathiri state of Seiyun in Saudi Arabia recently tried to exploit two groups of thematic collectors with one issue by bringing out a set featuring Churchill's paintings.

Another example of a State losing its philatelic reputation was when Tonga severed its link with the Crown Agents. Its philatelic policy degenerated and the first of a number of speculative issues, consisting of huge circular stamps, now known as the Tonga beer-mats, was made to commemorate the introduction of a gold coinage on the island. In spite of such flagrant exploitation by a growing number of postal authorities there always seem to be enough undiscriminating collectors to make it worth their while.

CONDITION: This is the hardest factor to assess and is increasingly important as the competition for fine material becomes more fierce.

(a) *Unmounted mint.* The stamp must be in a perfect state as it left the printer. The gum must be impeccable, never having been stuck to the page of an album. It must be clean and fresh without stains, creases or thinnings and with its perforations intact.

(b) *Mounted mint.* As (a) above but with minute traces of earlier hingeing or stamp mount.

(c) *Unused, part original gum.* A stamp that has been heavily mounted but still retains part of the original gum.

(d) *Unused, without gum.* An unpostmarked copy that had at some time been stuck down so that in soaking it off the paper its gum has been removed.

224

(e) *Fine used.* A stamp with the lightest possible postmark and otherwise intact.

Serious collectors should only buy stamps falling within categories (a), (b), and (e). Argument has raged in philatelic circles over the status of the gum on a stamp. Some experts insist that original gum is an essential characteristic of an unused stamp while others regard it as quite incidental to the stamp. Stamps dating from before 1880 are very rare in conditions (a) or (b) because, before mounts and hinges came into use, stamps were usually quite simply stuck down on the page of an album with gum, paste or glue. The pochettes or strips now in general use avoid the need to use any kind of adhesive.

As collectors continue to debate the merits of original gum, a strange situation has developed in which some curators of museum collections, taking the view that the stamps in their care will never be put up for sale, are now washing the gum off old stamps to prevent it cracking the paper while a busy group of forgers are regumming old stamps to gratify the needs of the more 'discerning' collectors.

The perforation of a stamp is almost as important as imperforation. If a stamp is valuable in its own right without any freakish characteristics, all the teeth of the perforation should be present and the image perfectly centred between the margins. Imperforation is an extremely rare condition, and it is generally realised that imperforation can usually only be established when no holes exist between adjoining stamps. Foxing or rust-stains caused by iron impurities in the paper can also reduce the value of a stamp although these can often be removed with chemicals.

METHOD OF PRODUCTION: The line-engraving method of printing used for the earliest stamps gives a finer result than any method used since. As demand for the lower denominations increased, many countries found it necessary to resort to the cheaper rotogravure, offset litho and letterpress methods with a consequent drop in printing quality. Some countries, including the U.S.A., France, Austria and Czechoslovakia, still use intaglio printing for all their issues and many others print only the higher values (for which demand is lower) by the more expensive method.

RARITY: This is judged in absolute terms by the number of stamps comprising an issue, yet more important is the rarity of a stamp relative to the number of collectors of the country. If the U.K. issued a commemorative stamp and printed one million only, this might turn out to be a good investment because there are many more than one million collectors of the stamps of Great Britain round the world. If, on the other hand, a country of relatively little interest to collectors such as Fiji made an issue of a million, it is unlikely that there would ever be enough collectors to raise the price above its face-value and the sheets would very probably have to be sold later at a discount.

The quantities of an issue are publicly announced in the U.K. and the U.S. and in many other countries but this does not deter many badly-informed Americans from investing in sheets of commemoratives whenever they are issued and in whatever quantities and putting them away against a rainy day. When the rainy day comes, they take the sheets of stamps to a dealer who, to their great indignation, will make an offer far below their face-value. Such stamps having originally been issued in billions could never have been expected to sell at a premium.

Of the 1000 1d. vermilion and 2d. blue Mauritius Post Office stamps originally issued, twenty-five are thought to have survived. An envelope bearing two of the one-penny stamps was auctioned by Harmers of London in New York in 1968 for $380,000, still a record for any philatelic item. Curiously enough there are cases of other stamps equally rare but valued at only $200. Absolute rarity in a stamp does not guarantee any particular value; the stamp must also have a special significance in postal history or for some other reason catch the imagination of collectors.

Buying and selling

Collectors not only define their speciality by area and subject but also by period. The three principal periods of stamps production are (1) those issued up to 1900 known as classics; (2) the period up to the mid-thirties known as the middle issues; and (3) the modern period.

The classics include the rare first issues of any country often hand-printed by the line-engraving process as well as those printed after 1860 by the faster methods of lithography and rotogravure that came to be needed. The middle issues are typified by the rather monotonous key-plate designs of the British colonies and the portraits of rulers surrounded by heraldic devices. The modern period really began when commemoratives started to be issued more frequently – often designed in two or more colours and printed by the photogravure process.

Stamps are often bought and sold in very shrewd as well as very foolish ways. Dealers have a saying that they make profits out of collectors to recoup the losses they make to philatelists. This is another way of saying that most dealers do not have the time to become really knowledgeable in more than one or two fields although they have to carry stock covering a far wider range. It follows then that anyone who makes a deep study of one subject will very probably come to know more than the majority of dealers and so be able to recognise value where they have not.

There are several ways of acquiring stamps. Philatelic agencies are the intermediaries between the issuing country and the stamp-collector. Their job is to maximise the revenue of the issuing country and to make it easy for collectors to buy. The oldest of these is the Stamp Bureau run by the Crown

Agents in the U.K. whose association with stamp production goes back to 1848. New issues can be bought from philatelic agencies in most countries although those who buy such issues consider it pays a collector to pay the extra 15–25% to have a standing order with a reliable dealer who will be able to supply all the new issues even when the number released is restricted. Many collectors acquire stamps by swop arrangements with collectors in other countries or from business connections with overseas traders.

Another important way of acquiring stamps is by the exchange packet. Most philatelic societies arrange for members to mount duplicates or other unwanted specimens in club booklets marked with the prices asked and catalogue numbers. The Secretary arranges for these to circulate to members in turn, who remove whichever stamps they wish to buy, sending the money to the Secretary and the booklet on to the next member. Many European Post Offices accept prepayment of parcel postage by having the sender stick stamps to special cards rather than on to the parcel. These are then sold to dealers by the kilo from which they are known as kiloware.

There are many specialist dealers more in the nature of brokers who will advise richer collectors on a buying and selling strategy, on mounting and arranging the collection and will even have it professionally written up by a calligrapher and entered for competitions. For the ordinary collector, there are ordinary dealers whose prices are invariably compared with the prices shown in the great catalogues.

It is true that these catalogues, Stanley Gibbons in the U.K. and Scott in the U.S., form the basis of all dealing yet it is important to recognise that, at their lowest, they are no more than dealers' price lists. They are mines of information on philately too but the prices they show are not necessarily the open market prices for those stamps. Where interest in a stamp has waned and the market price has fallen off as a result, the catalogue price will continue to reflect rather the price the dealer-cataloguer has paid for the stamp plus his profit margin; in other words, the price at which he hopes to sell it. For this reason big discounts off catalogue prices do not necessarily represent good value. Quite apart from the possibility that the catalogue price may have been inflated by past speculation, great care should also be taken that a stamp is not being offered below catalogue price because it is worn, thinned or repaired. It is seldom sensible to buy stamps in such poor condition but if a collector decides to, the discount should be at least 70%. Bidding at auction, either in person or by leaving a bid with the auctioneer, is a good way to buy although it is unwise to go too far above the estimate made by the saleroom. London is the world centre of the stamp-trade with regular auctions being held by Harmers, Robson Lowe, Stanley Gibbons, and Puttick and Simpson as well as some twenty smaller auction-houses throughout the U.K. The catalogues of the leading auction-houses offer meticulous descriptions and often fine illustrations too. A pamphlet called 'Philatelic Auctioneers Standard Terms and Conditions of Sale'

227

is essential reading, particularly the section headed 'Extensions' which deals with a purchaser's rights to reject a stamp sometimes within an agreed time if he can prove it, in the opinion of an expert committee, to be a forgery.

A good collection is occasionally best sold privately if the seller has a real knowledge of current values. Otherwise it is wisest to put the best material into an auction and hawk the rest around in a philatelic society's exchange packets. Stamp-dealers will normally only offer between 25–50% of catalogue price making them the least competitive outlet although their prices will come closer to catalogue prices if they are allowed to pick out what they want.

Fakers have become so ingenious that it is wise to have valuable stamps 'expertised' before buying and also, because it raises their value, before selling. In the U.K., expert committees are formed by the Royal Philatelic Society and the British Philatelic Federation. Although each has been known to grant certificates of genuineness to stamps turned down by the other, they are widely respected. Similar certificates, usually on paper bearing a photograph of the stamp in question, are issued by the Philatelic Foundation in New York and other official bodies throughout Europe.

Forgeries and fakes

There are two main kinds of stamp forgery – the first, known as a postal forgery, which is produced to defraud a postal authority, and the second known as a philatelic forgery produced to deceive a collector. Examples of the first kind were circulating in Italy in the 1860s. Some famous examples were of the French Sower type made in the 1900s and the 2d. Sydney Harbour Bridge of 1932. Postal forgeries such as these are rare and eagerly sought after by collectors. Philatelic forgeries are much more common and some collectors make it their speciality.

One of the greatest forgers of all time was Samuel Allan Taylor who first began to deal in stamps in Montreal in 1862. Experiencing difficulty in meeting the demand for local stamps, Taylor decided to print his own, beginning with the wholly fictitious 5 cent Bancroft's City Express and later a 2 cent Bell's Dispatch. Moving on to Boston in 1867, Taylor arranged premature first issues for Guatemala, Santo Domingo and Paraguay, forging as well a number of documents purporting to prove them genuine.

Another brilliant forger was Jean de Sperati who operated in France where the law allowed reproductions of works of art, including stamps, to be sold provided they were openly sold as such. The problem was that dealers from all over the world came to Paris to buy these reproductions but were less than scrupulous over their description when they came to sell them. Sperati even produced his forgeries or reproductions on genuine water-marked stamp paper by bleaching out the genuine impression from a common old stamp and then

228

Allied war-time propaganda forgery infiltrated into Germany. The stamps show Himmler's head and were intended to give the impression that Hitler was either dead or deposed.

Forgery of another Allied propaganda forgery (which have become quite valuable). The Hitler 'skull type' with the legend 'FUTSCHES REICH'. The Germans infiltrated a number of forged British stamps overprinted 'Liquidation of the Empire'.

imposing his own photo-lithographic impression. In 1953 Sperati felt his eyesight was no longer equal to the demands of the finest work and he looked out for a successor. At that stage, the then British Philatelic Association stepped in and bought up all his equipment and records for fear they might fall into more dangerous hands.

Fakes are stamps that have been altered for sale to collectors in upgraded conditions. It is now possible for stamps to be regummed, reperforated, have penmarks removed and be supplied with fine margins all round. Some consider it legitimate to improve the appearance of a stamp by boiling, washing and ironing and even treating a sulphuretted stamp with hydrogen peroxide to remove the sulphurisation, but to use a chemical that would change the colour of the stamp would be outright faking. The obsession many collectors suffer from about condition has given a fillip to this branch of forgery.

The first work on philatelic forgeries was published in 1863 and a considerable literature on the subject has built up to help collectors. This literature is, of course, no little help to the fakers themselves who can study the details by which their productions gave themselves away and take steps to correct them.

Many crimes other than forgery have been committed for the sake of stamps. Gaston Leroux, a well-known philatelist, was found murdered in his Paris home in 1892. A large sum of money lay untouched and the police could not at first propose a motive. A week after the body had been found, an alert detective looking through Leroux's indexed stamp collection noticed that a Hawaiian 2 cents of 1851 was missing. Suspicion fell on Hector Giroux, a keen collector of 'Missionaries' – so called because most of the letters mailed from the islands were sent by missionaries. After several weeks, Giroux was persuaded by the detective, now posing as a fellow philatelist, to show him his collection. There among the early issues lay Leroux's Hawaiian 2 cents 1851. Giroux was arrested the following day and confessed at his trial that he had murdered his friend for the sake of the stamp.

229

Why do people collect?

What rational explanation, if any, can be offered for stamp collecting? As with coins, collectors themselves most frequently advance the theory that stamps actually teach them history and geography. This account is not very convincing since an hour spent with a history or geography book will plainly be more instructive than an hour looking at stamps. What collectors must mean is that stamps are in a modest sort of way historical documents or at least have the power to evoke a sense of history. Collectors of British Empire issues could, as it were, do their own empire-building without stirring from their own homes. The stamps were symbols of great imperial possessions. They also bore in numbers or letters, sums of money denoting their value in buying a postal service but even when they were cancelled many people must have found it hard to convince themselves that a black mark, sometimes quite light and small, could utterly rob them of their value.

Anti-vaccination propaganda cover, 1849.

It is no doubt true that in the 1840s and 1850s, stamps symbolised for some people the right to private correspondence but that aspect of stamp collecting is no help in explaining the pursuit today. It was also no doubt more true in the early days of postage, when to travel long distances was open to very few people, that collectors enjoyed a vicarious experience of travel although the design of most stamps could not be said to be very informative other than to suggest the presence of, perhaps, palm trees or elephants in the issuing countries.

Although many stamps are very finely printed, another favourite argument

230

in favour of collecting stamps – that they are miniature works of art – would surely hold up better if a single great artist had ever chosen to work in the medium or if the artists or designers of stamps had ever become celebrated outside stamp-collecting circles. Even the stamps which are hailed by many collectors as the most beautiful ever produced show a head of Queen Victoria taken from the portrait in oils by A. E. Chalon, while the Penny Black itself was based on the medal by William Wyon.

Another problem with the miniature work of art argument is that what entrances many collectors most is a stamp on which part of the design has been accidentally omitted. The pre-occupation with errors that is shared by so many collectors is what makes it difficult to take stamp collecting seriously as a branch of the arts – for in no art-form is faulty workmanship ranked as desirable in itself. No one knows how the fascination with errors started but it was already a feature of stamp collecting by the 1880s. Flyspeck philately or the preoccupation with minute errors which excites some collectors to study, for example, 'a tiny dot on the King's cheek' as a result of a piece of grit sticking to the printing cylinder, is now in decline although water-mark errors and even gum errors are keenly studied. Dealers tend to ask very high prices for colour shift errors they discover in their own stocks but are reluctant to pay a good price to anyone having bought one by luck at the Post Office.

To an investor, errors are less reliable than straight stamps. Stamp collecting is an irrational activity; so to invest money in stamps carries with it the risk that one day their intrinsic worthlessness will be reflected in their market price. To

A Valentine cover of *c.* 1855. Philatelists' interests now range over all fields related to postage.

invest money in errors which is the extreme form of an already irrational activity can only be more hazardous.

It is well understood that children are fascinated by objects on an unfamiliar scale, such as dwarfs and giants, and love to play with miniature trains, cars and animals. A child's propensity to control is seen in its preference for such miniature objects with which they undoubtedly feel safe yet powerful. It is to the controlling urge in children and adults that stamps often appeal. Stamps also symbolise authority often by bearing a representation of a king or queen, a small part of whose authority may be felt to have transferred itself to the owner. Stamps are now universally recognised as objects of value – each one is denominated by value – and to a child, they seem to be priced in the same way as goods in a shop. They are even referred to not by their colour or size but by their value. By the time a child has learnt that their values when used are no longer as printed on the faces, he will also have learnt that although they no longer have a value in buying a postal service, they do have another sort of value, sometimes very high, to people who collect them. There has never been a time when these little pieces of paper have not been closely associated in people's minds with money and, in a way, stamp collecting has ceased to require any further explanation. It is no longer possible to look at them with an innocent eye and estimate their natural appeal free from all associations.

Price trends

The most remarkable rise in value since 1950 has been that of the classic issues of Great Britain. Every serious philatelist and dealer knows that the best bets for a sound investment are the classic issues of any country yet, in spite of this, many dealers continue to recommend collectors to buy new commemorative issues. Many of these commemorative sets are issued ten million or more at a time and it is difficult to see how the word rare can sensibly be applied to anything of which there exists such an enormous supply.

No one really knows how many stamp collectors there are in the world. Some estimate two million in the U.K., five million in West Germany, ten million in the U.S.A. and so on. If those figures were about right, and a large figure were added in for collectors elsewhere, there begins to develop a picture where at least theoretically a large commemorative issue could actually become scarce and so command a premium over its face-value. But dealers have an obvious motive in recommending these issues in that they usually take a profit of 15–25% on the face-value charged them by the philatelic bureau of the issuing country. In buying endless sets of commemoratives, many collectors are simply enjoying themselves although the majority undoubtedly expect the stamps to be worth more when they try to sell them. Others seem to suffer from a residual obsession with completion. They feel they just have to have the new set

otherwise there will be a gaping hole in their collection and it is of this anxiety that many postal authorities take full advantage.

A leading London auction-house recently received a letter from a bank stating they had a customer who wished to liquidate his 'stamp investment'. His collection turned out to consist entirely of commemoratives, none earlier than 1969, including many Channel Islands issues. Its value at catalogue prices was $1,700,000 yet the auction-house had to reply that it was totally unsaleable except over a period of several years and even then the owner could only expect the stamps to fetch wholesale prices way below what he had paid for them.

One effect of the steep rise in British prices was to make it impossible for collectors of moderate means to continue with this speciality at all. They switched their attention to neglected areas where they could get the same enjoyment at a fraction of the cost. Countries that quickly grew more popular included Central and South American states. Whereas in 1960 mixed specimens of these areas dating from 1890 onwards could be bought for about a cent a dozen, the same material is now fetching $10 a dozen. Another area that for the same reason came up very strongly, particularly over the last ten years, was the States of Australia which issued stamps independently before the system was unified in 1913.

Stamp values of different countries obviously rise and fall according to collectors' demand. That demand is shaped by the currency, economy, philatelic policy and political stability of each country. In Japan, stamp

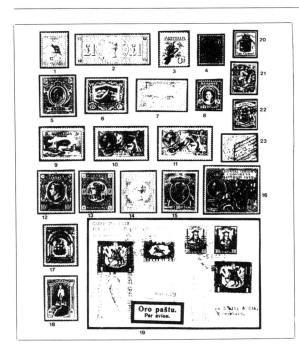

A selection of stamps
1 Australia: 1913 £2 black and rose
2 Great Britain: 1887–1892 £1 green
3 Australia: 1913–14 6d. claret
4 Antigua: 1921–29 £1 purple and black on red
5 Montserrat: 1903 5/– black and scarlet
6 Zanzibar: 1913 20r. black and green
7 Montserrat: 1932 Tercentenary 3d. orange
8 Bahamas: 1863–80 1d. red
9 Australia: 1932 Sydney Bridge 5/– blue-green
10 Great Britain: 1913 10/– indigo-blue
11 Great Britain: 1913 £1 green
12 Great Britain: 1939–48 10/– dark blue
13 Zululand: 1888–93 5/– rose
14 Great Britain: 1880–84 10/– ultramarine
15 India: 1911–22 10r. green and scarlet
16 Great Britain: 1929 Postal Union Congress £1 black
17 Antigua: 1932 Tercentenary 5/– black and chocolate
18 Australia: 1937–49 thick paper 10/– dull purple
19 Lithuania: 1932 Zeppelin Flight cover to Brazil
20 Switzerland: Geneva: 1857–58 5c. on yellow-green ⎫
21 Germany: Saxony: 1855–63 10ngr. blue   ⎬ Sperati
22 Germany: Oldenburg: 1859 2g. black on rose   ⎪ Forgeries
23 Italy: Papal States: 1852–64 50b. dull blue   ⎭

A set of the German
occupation 'Swastika'
overprinted stamps of
Jersey.

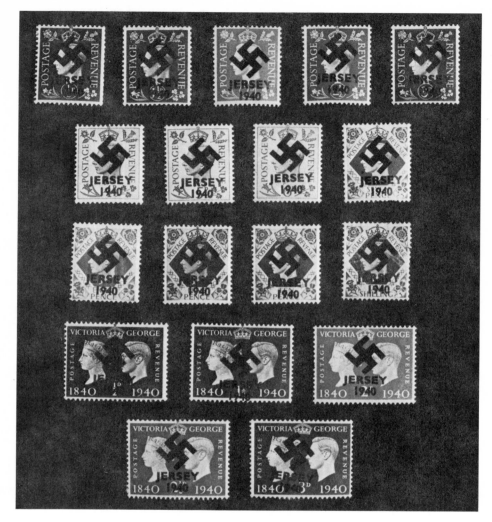

collecting is an important pursuit, with large numbers of collectors specialising
in their own and other oriental issues. Growth in disposable income has a
significant effect on demand for stamps and the great economic strength of
Japan has underpinned the steady rise in oriental values. The same growth has
been experienced in varying degrees by German, Swiss and American issues.

On the other hand certain issues of the South African Provinces before the
Union in 1910 would have proved fairly disappointing investments. Apart from
being visually rather uninteresting, two reasons for this suggest themselves.
The first is that the widespread abhorrence of the political régime has prevented
a normal increase in interest outside the country. The stamps of the Soviet
Union have won a similar unpopularity. The second reason is that South
African stamps have been used extensively as a means of bringing blocked

currency out of the country and the regular supply arriving in the outside world has tended to prevent any scarcity developing.

The stamps of newly independent countries always arouse a great deal of interest when first issued which may or may not last depending on the sort of philatelic policy that is followed. Ghana and Sierra Leone are just two of the countries that have just about alienated collectors altogether. Such streams of 'wallpaper' were issued that all but the most tenacious seekers after completion refused to go on buying and wisely put a final date on their collections.

'Dead' countries such as Tibet which have ceased to issue stamps were often of little interest to collectors although there were exceptions such as Tristan da Cunha which was suddenly in demand when it became known that the island was to be evacuated.

Other 'dead' countries in which there used to be very little interest were the Balkans which over the last five years have shot up in value. It is quite possible that renewed interest will develop in all 'dead' countries, one major attraction being that completion is at least theoretically possible since there are no streams of new issues to cope with.

Italy is looked upon as the most investment-conscious country of the stamp world. Dealers there have operated large-scale investment drives offering stamps at ever-increasing prices and even with guarantees to buy them back at a profit. These speculative schemes have ended, as they were bound to, with large numbers of burnt fingers and much bad feeling towards the stamp trade.

In the U.S.A., the ring tries to operate at auctions but the intentions of the few dealers who make a bidding agreement are usually frustrated by the numerous postal bids and the bidding of non-ring dealers. The standard of cataloguing varies widely from one auction-house to another, some are completely dependable, others are full of over-described conditions, undetected (perhaps deliberately) reperforations, re-gums, etc. Re-gums can easily be arranged for $2 a time but it takes an experienced eye to identify the best work.

Stamp collecting in the U.S. is a serious business. There are hundreds of clubs where collectors meet and swap nickel stamps to and fro all evening. But there are bigger-time collectors spending millions of dollars in putting together award-winning collections. There are mug-hunters in every hobby but in philately they proliferate. Every philatelic exhibition will award for each country a large gold medal, a gold, vermeil, large silver, silver, small silver, bronze and even a certificate of participation. The judging of entries is based, on a number of well-established points such as philatelic knowledge, original research, neat lettering, precise but not overwritten descriptions, pleasing layout, etc. One collector who had often shown some fine German material but never got a higher medal than a bronze asked a leading New York dealer to help him improve the descriptions and layout. At the next show the gold medal was duly won and the dealer found himself smothered in kisses by the delighted collector. Such is the strength of feeling aroused by these events.

The dividing line between philatelist and eccentric is quite easily drawn. Philately is about collecting stamps which by means of their water-marks, surcharges, cancellations, covers and so on throw light on some facet no matter how obscure of postal history. Whereas a typical example of an eccentric's collection was recently brought to a New York dealer to dispose of. It consisted of one Red Cross stamp of which a man had collected 446 corner blocks of eight and 381 corner blocks of 4, each block showing on its margin a different printer's serial number. The collector thus had 827 numbers out of a possible 1920. Catalogue value was $2900 and saleroom value, in the absence of like-minded eccentrics, perhaps $100.

Demand for stamps of different nations varies with the ethnic groupings in different cities of the U.S. Polish and German material that you can barely give away in Los Angeles, they will beat you over the head for in Chicago. Dealers will also manipulate the markets in the stamps of countries of which they have large stocks. Recent issues of Israel and the Vatican were put into phoney auctions and the 'big increases' publicised in the philatelic press. For all the hustling in the lower and middle price-ranges, the price of the greatest U.S. items – the rare Postmaster Provisionals for example – is considered low by international standards, around half the price of European items of comparable rarity. As a result, some of the best U.S. material is now finding its way into European collections.

London salerooms receive so many postal bids before their auctions from all over the world that it is impossible for the ring to function at all effectively. There is no need therefore for a private collector to pay a commission to a dealer to act for him. Quite frequently, both dealers and collectors prefer to leave their bids with the auctioneer so that their bidding is not used as a guide.

Although the Philatelic Traders' Society, which has about four hundred members in the U.K. and about four hundred in sixty-five other countries, has a strict Code of Conduct and from time to time expels members who fall short of the required standard of behaviour, the feeling among the most reliable members of the trade it that there are serious abuses which have increased over the last ten years as less reputable dealers have taken advantage of the investment boom. It is not that stamps are necessarily bad investments – with knowledge, experience, foresight and preferably some luck, very large gains can be made – it is rather that many stamp dealers are selling stamps to non-philatelists at prices which are impossible to justify.

One provincial firm of auctioneers in the U.K. which offers free advice to investors uses another company in the group to buy stamps in London which they then offer for sale at their own auctions. They will then bid on behalf of investors whom they have 'advised' to pay a given sum. In this case, a company is in effect selling its own stamps and buying them back at an inflated price on behalf of their clients and using a public auction as a front to give the appearance of a real market price. Another form of abuse is where a dealer either directly or through a private philatelic agency controls the stamp-issuing policy of some small state. This can lead to unacceptable practices where the dealer has a number of investment clients whose portfolios will be stuffed with all the new issues of that state although their prospects of growth are very poor.

Stories of investors being hustled are not often heard, partly because people do not like to advertise their mistakes and partly because if a man spends $10,000 on stamps and five years later finds they are only worth $4,000 he may go back to the dealer, demand his money back and actually get it. In such a case, rather than risk bad publicity, the dealer many prefer to refund his customer the full $10,000 and get back his stamps which may have risen in value above his original cost. The dealer will have enjoyed in effect an interest-free loan for five years which he has repaid with devalued currency and often the investor will be delighted to have his $10,000 back and feel that he has been quite well treated.

A favourite kind of hustle in the U.S.A. is where a dealer will buy perhaps a hundred specimens of a stamp catalogued at $10 and then advertise in the press that he is making a market in the stamp, bidding $18 and offering them at $20. Anyone coming in to sell will have his attention drawn to some trumped-up defect in the stamp which reduces the value to $2 and go away disappointed, while the others will quickly secure a specimen before there is another 'big rise' in the price.

Basic information

1. Collect countries that have a strong economy and a large and prosperous middle class.

2. As soon as demand for modern issues of any particular country can be seen to be rising, take care to buy the earlier issues of that country and any items of postal history because interest in these will quickly follow.

3. Do not buy common definitive stamps nor low value commemoratives issued in large quantities.

4. Try to distinguish, by asking around, between real collector demand and speculative buying.

5. Pay top prices for specimens in the best condition whether used or mint. The obsession with condition is of long-standing and evident in every field of collecting. The premium paid for best over second best has been growing and is likely to continue to do so.

6. Buy stamps that are easy to sell rather than easy to buy.

7. Study the chosen speciality in depth. Thousands of titles covering every speciality are in print and the more knowledge goes into a collection, the more valuable it will be to another collector when the time comes to sell.

8. It can be helpful and interesting to join a society. The tendency now is for collectors to form themselves into societies based on a shared speciality rather than the fact of merely living in the same area.

Important public stamp collections

U.K.	Birmingham	City Museum and Art Gallery
	Halifax	Bankfield Museum and Art Gallery
	London	British Museum
		British Red Cross, 14 Grosvenor Crescent, S.W.1. (by appointment)
		Bruce Castle, Lordship Lane, Tottenham, N.17
		Imperial War Museum
		National Maritime Museum
		National Postal Museum
		Science Museum
U.S.A.	Boston	Cardinal Spellman Museum
	Washington	Smithsonian Institute

Trade organisations

American Stamp Dealers Associations Inc., 595 Madison Avenue, New York, N.Y. 10022

British Philatelic Federation, 1 Whitehall Place, London S.W.1.

Philatelic Traders Society, 27 John Adam Street, London W.C.2.

Book list

MACKAY, JAMES. *Stamps* (Source Book Services) (Illus.) 1974, International Publications Services

NEW, ANTHONY S. *The Observer's Book of Postage Stamps* (Pub. by Observer Books) (Illus.) 1977, Scribner

NARBETH, COLIN. *Collecting British Stamps: A Beginner's Guide* 1977, British Book Center

SUTTON, R. J. *The Stamp Collector's Encyclopedia* (Illus.) 1972, Arc Books

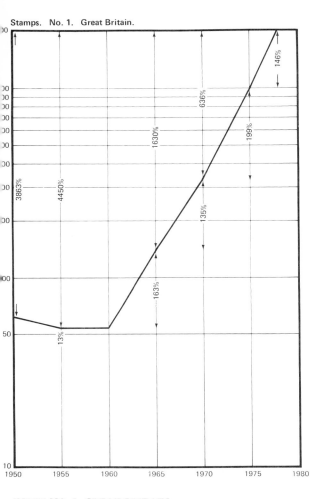

Stamps. No. 1. Great Britain.

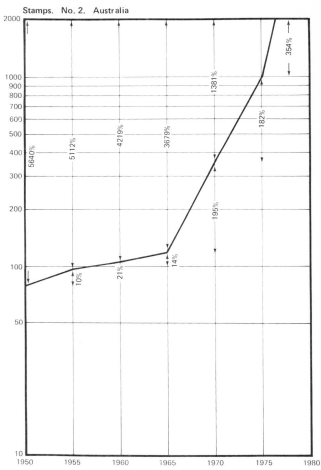

Stamps. No. 2. Australia

INDEX NO. 1. GREAT BRITAIN.

1. 1867–83.   £5 Orange on white paper.

2. 1884.   £1 Brown/lilac.

3. 1911–13.   £1 Printed by Somerset House.

4. 1913.   £1 Sea-horse. Dull blue-green.

5. 1929.   £1 Postal Union Congress. St George & Dragon.

6. 1935. $2\frac{1}{2}$d Prussian blue. (normally ultramarine).

Condition – Mint, part original gum.

INDEX NO. 2. AUSTRALIA.

1. 1913.   £2 Kangaroo.

2. 1932.   5/– Sydney Harbour Bridge.

3. 1937–49.   5/–, 10/– & £1 Robes. Ordinary paper.

4. 1948–56.   5/– to £2.

Condition – Mint, part original gum.

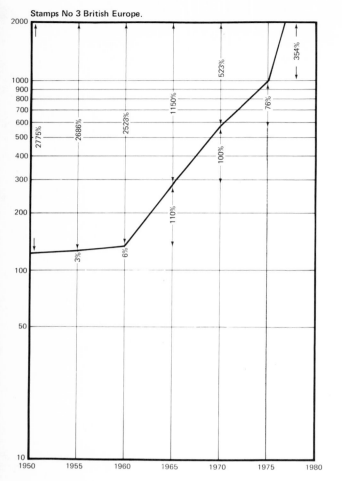

Stamps No 3 British Europe.

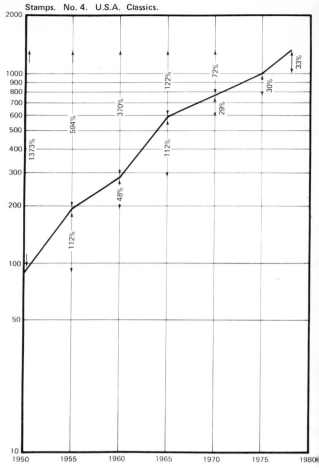

Stamps. No. 4. U.S.A. Classics.

INDEX NO. 3. BRITISH EUROPE.

1. Malta.   10/– Multiple crown & C.A. (Crown
                 Agents). 1919.

2. Cyprus.   £5 George V. 1924.

3. Gibraltar.   £5. 1925–32.

Condition – Mint, part original gum.

INDEX NO. 4. U.S.A. CLASSICS.

1. 1857–61.   90 Cents.

2. 1870–71.   90 Cents.

3. 1893. $5 Columbus.

4. 1898. $ Omaha.

5. 1902–03. $5 'Series 1902' issue.

Condition – Mint, part original gum.

240

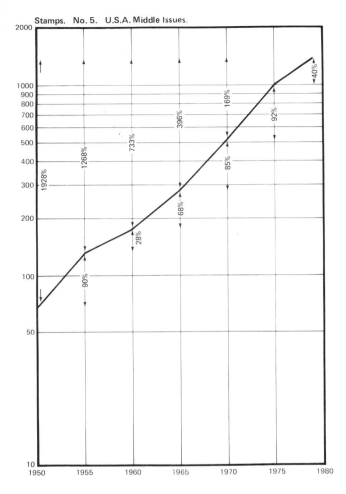

Stamps. No. 5. U.S.A. Middle Issues.

INDEX NO. 5. U.S.A. MIDDLE ISSUES.

1. 1901.   Pan-American Exhibition. Set of 6.

2. 1913–15.   Pan-Pacific Exhibition.

3. 1918–20. $5 Franklin.

4. 1926.   White Plains sheet.

5. 1930.   Zeppelin Set.

Condition – Mint, part original gum.

French Wine

Although wine was being made in the Middle East by about 4000 B.C. and possibly even earlier, the first golden age of vintage wines did not start until about 700 B.C. when the wine-grower first recognised and acquired the two pieces of equipment without which fine wine cannot be made – a pruning knife and an airtight earthenware container. The verse of Homer and Ovid provides many insights into the culture of vines, the variable bouquet and strength of the wines and the time needed to reach maturity.

Fine wines can only be made from vines pruned back to within five or so feet of the ground so that the bunches of grapes can be ripened not only by the direct heat of the sun but by the heat refracted from the baked earth. Wine can be made from unpruned vines but it tends to be light and acidulous.

Pliny describes such a vintage in a wild Campanian vineyard where the vines had climbed to the tops of poplar trees and the gathering of the grapes was considered so dangerous that labourers could only be hired if a free funeral, whenever necessary, was included as a perk. The amphorae in general use in Homer's day were sealed with terracotta stoppers bound with twine and daubed with clay or pitch. The Romans used a cork bung covered with an adhesive cement called pozzolana from the volcanic ash of Pozzuoli. When a wine-boat sunk off Marseilles in 80 B.C. carrying 2000 amphorae of wine was recently raised, it was found that the stoppers were still in position although the wine was not surprisingly past its peak.

This golden age of fine wines lasted about a thousand years until the fall of Rome and extended to many parts of the world then known. The Greeks had planted vines in their colonies from the Black Sea to Spain and the Romans had introduced the vine to the Moselle, the Danube and the Rhine. When Rome fell in A.D. 476, it was the beginning of the dark ages for wine too, largely because the amphora was replaced by the cask. The staves of a cask allow too much oxygen to penetrate to the wine to allow it to reach maturity. Earthenware containers survived in parts of Europe – the dolium survived in Spain and bore a close resemblance to the huge earthenware *tinajas* still used in Montilla but, for the most part, the experience of drinking great wines and the art of making them was lost.

In the 4th century A.D., Ausonius, who was a native of Bordeaux and whose name is remembered in Château Ausone, was tutor to the Emperor Gratian and was later rewarded with great wealth and high office. He had a villa called

Pauliacus – in an area later known as Pauillac the home of Château Lafite and Château Latour – and considered himself a *bon viveur*. He was fond of oysters and in his poetry he devoted seven hexameters to the glorious Médoc natives yet he was not inspired to write a single word on the subject of wine which suggests that it may not have been all that fine.

After the fall of Rome, the history of wine becomes closely interwoven with that of the Christian Church. Not only was wine an essential part of the communion service, its cultivation was very profitable. These aspects of wine were perfectly acceptable to the church but that it was intoxicating and also extremely pleasant to drink ran contrary to the spirit if not the vows of privation, poverty and abstinence that characterised many religious orders. The consumption of wine and even its cultivation has weighed heavily on the Christian conscience ever since.

In the mid-12th century the Benedictine monks of Cluny in the heart of Burgundy were reproved by St Bernard for their excessive drinking, and some had set out to establish a new more ascetic order calling themselves the Cistercians after the *cîteaux* (marshland areas) round Beaune. But on the slope of the hills they found that the vine grew best and it was here that they planted the great Clos Vougeot and other now famous vineyards. What the Cistercians were to Burgundy, the Benedictines were to Médoc. Few of the great vineyards of France (and of many other European countries) have not at one time or another been in the hands of the Church and many in France remained so until the Revolution in 1789.

But even wine from the best medieval vineyards was being drunk young from the cask. The many literary references to wine-drinking show that men who were in a position to buy the best wine were valuing it for its alcoholic effect rather than its taste. John of Salisbury, the great scholar and biographer of Thomas à Becket, states that he drank both wine and beer, 'nor do I abhor anything that can make me drunk'. Falstaff had nothing good to say of Sack other than to praise its effect on his brain and the warming of his blood. Since the secret of making great wine was lost, attempts were made by apothecaries to recapture by the addition of spices the qualities over which classical authors had rhapsodised. In England the best-known recipes were Hippocras and Clarry which were added to Vernage, a wine made from the Vernaccia grape. Chaucer describes old January as he prepares for his wedding night.

'He drinketh ipocras, clarree, and vernage

Of spyces hote, t'encresen his corage.'

As cocktails originally came into use as a means of disguising the evil taste of the Prohibition era spirits, so these recipes served a similar purpose for medieval wine.

In the 15th century, several German princes began to vie with each other to see who could build the largest wine tun or cask. The first of the vast receptacles was the Strasburg Tun of 1472 but this was soon beaten by the Great Tun of

243

A woodcut from a treatise on wine showing racking in progress, *c.* 1500.

Heidelberg which could hold 37,000 gallons or 19,000 dozen bottles. Eventually all records were beaten in 1725 by the Königstein Tun which held nearly a million gallons. These developments at least showed that the need for wine to mature was beginning to be understood. Although oxygen penetrated the dry staves at the top, the tuns were topped up as frequently as possible and the oxygen only gradually reached the wine lower down. In this way was the classical tradition of allowing wine to mature rather accidentally revived.

In 1775 Sir Edward Barry wrote *Observations, Historical, Critical and Medical on the Wines of the Ancients* in which he recognised that, by preserving their

244

wine in large earthenware vessels covered with pitch, the ancients enabled their wine to resist better the frequent changes in the air. He was also aware that wine matured better the larger the bottle. At about the same time, the port-shippers of Oporto were experimenting with a cylindrical bottle which allowed the wine to be binned away horizontally with wine in contact with the cork. This prevented the cork from drying out and allowing too much oxygen to pass through the cork and into the wine.

Until then the role of the glass wine bottle was a humble one. It was squat, bulbous and broad-bottomed so that it could sit safely on the inn table. Its only job was to convey wine from the cask to the wine-cup and if it still held wine at the end of the evening a cork might be stuck in it to keep out the dust. The evolution of the shape of the wine bottle and the development of the airtight cork too can be traced to the Portuguese and it is thanks to them that a new golden age of vintage wines was made possible.

The Phylloxera blight in the 1860s and 1870s was the most serious interruption to the great age of wine in which we still live. The tiny beetle *Phylloxera vastatrix* first reached Europe from America in 1863. Although it multiplied at the rate of one generation a month, its attack on the roots of the vine took time to develop. Between 1869 and 1873 French wine production fell from 70 to 36 million hectolitres. The Ministry of Agriculture offered a prize of 300,000 francs to anyone who could produce a successful cure. Every kind of remedy from fumigating to flooding was tried and the eventual solution, which was to graft French vines on to resistant American root stock, was not found until 1871. The idea was badly received since American vines tended to produce a foxy-tasting wine (*goût de renard*) and it was feared that the glorious tastes of French wine would simply pass out of existence. Such fears proved to be unfounded, although nostalgic talk of the good old days of pre-phylloxera wine is sometimes heard even today. The argument over the relative quality of pre- and post-phylloxera wines can not now be conclusively settled because although some pre-phylloxera wines are still in apparently perfect condition, tasting notes of early dates can not accurately convey their character nor pinpoint the moment of their prime.

There are about forty species of vine throughout the world of which only one, *Vitis vinifera*, will produce good wine. There are some 5000 varieties of this vine and the transformation of its fruit into wine consists of a series of natural chemical processes regulated by man according to principles that have been evolved over several thousand years. There are three basic stages in wine-making.

1. Crushing the grapes to obtain their juice.

2. Fermenting the must (the grape-juice and pulp with or without the stalks, pips and skins depending on what wine is to be made) to produce the wine.

3. The maturing of the wine firstly in cask and then in bottle.

The taste of wine will depend upon the variety of grape used, the

245

One of a set of tapestries at Ham House, Richmond, *c.* 1710.

246

geographical postion of the vineyard, the composition of the soil and subsoil, the weather conditions in the year of growth and the vinification – that is, the way the wine is treated before, during and after fermentation.

It may take five or ten years before newly-planted vines will produce grapes from which fine wine can be made. In parts of France, the *viticulteur* superstitiously arranges much of his work according to dates of national or religious significance. All pruning must be done by January 22nd, the feast of St Vincent the patron saint of wine-growers. The planting of new vines must be over by Easter whenever that may fall and the spraying of the vines must not take place after July 14th, Bastille Day. The timing of the harvest upon which so much depends will take place some time in October although the date is not apparently a matter on which divine guidance is sought.

When the grapes have been gathered, the stalks are removed either by machine or by hand and the must is placed in a vat where, within forty-eight hours, it will naturally begin to ferment. Depending on the type of wine to be made, the juice may be left to macerate with the skins for two or even three weeks, for as the must ferments the alcohol draws colour out of the skins as well as tannin and other substances which are important to the character of the wine. Most rosé wines are made by leaving the must with the skins for just twenty-four hours so that only a small part of the colour in the skins can be drawn into the wine. In the case of white wine the whole bunches of grapes, stalks and all, go straight into the press and the juice drained off so that the wine-to-be is in contact with the skins for only the shortest possible time.

The actual fermentation process comprises a number of chemical changes, the most important of which is the transformation of grape sugar into ethyl alcohol and carbonic acid gas. The catalyst in this process is a yeast that forms on the bloom on the grape-skins called *Saccharomyces ellipsoideus*. This accounts for about 80% of the active ferments in the making of wine although other chemical reactions are taking place depending on the composition of the must. But the principal reaction concerns the grape sugar which is made up of carbon, hydrogen and oxygen and arranged in groups of molecules known as dextrose and fructose. It is these that are reorganised during fermentation into alcohol and carbon dioxide. The rest of the grape-juice consists of other vegetable and mineral substances which are affected in different ways by the other enzymes and catalysts present and by the temperature of the fermentation.

Temperature is an important consideration. Yeast cells become active at about 59°F but die if the heat reaches 100°F. As fermentation goes on, the temperature of the liquid rises and in hot autumn weather there is a danger that the process will simply stop due to the death of the yeast cells. The result would be a wine comparatively weak in alcohol and strong in unconverted sugar and particularly' vulnerable to various bacteria which can sometimes begin the transformation into vinegar. Two principal methods are used to cool the wine during hot weather fermentation to below the danger point either by pumping cold water through pipes in the vats or by pumping the wine itself through cooling compartments into another vat.

Wine contains 97% by volume of water and ethyl alcohol, the remaining 3% being made up of glycerine, acids, alcohols (other than ethyl) and esters which are in their different ways responsible for the taste and smell of wine. First among the acids is succinic which according to Pasteur, who first tackled the complex chemistry of wine in the 1850s, appears to be equal to 0·61% of the grape-sugar present in the must. This is the most important acid because it gives wine its *saveur* or most characteristic winey taste. Acetic acid should also be present in minute quantities although, if the flavour is too pronounced, it means that the ethyl alcohol is becoming oxidised and the wine is on the road to becoming vinegar. The bouquet or aroma of wine arises from the esters formed by the other alcohols (e.g. propyl and butyl) with the other acids (e.g. acetic, proprionic, valerianic, etc.).

So it is that only 3% of a bottle of wine accounts for the difference between a great wine and an undrinkable one. Recent research suggests that the quantities and proportions of the esters and acids that finally remain in the wine depend upon the varieties of *saccharomycetes* and other micro-organisms present in the grape-juice or added later on.

Until around 1950 it was traditional to leave the fermented wine on the skins, pips and pulp for some time to allow it to draw off more colour, a higher tannin content and 'nourishment'. The extra tannin which produces a harsh taste in young wine ensured that the wine would have long life while the extra nourishment gave the wine the wherewithal to develop during that long life. The result was bigger, stronger, more fully developed wines, but wines that were not bottled until perhaps after three years in cask and then not drunk until between ten and twenty years after bottling.

In the more competitive atmosphere of the wine-trade that developed in the fifties, it suited wine merchants to speed up their turnover and the winemakers were only too pleased to be able to do the same. Most wine-drinkers too, whether for reasons of money or space, were unable to lay down wines for long periods. Consequently the vinification processes that have since then become quite prevalent allow wines to be left in cask 12–18 months and to be drunk after three or four years in bottle. Such wines may well have reached their peak but that peak will be far below the one they might have reached had the wine been allowed to remain just a few weeks longer in the vat.

In buying wines for investment, it is essential to know what method of vinification has been used and therefore when the wine is likely to reach its peak. Old age in wine has no value in itself. Once a wine has reached its peak it may hold it for a few years, lesser wines for a year or two, great wines for five years or very much more. And thereafter they may decline in quality at a rather faster rate then they improved. It is of course impossible to prophesy when a wine will reach its peak for wine contains living organisms whose behaviour will determine the life-cycle of the wine. To buy a young wine from a great vineyard as soon as it is bottled involves two hazards – firstly that no one can tell precisely how it will develop and secondly that the next five vintages may turn out to be even greater and more abundant which can only affect the demand for the wine already bought.

Once the wine is in cask, it still has to be carefully supervised. The staves at the top of the oak cask that are not in contact with the wine dry out and allow oxygen to enter the cask and some of the wine to evaporate. The refilling process, known as ullage, which prevents a pocket of air containing dangerous bacteria forming above the wine is carried out every few weeks. Other operations such as racking, where the wine is drawn off the lees into a clean cask and fining where an agent, usually bentonite nowadays which has replaced egg-white or fish-tails, is poured into the wine which absorbs and sinks all the solid particles that may still be swimming around. Other special fining agents can now be used to remove excess tannin or colour.

The naming and description of French wines is exceedingly complicated and there are very good reasons why this has to be so. In 1855 some of the best Bordeaux wines were included in a great Paris Exhibition. Of the five great wine-growing districts of Bordeaux only two, Médoc and Sauternes were dealt with in what was called the Official Classification of the Great Growths of the Gironde. The sixty-five best wines of Médoc were divided into five growths or *crus* known as the classed growths or *crus classés*. After these came the *crus bourgeois* numbering about 2000 growths of the minor *châteaux*. These provide the basic output of the *vin de garde* or wines which are fine enough to be worth keeping in bottle for some time before being drunk as opposed to *vins de consommation* or *vin ordinaire* such as is kept in cask in restaurants and cafés and some private houses and drawn off as it is needed. And after the bourgeois growths come the artisan growths, *crus artisans*, and peasant growths, *crus paysans*.

Of the three other wine-growing areas of Bordeaux, the best wines of Graves were divided into two classes for red and one for white in 1953, the best growths of St. Emilion into three classes in 1955 and although the wines of Pomerol have never been officially classified, a list of principal growths is generally accepted as are the ten exceptional ones appearing on it.

These classifications are important and useful but carry no legal force. The French Government, partly to prevent fraud and partly to maintain the standard of wines which were regarded as one of the glories of France, set up the Institut National des Appellations d'Origine (INAO) to administer a series of regulations known as the *Code du Vin*. Two classes of wine are controlled, each accounting for 10–15% of total national production. The higher group known as Vins d'Appellation d'Origine Contrôlée (A.O.C.) and the lower Vins Délimités de Qualité Supérieure (V.D.Q.S.).

Wine-growing areas designated A.O.C. are those which over the years thanks to the soil, careful methods of vinification and so on have produced wines of a particular quality or character and hence those whose standards the State wished to see maintained. The A.O.C. laws dictate the number of vines that may be planted per hectare, the way in which they may be pruned and also the variety of vine that may be planted. Further regulations set the limits for acidity, alcoholic content, etc. These A.O.C. laws apply to certain of the best areas of Bordeaux, Burgundy, Côtes du Rhône, Loire, Champagne and Alsace and to other less familiar areas.

The second group of wines designated V.D.Q.S. come from areas which have established a reputation for good sound wines. The purpose of the law is partly to enforce standards and partly to prevent other wine-growers who produce similar but less good wines passing them off with fraudulent labels as coming from areas of better reputation.

Most authorities agree that all white wines, including champagne but excluding the sweet wines of Sauternes, should be drunk before they are ten years old and in many cases a good deal earlier. This is because white wines develop faster and have a tendency to maderize. Maderization is the process which eventually turns wine the dark brown colour of Madeira and is caused by the presence of excessive sugar coupled with lack of acidity. Also known as oxidation, it gives the wine a disagreeable musty flat taste. Such wines are by no means ideal for investment because their life-span and peak drinking period is relatively short and the tendency to begin to maderize without warning amounts to an unnecessary risk. These factors also restrict the choice of times at which they can be disposed of and may actually necessitate a sale at an unsuitable moment.

The wines that do lend themselves to investment are those which from the moment the grapes are picked have undergone treatment such that a period of continuous improvement of at least twenty-five years can be expected. A portfolio of wines for long-term investment would have to be chosen from among the great wines of the five districts around Bordeaux and from the great *domaines* of Burgundy.

The Bordeaux area has 200,000 acres of vines and produces around 500 million bottles of A.O.C. wine a year. The overall quality is higher than in any other region of France and the exceptional variety results from the many different soil conditions – clay, lime, sand, gravel and flint occurring in positions with different exposures and altitudes. Four main varieties of grape are used for the red wines, the Cabernet, Merlot, Malbec and Verdot; and three for the white, Sémillon, Sauvignon and Muscadelle. The red wines of Bordeaux, now known to the English-speaking world as claret – originally *clairet* because of its light colour – were first exported to England seven hundred years ago when Gascony was an English possession.

The nucleus of any wine investment might well be the four châteaux classed as first growths in the 1855 classification, Lafite, Latour, Margaux, Haut-Brion (actually in Graves but included because of its excellence) and Mouton-Rothschild which was officially added to the list in 1973. The names of these growths are now so famous that demand from all over the world is consistently high. Indeed such is the snobbery of the wine-world that a poor year of a first growth will command a higher price than a better wine classed in the fifth grade or even in the *crus bourgeois supérieures*.

Many of the people who drink very expensive wines do not have much knowledge or experience of wines and tend to take a good close look at the label before offering an opinion on the wine they are drinking. Names and labels then must be considered very important by the investor. It is not possible for him to play the wine market like a stock market. There is no money to be made buying a *cru bourgeois* he believes to be undervalued in the hope that the market will re-rate it. The classification of 1855 was based on the prices the wines had fetched over the previous one hundred years and it is still widely accepted today. A few wines sell at prices quite out of line with the others in their *cru* such as Château Meyney but on the whole re-ratings do not take place. Until 1820, the Bordeaux wine trade recognised four main grades of wine and their practice had been to weight their values broadly at 100 for the first growths, 75 for the second, 60 for the third and 50 for the fourth. Over the years the differentials have widened especially at the top end so that the broad average today would be 100 for the first growths, 50 for the second, 40 for the third, 30 for the fourth and 20 for the fifth.

The French, it seems, have a passion not only for food and drink but for classifying it as well. The wines of Bordeaux were first classified in the 15th century and nowadays all kinds of foods such as oysters, truffles and even artichokes have their special *crus*.

251

Médoc

The Médoc area is the eastern half of a peninsular formed by the Gironde and the Atlantic Ocean about ten miles wide and sixty long. The central section contains the finest wine-growing areas and of the four main communes of the Haut-Médoc, Margaux, Pauillac, St Estèphe and St Julien, Château Latour, Château Lafite and Château Mouton-Rothschild are in Pauillac, Château Margaux at Margaux while Château Haut-Brion is at Pessac, strictly speaking in the Graves area.

Château Margaux, sometimes known as *le roi de Médoc* produces about $32\frac{1}{2}$ tonneaux (1 tonneau = 4 barrels = 96 cases) or about 150,000 bottles a year. All the Margaux wines are known for their distinctive bouquet. André Simon described it as reminiscent of wild violets and amber but words cannot fully convey the subtleties of taste and scent although the attempt to do so leads wine enthusiasts to use all kinds of exotic analogies. The château itself is a grand neo-classical building which stands in a large park but the total production of wine comes from only about 150 acres of vines. The quality of production was consistently high throughout the 19th century and until 1930 when it began to decline. The present owner replanted the vineyards in the late 1930s and early 1940s and since 1945 the quality has usually been excellent. The huge white-washed *chais*, where banquets are held every year for as many as 1500 people, are kept spotlessly clean as protection against bacteria.

Château Latour produces 50–100 tonneaux of really reliable wine usually considered the second or third best of the *premiers crus*. No château remains there, having been burnt down when Bordeaux was captured from the English by the French in 1453 but the *chais* are among the most elegant in the Médoc. Since 1964 the wine has been fermented in stainless steel vats and the new oak barrels are scrubbed to perfection to prevent any dangerous bacteria coming into contact with the wine. Latour has the reputation of making exceptionally good wine even in bad years, although on the very rare occasions when the vintage, in the owner's opinion, is below standard the wine is sold to shippers simply as Médoc so that the vineyard's reputation is maintained.

Château Mouton-Rothschild was formally admitted to the *premier cru* class in 1973 thanks to the exertions of its owner Baron Philippe de Rothschild who had been gradually improving on the quality of its wine since he took over the management in 1922. This wine has the power of a great burgundy and the subtlety of the finest claret. The vineyard covers 125 acres and produces on average 190 tonneaux. Brand new casks of young oak are used every year from which the wine draws tannin that helps it survive and develop over such long periods. A peculiarity of Mouton-Rothschild since 1945 has been to commission a famous artist to design the label each year. Kandinsky, Braque and Salvador Dali for example have each produced labels which have helped to give the vineyard the cachet it has always sought.

Across a cart-track at the north end of the vineyard stands Château Lafite the other Rothschild-owned *premier cru*. This 200-acre vineyard produces about 200 tonneaux of wine a year, less reliable than the other *premier crus* but also more delicate than its rivals. The great vintages here seem to occur less frequently than for the other *premiers crus* although 1949, 1953, 1959 and 1961 are regarded as unsurpassably great – in fact, the perfect wine.

The fifth of the *premiers crus*, is Château Haut-Brion over the border in Graves. This American-owned vineyard installed stainless steel vats in 1960 to achieve better control of temperatures during fermentation. Its 100 acres, standing more or less in the suburbs of Bordeaux, produce around 120 tonneaux of great wine. Cyrus Redding wrote in 1834 that its flavour resembled burning sealing wax, hardly a strong selling point, although its bouquet reminded him of violets and raspberries. Graves is so-called because of its gravelly soil and the presence of gravel down to sixty feet at Haut-Brion is thought to be one of the reasons why the vineyard is able to produce good wine even in bad years; the heat reflected from the pebbles helps to ripen the grapes in years of little sunshine and the pebbles allow the soil to drain fast in rainy years.

Sauternes is one of the greatest white wines of the world. In the 1855 classification, the best white wines of the five Sauternes communes were graded into first and second growths but with Château Yquem standing in a class by itself ahead of the first growths. When the grapes in these vineyards are ripe, they are not picked but left to rot. *La pourriture noble* or noble rot is caused by a special mould, *botrytis cinerea*, which draws water from the grapes and accounts for the greater sugar content in the grape-juice. It also causes minute changes in the constitution of the grape-juice which eventually gives the wine its distinctive character. The grape-pickers go round with long pointed scissors snipping off the grapes that are brown and shrivelled. As many as ten times the pickers may return to the same bunches during the course of the harvest looking for the grapes that have rotted to exactly the right stage. The Sauternes area has eleven first growths and twelve second growths which represent exceptional value to the drinker since sweet wines are still so unfashionable. But for the investor the cachet attached to Château d'Yquem makes it unquestionably the first choice.

Burgundy

The wine-growing area of Burgundy which stretches from Chablis in the north to Villefranche-sur-Saône in the south produces on average 120 million bottles of wine a year. It is said that wine has been made there since 600 B.C. and over the years experiments with vines have shown the best red wines are to be made from the Pinot Noir grape and the best whites from the Pinot Chardonnay. In the southern part of Burgundy, where the less grand wines are made – the Chalonnais, Mâconnais and Beaujolais – the Gamay Noir is grown for red and the Gamay Noir and Aligoté for white. The Gamay was brought back from the Middle East in the 12th century and many Burgundians maintain that this was the real purpose of the Crusades.

The area producing the best red wines in Burgundy is the Côte d'Or, now divided into the Côte de Nuits and the Côte de Beaune. Here there are very few big estates and most of the vineyards belong to peasant proprietors whose average holding is about 1½ acres. The great wines of the area come from only about 20 square miles and much blending of bad wines from the Rhône and Algeria with good Burgundy takes place in order to increase the quantity of wine that may be sold as Burgundy. Indeed many good wines all over France are lost in *la grande sauce*. The wine trade lives on blending or *coupage*, that being its only contribution to wine production.

Considerable confusion over the naming of Burgundy existed until 1936 when the first controls by the I.N.A.O. were introduced. There is no classification of the kind that exists for Bordeaux. Some wines are produced in such tiny quantities that they are sold by the name of the village followed simply by the words *premier cru*. Although such wines may be totally different in character, if they happen to share the same nearest village they may carry identical labels. A wine-producing village or parish in Burgundy may be known as a *finage* and each vineyard within it is known as a *climat* meaning literally climate. It is often thought that to claim to be able to recognise a wine and identify the actual vineyard of origin must be the height of affectation, yet the use of the word *climat* in this context highlights the fact that a distance of only ten metres between two vines living in quite different conditions from the point of view of exposure to sun, drainage, soil, etc. really can produce wines of quite different character.

It is on the acceptance of a great multiplicity of characteristics that the Appellation d'Origine laws are based. Local committees first define an area of their region, its soil and subsoil and then set minimum standards for the tannin, acid and alcohol content. In some areas, where the slope changes to flatland, the exposure of the vines to the sun will be affected and this will be taken into account in fixing the various minimum criteria. Original and acquired bouquet too are defined.

The resulting laws of Appellation d'Origine are confusing to say the least. Yet, by wisely recognising the need for different standards, the French have managed to maintain the distinction of their greatest wines. A further complication in the naming of Burgundies is the practice sanctioned by the *Code du Vin* of adding to the name of a village the name of its most famous vineyard. So the village of Gevrey becomes Gevrey-Chambertin, Aloxe becomes Aloxe-Corton etc. There are, unfortunately, exceptions as for instance when the best vineyards at Gevrey, apart from Chambertin, use their own name e.g.

Latricières or Charmes and add Chambertin for good measure so that a Latricières-Chambertin or Charmes-Chambertin may not be as good as a Chambertin but it will be very much better than any Gevrey-Chambertin which means no more than a *vin ordinaire* grown within the boundaries of the village.

The Burgundian advice amidst all this confusion is *'respectez les crus'*. In other words, learn the names of the actual vineyards and forget the rest.

Most of the *communes* or *finages* of Burgundy arrange their best wines in four classes. Firstly *tête de cuvée* signifying the best growth in the area and followed by *premièrs cuvées, deuxièmes* and *troisièmes*, and after these the unclassified *vins ordinaires*. Because the parcels of land are often so small in Burgundy, much of the wine has to be blended by the *négociants* or shippers whose reputations are therefore of the greatest importance. But, as in Bordeaux, it is wiser for the investor to stick to wines bottled on the *domaine* by the *vigneron* himself rather than take a risk on a reputation that could change.

Four great wines are chosen to represent the Côte d'Or – three from the Côte de Nuits and one from the Côte de Beaune.

Chambertin-Clos de Bèze is one of the two great vineyards in Gevrey-Chambertin. The 37-acre vineyard was planted in A.D. 630 by the monks of the Abbaye de Bèze and now produces wine of remarkable qualities. Bouquet is too delicate a word to use here and the Burgundians speak of the wine's tremendous nose. Its deep red colour brings out ecstatic comments while the taste is variously described as balanced, powerful and majestic.

Romanée Conti is one of the five *têtes de cuvée* of the Vosne-Romanée commune. The vineyard is only $4\frac{1}{2}$ acres and produces what for many people are the most glorious wines on earth and for everyone the most expensive.

Le Saint-Georges is one of the ten *têtes de cuvée* of Nuits-Saint-Georges. The wines of this commune are known for their firmness. People refer to them as *mordant* meaning that their texture is so full that they feel as though they can be bitten. They mature slowly and are remarkably consistent in old age.

The Hospices de Beaune is a charitable institution founded in 1443 by Nicolas Rolin a tax-collector for Louis XI. Its sole revenue is from the sales of wine made from its vineyards scattered over 125 acres. This wine is sold each year at public auction on the third Sunday in November. Buyers from all over the world attend the auction held in the great hall of the Hospices and the prices paid are the first and usually very accurate guide to the overall quality of the Burgundy vintage.

Château and estate bottling

For much of the 19th century, claret was not considered alcoholic enough for the English taste and the first growths of the Médoc were almost always blended with Hermitage, a strong Rhône wine, or Beni Carlos, a powerful deep-red Spanish wine from Valencia. Alcohol too was added, by which time the flavour and bouquet of the wine were almost completely ruined, so attempts were made to revive them with orris root and raspberry brandy. It was difficult to get hold of 'unimproved' clarets but demand was growing for those which had not been 'cut' or blended. A few wine merchants, who were keen to offer wine with good credentials, demanded that the wine of Château Lafite be bottled at the château and this was done for the first time in 1869.

The practice has grown throughout Bordeaux to include almost all the *crus classés* and in these cases the corks are branded with the year of the vintage and the words '*Mise en bouteille du château*' or '*Mis en bouteilles au château*'. These words will also appear on the labels when the bottles are dressed.

In Burgundy, estate bottling is the equivalent to château bottling in Bordeaux and the label will bear the name of the grower (*vigneron*) as well as the vineyard and commune together with '*Mis au domaine*' or '*Mis en bouteilles par le propriétaire*' (bottled by the owner) or some other unambiguous form of words. French law gives the protection that an estate-bottled wine must be one where the bottler is the owner of the vineyard and holds a licence to bottle his own wines and no others.

But misleading statements are often seen such as '*Mis en bouteilles dans mes caves*' (bottled in my cellars). If the owner of the vineyard is not the same man as the bottler and since all wine it bottled in cellars the statement may be quite meaningless. Again '*Mis en bouteilles au Château X*' is ambiguous since some shippers maintain offices in a château which also allows them to bottle on their premises wine bought outside.

The future

The outlook for the supply of fine wines is much easier to assess than the demand. There is hardly an acre of France that has not been planted with vines at one time or another and the areas now producing fine wines may be said to be the only ones capable of doing so. It is possible that identical conditions prevail in some remote corner of the world and there is no reason why prospectors should not identify, as has happened in the Napa valley and other areas of California, suitable locations for vineyards by reference to soil, weather and so on in the same way the geologists can pinpoint diamond-bearing structures without needing to dig the hole. Yet no one has fully succeeded in the case of vines and if the perfect location were to be found, it would be six years before the vines were able to produce grapes suitable for fine wines and several more before the wine made from them could be properly assessed. So the supply of fine wines may be regarded as static for practical purposes except in so far as the size of the harvest as with any other crop will vary according to the weather.

The demand for fine wine is very difficult to forecast and any attempt to do so cannot be much better than a guess. The very high prices have already produced strong resistance among 'private drinkers' in many countries. As the prices of fine wines rise, it follows that without a corresponding rise in the prosperity of existing wine-drinkers, fewer and fewer people will be able to afford to drink them. But here, as in other fields, it may be institutional demand – not in this case museums, universities and so on – but directors' dining-rooms, airlines, expense account restaurants and hotels which will sustain a rising trend in prices.

In other words, demand for fine wines will be set to a great extent by people who do not pay for them. In these conditions, it is hard to see what would stop business people drinking great wines when such extravagances may easily be justified by the call of prestige and the need to flatter customers. What after all is $200 for a bottle of wine if a contract with several more noughts hangs in the balance? Of all the *premiers crus*, it is estimated that between 50% and 75% is now drunk by people who do not pay for them. A great deal is still certainly drunk by very rich individuals but these are precisely the people who are most often able to charge such expenses to this or that business.

It is only quite recently that the delights of drinking great wine have spread at all widely. In the 18th century, the English squirearchy and nobility were the biggest consumers; in the course of the 19th century the Edinburgh lawyer and the prosperous Manchester businessman and the European nobleman were added to the circle. Between the two world wars, there was prohibition and depression in America and the circle did not grow significantly until the 1950s when the entire market changed. Now the whole world is after great wine and although wine merchants continually gasp at the opening prices being asked, it is evident that many countries whose currencies have not been battered by inflation and devaluation are still able to absorb the wine at the offered prices.

Everyone is agreed that the wine investment boom of 1971/2 drove prices to unrealistic heights. This was indirectly and partly the result of the rivalry between the two Rothschild-owned vineyards that had been simmering since 1855 when Château Mouton-Rothschild was classed as a second growth and the cousin's Château Lafite was placed in the first class. Baron Philippe de Rothschild, the owner of Château Mouton-Rothschild, who had tried unsuccessfully in 1970 to stop the spiralling in prices by offering his vintage at an artificially low price, seems to have done a *volte-face* in 1971 when he became determined that even if his wine was not officially classed as a first growth he would put one over his cousin at Château Lafite by offering his 1971 wine at a higher price and by showing that the market would stand it. A waiting game ensued which resulted in Baron Philippe capping Lafite's opening price of 110,000 francs per tonneau by 10,000 francs.

Much tut-tutting was heard in Bordeaux for these prices were about double the previous year's and about ten times those of the great 1961 vintage. But before long the *négociants* and *courtiers* (brokers) of Bordeaux were asserting 'if

257

Château Mouton-Rothschild is worth X, Château Y must be worth at least Z' and with that the whole structure of wine prices, right down to the *crus paysans*, was soon hoisted to new heights. The Bordeaux bubble burst when the original opening prices of the *premiers crus* were seen to be even higher for 1972 than 1971 even though the vintage was much inferior.

That Christies in 1966 resumed their wine-auctions after a break of twenty years and that Sotheby's followed them in 1971 also contributed to the sharp rise in prices by providing the sort of market where new price levels attracted the maximum publicity. Another important factor was the boom in world stock markets which gave wine-buyers more money to spend as well as causing investors to search out any neglected sector.

Although it is possible to negotiate the purchase of wine in cask in Bordeaux and Burgundy, there are many reasons why it is ultimately safer and cheaper to deal through a reliable wine merchant. There is first of all the cost of travelling and staying in France, although for many people the cost of doing so would be justified by the pleasure and therefore would not need to be considered part of the basic cost of the wine.

Most of the important châteaux have standing arrangements with agents in different countries who would be understandably put out if they knew their suppliers were selling wine more cheaply to their own customers. So although most important châteaux will refer enquiries to their agents, quite a number of the minor châteaux and domaines will be very pleased to do business with any takers. Almost too pleased, really. For most of the *vignerons* and *négociants* are accustomed to dealing with hard-nosed professionals only. There are many amateurs throughout the world who have deep knowledge and experience of fine wines but this would be of little use to them in Bordeaux or Burgundy because to taste immature wines which may be harsh and unpalatable in their early stages of development and to be able to anticipate their style and character many years hence, requires knowledge and experience of a kind usually possessed only by people in the wine-trade.

For all the talk of wine lakes in the E.E.C., it is worth remembering that there is never a problem selling good wine – the difficulties start when trying to dispose of the mediocre grades. The appearance then in Bordeaux in 1971/2 of parties of 'wine speculators' was a thrilling sight for the *Bordelais*. Many unfortunates were sold large quantities of the lowest grade wine at the highest prices and only became aware that they had been ripped off when they tried to unload their acquisitions in 1973 and later.

The buying of immature wine is a very difficult business even for the expert. Most wine merchants would prefer to buy wine after it had been in cask for two years, yet such is the competition to get hold of good wine that many are prepared to take a view after only one year in the cask or even before the malolactic fermentation has taken place – usually the spring after the grapes are picked but sometimes even earlier. In the sixties there was a small futures market in Bordeaux which enabled certain *courtiers* to offer tonneaux of wine *sur souches* (on the vines) but the risks were too great for most people in the trade and such offers are no longer made.

There are now two main U.K. auction-houses handling wines of all classes – Christie's and Sotheby's, which between them hold about eighty sales a year, of which more than half take place at Christie's. Of the fine wines they handle, almost all are ready for immediate drinking because the U.K. wine trade is still very much in control of the laying-down or immature wine business. No buyer's premium is charged by any of the auction-houses and in one respect it is safer to buy wine for investment when it has developed far enough to enable experts to be fairly confident of its future. There were times in 1971 and 1972 when auction-room prices shot ahead of those on wine merchants' lists and certain clients of Berry Bros, the famous St James's Street wine merchants, placed large orders with instructions to deliver direct to Christie's round the corner. The position was reversed in 1973 when auction-room prices plummeted and wine-drinkers found they could buy there more cheaply than from their wine merchant. The auction-houses at that stage became unpopular with the trade although it is difficult to see how they could have affected prices directly. Indeed, many wine merchants, on seeing the sharp upward movement in prices in 1971, bought twice their normal quota driving prices up even higher.

There is still a highly sophisticated wine trade in the U.K. and U.S.A. although the number of independent merchants dwindled a lot in the 1960s as the hotel and brewing groups took them over. It would not be a good idea to buy wine for investment by going into a famous wine merchant, securing a good discount on $10,000 worth of great wines and walking out again. This would almost certainly unbalance the merchant's stock and even after a 10–20% discount would be a relatively expensive way of buying wine. It would be more sensible to plan the investment with the wine merchant who might advise waiting for the next good vintage or at least until he is next in Bordeaux or the Côte d'Or when he will buy on your behalf $10,000 worth of fine wine over and above his normal requirements. For this service, he may charge as little as 10% which would establish as low a base price for the investment as could be hoped for.

At a recent seminar in Bordeaux, it was estimated that about 10% of all claret is now sold direct to the public while in Burgundy the percentage has grown rapidly since the construction of the motorway which can bring a Parisian right into the vineyards in two hours and estimates of Burgundy sold direct range up to 50%. Even if these figures were accurate, they would tell nothing about the price or quality of the wines changing hands. There have been repeated attempts to cut out the various middle men in the wine trade, retailers, wholesalers, brokers and shippers and the fact that they all continue to exist may suggest that they perform a real service.

Investment in wine involves as it were a double sterility – the first conventional one that it produces no interest, dividend or rent and the second that there is no benefit or pleasure to be derived from the contemplation of it as is the case with most other alternative investments. For wine-bottles have no generally recognised aesthetic value otherwise they would not be thrown away when they were empty and if the anticipation of the pleasure of drinking the wine is regarded as a benefit or pleasure, this can hardly apply to the investor since he will be selling the wine not drinking it in any case.

The new faster method of vinification may well be a benefit to wine-drinkers because to tie up capital in a wine for say fifteen years with inflation and interest running at high rates means that the wine must be a very considerably better wine at fifteen years of age than it was at five to justify the difference in cost. Supposing a wine, made in such a way that it would reach a peak of maturity in five years' time, were sold at the time it was made for $10, the real cost of drinking it at its peak, assuming interest rates of 10%, would be around $17. If it had been made in such a way that it was expected to reach its peak in fifteen years' time, then the real cost of drinking it then with interest rates at 10% would be nearly $30.

In other words, a man opting for a wine whose method of vinification requires a wait of fifteen years before it reaches its peak rather than one requiring just five years is saying, in effect, that it is worth paying 75% odd more for the slow-maturing wine. Or to put it differently, he would prefer to drink six bottles of it in fifteen years' time than ten bottles of the same wine matured faster in five years' time. Very few people would agree such a price differential between the two wines was warranted and market prices do suggest that the 'long haul' wines are not accorded the rating they deserve. In other words, the investor in slow-maturing wine is not adequately compensated for his notional financing cost. It does not follow however, that he would not be able to make similar gains if the market as a whole moved upwards.

French words commonly used in describing the various characteristics of wine

Aigre	Sour. On the way to becoming vinegar (*vin aigre*).
Bouchonné	Corked. Where the wine has taken on the taste of a defective cork.
Capiteux	Heady. Of wine with unusually high alcoholic strength.
Chambré	Brought to room temperature.
Charnu	Fleshy. Fat-bodied wine.
Corsé	Well-built, full bodied and with high alcoholic strength.

260

Coupé	Blended.
Crémant	Sparkling.
Dur	Hard due to excess tannin.
Finesse	Supreme delicacy or elegance.
Goût de bois	Tasting of wood.
Goût de paille	Tasting of wet straw.
Goût de pierre à fusil	Flinty.
Goût de renard	Tasting foxy or pungent.
Goût de terroir	Tasting of the earth of the vineyard.
Mâché	So big, round and full that you can almost chew it.
Mou	Flabby, unattractive.
Mousseux	Sparkling.
Nerveux	Strong and sinewy.
Pétillant	Slightly sparkling.
Piqué	Tart. On the way to becoming vinegar.
Plat	Flat and dull.
Soyeux	Silky and smooth. Free of all traces of acidity.
Usé	Worn. Kept too long.

Book list

LICHINE, ALEXIS. *Alexis Lichine's Encyclopedia of Wines and Spirits* (Illus.) 1967, Knopf

—*Alexis Lichine's Guide to the Wines and Vineyards of France* (Illus.) 1979, Knopf

SIMON, ANDRE L. *All About Wines* 8 Volumes Shalom

French wine. No. 1 Bordeaux first growths

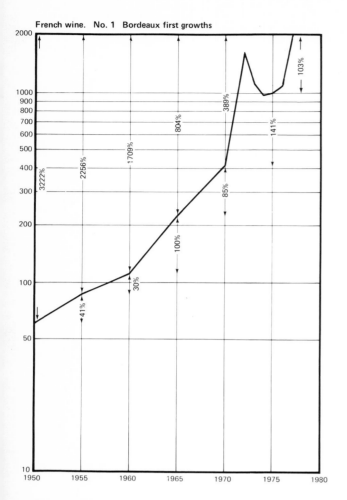

French wine. No. 2 Burgundy têtes de cuvée

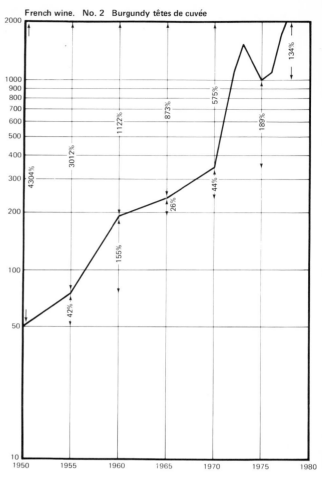

INDEX NO. 1. BORDEAUX FIRST GROWTHS.

1. 1945 Château Lafite.

2. 1947 Château Margaux.

3. 1947 Château Mouton-Rothschild.

4. 1949 Château Latour.

5. 1949 Château Haut-Brion.

INDEX NO. 2. BURGUNDY TETES DE CUVEE.

1. 1947 Vosne-Romanée. Romanée Conti.

2. 1947 Nuits-Saint-Georges. Le Saint-Georges.

3. 1947 Chambertin. Clos de Bèze.

4. 1947 Hospices de Beaune. Aloxe-Corton. Cuvée Dr Peste.

262

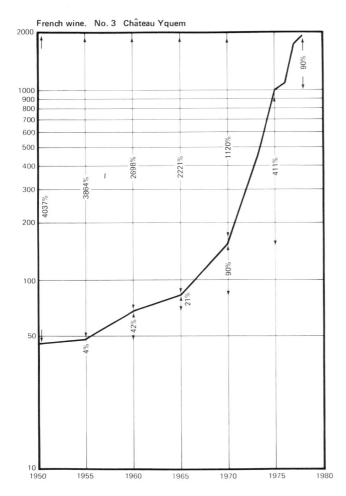

French wine. No. 3 Château Yquem

INDEX NO. 3. SAUTERNES.

Château Yquem 1921, 1937, 1943, 1947.

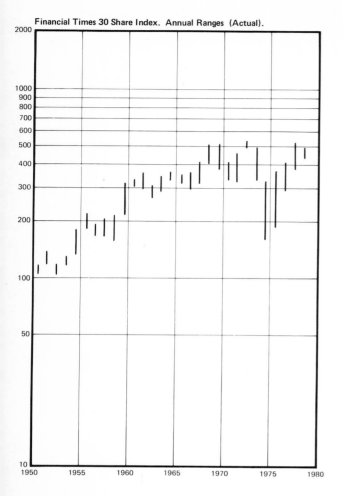

Financial Times 30 Share Index. Annual Ranges (Actual).

FINANCIAL TIMES 30 SHARE INDEX NO. 1.

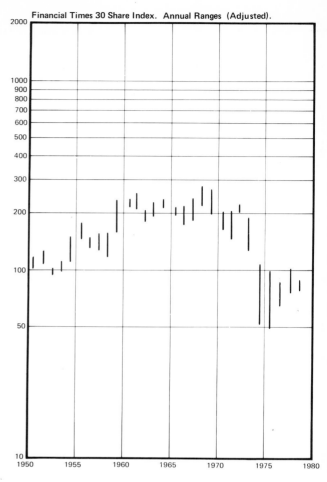

Financial Times 30 Share Index. Annual Ranges (Adjusted).

FINANCIAL TIMES 30 SHARE INDEX NO. 2. IN REAL TERMS.

Annual ranges adjusted by the Consumers Expenditure Deflator 1950–62 and the General Index of Retail Prices 1962–78.

264

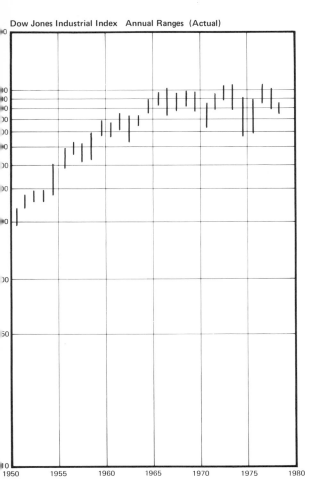

Dow Jones Industrial Index   Annual Ranges (Actual)

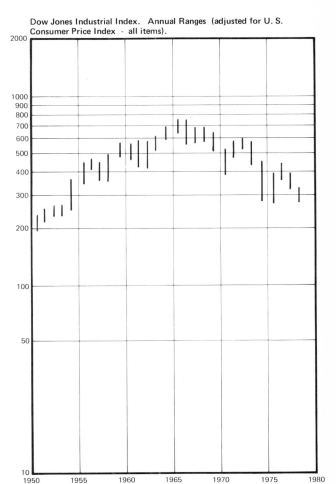

Dow Jones Industrial Index. Annual Ranges (adjusted for U. S. Consumer Price Index - all items).

DOW JONES INDEX Industrial Average No. 1.

Annual ranges.

DOW JONES INDEX Industrial Average No. 2.

Annual ranges adjusted by the U.S. Consumer Prices Index (all items).

265

Index

Folios in *italic* indicate illustrations